KU-667-495

An Irish Doctor's
ODYSSEY

DOM COLBERT

ABOUT THE AUTHOR

Dr Dom Colbert has worked as a volunteer in developing countries since 1960. He worked in many disaster areas, including Biafra, Ethiopia and Bosnia to mention but a few. He is currently an honorary Senior Clinical Lecturer in the Department of International Health and Tropical Medicine in the Royal College of Surgeons, Dublin, and invited lecturer in Tropical Medicine in National University of Ireland Galway (NUIG), where he taught Applied Physiology for many years. He is the co-founder of the thriving Travel Medicine Society of Ireland and the founder of the Volunteer Medical Doctor scheme and Voluntary Services Abroad – the 'VSA' – which sends trainee doctors from Galway to do electives in developing countries. The VSA has donated more than €1.5 million in medical aid since 1977.

Dr Colbert has lectured widely in Europe and the United States and has written extensively on medical topics. As part of a team sent to Africa by the Royal College of Surgeons, Ireland, he taught and examined young surgeons for the College of Surgeons of East, Central and South Africa (COSECSA), and was elected as a Fellow of COSECSA for 'outstanding service to surgery in Africa'. He lives in Galway, Ireland.

AN IRISH DOCTOR'S
ODYSSEY

THE SAINTS ARE IN HEAVEN

Selected memories of an Irish doctor

DOM COLBERT

ORPEN PRESS

Published by
Orpen Press
Upper Floor, Unit K9
Greenogue Business Park
Rathcoole
Co. Dublin
Ireland
email: info@orpenpress.com
www.orpenpress.com

© Dom Colbert, 2018

ISBN 978-1-78605-057-1

A catalogue record for this book is available from the British Library. All
rights reserved. No part of this publication may be reproduced, stored in
a retrieval system or transmitted in any form or by any means, electronic,
mechanical, photocopying, recording or otherwise, without the prior,
written permission of the publisher.

This book is sold subject to the condition that it shall not, by way of trade
or otherwise, be lent, resold, hired out, or otherwise circulated without
the publisher's prior consent in any form of binding or cover other than
that in which it is published and without a similar condition including
this condition being imposed on the subsequent purchaser.

Printed in Dublin by SPRINTprint Ltd

To Doreen

ACKNOWLEDGEMENTS

I thank Orpen Press for having faith in my work, my friends for urging me to write it and my family for believing that this is the best book ever written! I am also grateful to Vincent Holmes of the *Galway Review* for his constant encouragement when I faltered. But I could never have done anything without the inspiration of so many doctors, nurses, missionaries and students, who taught me all I know and who seldom, if ever criticised, my imperfect efforts. Finally, I owe a lot to the different presidents of the National University of Ireland, Galway (NUIG) and to my departmental colleagues for allowing me time off to work in crisis areas so often.

Contents

Preface   ix

1. The Early Years   1
2. Newbridge College   37
3. University Days   58
4. Lourdes   68
5. Doreen   71
6. The Real World   75
7. The Armchair Traveller   92
8. Nigeria, 1960   94
9. Liberia, 1965   128
10. A Caribbean 'Holiday', 1968   151
11. Another World   165
12. Khartoum   170
13. Tanzania, 1984   179
14. Jambo to Kenya   184
15. Loarengak/Lokitaung   220
16. On the Road to Kakuma   228
17. The Girl with No Hands   233
18. Tales from Canada   245

Appendix 1: Robbie and Mike   271
Appendix 2: Animal Encounters   281

Appendix 3: Tropical Hazards   299

Appendix 4: Overseas Aid   304

Epilogue   309

PREFACE

Neither this book nor its sequel, *No Tears Left*, are meant to be historical, geographical or literary masterpieces. Instead they are random personal memories of which my family knows little or nothing but which reflect times I lived through and my own changing view of life.

I tell things as I remember them now, but in so doing I am well aware that I may be distorting some events where my memory is faulty. I am certainly guilty of failing to mention many people and many events that have been important in my life for lack of space or simply because I have lost names, and I apologise unreservedly to anyone whom I have unwittingly offended in any way, for indeed no offence is intended.

Obviously, I do not always quote people verbatim. However, I do try to give whatever message they hoped to convey as accurately as my memory permits. I freely admit that my memory may be sometimes off-beam in this regard.

I wrote this book initially as a memoir for my family. Now I see it as a commentary on my generation and as giving the reader an insight into how an ordinary person – for indeed I am ordinary – can become more than a spectator at extraordinary events.

I hope you will enjoy travelling down the years with me and share some of the joys and sorrows that have been my lot in life.

Dom Colbert
Galway 2018

CHAPTER 1

THE EARLY YEARS

The Age of Innocence

On the afternoon of the 18 October 1934, St Luke's Day, Helen Colbert gave birth to a boy, her fourth child, in 'Chatsfort', Newtown, Waterford. The birth took place upstairs in my parent's bedroom, which had an uninterrupted view of the wide shrub-dotted front lawn that rolled steeply down to the massive iron difficult-to-close front gates. Chatsfort was an old and rather grand house spread across 3.5 acres, overlooking a sweep of the river Suir.

This fine river still flows majestically to merge with St Georges Channel, the southernmost portion of the Irish Sea. It loses its identity somewhere between Hook Head, in county Wexford, and Crooke, a small picturesque fishing village on the Waterford side of the estuary.

Hook head itself is perpetuated in the saying attributed to Oliver Cromwell who vowed that he would take Waterford 'by hook or by crook'. As one of the earliest lighthouses in the world, the kindly lamp on Hook was undoubtedly a welcome guide for early invaders of Ireland, including the Vikings, and later for Strongbow and the Normans.

But these were not the thoughts of Helen Colbert as she laboured for over 72 hours to give birth to a baby boy who by good luck eventually changed from a transverse lie – where a natural delivery is impossible – to a face presentation,

Leabharlanna Poibli Chathair Baile Átha Cliath

Dublin City Public Libraries

where natural delivery can occur, albeit slowly and painfully. Her mind was filled with those thoughts that only mothers in labour experience and to which no one is privy except the Lord. And among them must be the wrenching *cri de coeur* of 'When will it end? 'Will it ever end?' and, 'Oh! God help me,… Help me God… Help me Mary.'

In those days, confinements took place at home. My birth was no exception and my mother had Nurse Topping in attendance throughout, with Dr Ryan, the local general practitioner, at her side once the cervix was fully dilated. I do not know how poor people managed. Sepsis was rife, neonatal mortality high and irreparable damage to the unfortunate mother's perineum commonplace. Analgesia was minimal in 1934, but if the mother was lucky the nurse dropped ether or chloroform on to a gauze pad, which was placed over her mouth and nose. This may seem extraordinary to us nowadays, but even more extraordinary was the fact that the doctor often enjoyed a cigarette while the nurse poured these highly flammable fluids!

To make matters worse, there was a bright log fire burning all the time to keep the room warm, and the windows were closed tight to prevent damp air entering and giving the mother pneumonia or even consumption (which we now know as TB).

Outside the room – for no one else could enter – my father waited patiently, probably smoking non-stop and probably having a little too much whiskey for his own good. My two elder brothers, Neville and Norbert, and my sister, Sibyl, were really unaware of what was going on except that the doctor was bringing a new baby. Perhaps Hannah, my mother's mother, was there too. I was later to love my gran very much.

Eventually, it was all over. Nurse fussed my mother and removed all traces of birthing. Much hot water and soap were used. Sheets were changed. The housemaids ran to and fro making tea and preparing meals for nurse, doctor and 'the children'. Dr Ryan walked down the stairs with his doctor's bag under his arm. My sister Sibyl was sure the new baby was in the bag. He did not dissuade her.

It was St Luke's day – St Luke the physician, St Luke the patron of doctors.

Nurse Topping stayed in Chatsfort for six weeks following my birth. Six weeks was considered the normal time for a mother's puerperium, after which she was expected to resume her usual activities. In many ways, this rather old-fashioned notion was a good thing. It allowed the new mother time to recover both mentally and physically from what may have been a very difficult delivery. It provided breathing space for everyone to adjust to the new arrival or to pick up the threads of life where the baby had been still-born or died after birth.

Churching

It was also roughly the time when the mother was 'churched'. This ancient custom, based on Jewish practice, was performed as a special blessing, enabling the mother to go out into the world again. The idea of 'purifying the mother' derived from the purification of Mary, which was done 40 days after the birth of Jesus in accordance with the Mosaic Law. The belief that fairies might otherwise kidnap the mother was a later accretion, primarily in Ireland and the United Kingdom.

Churching is not done nowadays in the Western Church but is still practised in many parts of the East, where it certainly does not imply that the new mother is unclean in any sense. I accept it like the Easterners as a special blessing, and 24 years later, my own wife was churched in St Josephs in Galway after she gave birth to her first child.

I was christened Serright Dominic Thérèse Colbert in St John's Church, Waterford. It was my uncle Michael's first baptism. He had been ordained a Dominican the July of that year in Rome. My mother picked these unusual names before I was born on the assumption that I would be called Thérèse (after St Thérèse of Lisieux) if I were a girl, Dominic if a boy and Serright (later changed to Serryth) could be used for either a boy or girl. Hence I was known as Serryth for the first ten years of my life, until Gran persuaded my mother to call me Dominic or Dom, as she wanted me called after a Christian saint and not to be labelled with a meaningless made-up name.

At the time of my birth, my immediate family consisted of my father Tom Colbert, my mother Helen, my eldest brother Neville aged 6, my sister Sibyl aged 4 and Norbert aged 2. Two 'maids' completed the household (apart from Shep, our dog), a senior one and a junior one – who was also known as the 'scullery maid'.

The maids lived in, and had just one half-day off in the week. By week I mean seven days. They worked Sundays. Their wages were five shillings and two shillings and sixpence, respectively, per week.

But they were well fed, comfortably housed – each having a room of her own – and were provided with black dresses, white aprons and white caps. My mother took care of them if they were sick and was always concerned that they got enough rest. She enjoyed the stories of their love lives, saw they did their religious duties and generally advised them when they had any personal problem.

They addressed us as master and miss and mothered us when we were infants. I was told later that Annie, the senior maid, used to pick me up as a baby and waltz around singing 'I'm in heaven…when we're dancing cheek to cheek'. Clearly, she was a fan of Hollywood and of Fred Astaire, in particular. I must have loved her in return as one day; perhaps when I was two and a half, a panic arose when no one could find me. Eventually, I was found fast asleep in her bed. The last place anyone would look. I was quite unaware and unconcerned that everyone was searching the house and garden for me.

I know that as a child I was a wanderer, always getting lost and quite unconcerned that anyone would either miss me or search for me.

Indeed, my inclination to stray was so marked that when I was six years old my mother bought me a startling red blazer, so that she could identify me quickly at mass or in a crowd. This worked against her on one occasion when I strayed on the Woodstown Beach. It seems that red blazers were all the rage that summer as every second child on the strand wore one that day, much to my mother's confusion. She had much pleasure in recounting this episode on many subsequent occasions.

Apart from getting lost so often, two other, rather simple things stand out in my mind from these early days.

One was the fact that I regularly left bits of chocolate behind a statue of Our Lady in the breakfast room expecting that she would eat it during the night. She regularly obliged, but, of course, the beneficiary was my eldest brother Neville who not only enjoyed the spoils but also fulfilled my wish of pleasing the mother of the God.

The other thing I remember is the 'man in the trapdoor'. This mythical man was the invention of my sister Sibyl who would bring me back a little piece of cake or chocolate, telling me that she got it from 'the man in the trapdoor'. Sibyl used to cycle to St Anne's National School in Ballytruckle each day and told me that sometimes on her way home a trapdoor would suddenly appear in the road and a little man pop up and give her 'something for Serryth'.

It was, of course, Sibyl's own treat that she had been given for her lunch break in school.

I believed her implicitly and on one occasion sneaked off on my own to thank the man in the trapdoor but failed to find him.

My early days were full of sunshine and happiness. I was a little scamp who played in the fields and garden. We had a wood behind the house filled with wild flowers, trailing ivy and gnarled deadwood. There were hidden dark corners where we imagined gnomes, pixies and evil sprites held court at midnight. There was a grassy lane skirting the wood leading to the main road, which my sister Sibyl christened 'the raiders road'. That road filled me with awe and excitement, and often fear.

Chatsfort had a fine, if somewhat neglected, kitchen garden. This was oddly placed so that you came across it suddenly, unexpectedly, at the end of a narrow path which ran between thick wild bushes. It reminds me now of the dazzling excitement one gets when emerging from the pathway that leads to the Treasury in Petra. Fortunately, for us children, the kitchen garden was neither neat nor orderly. It always seemed to me to consist of a haphazard collection of rhubarb stalks, limp lettuce plants, wild strawberries and consistently disappointing apple trees.

There was also one stunted pear tree that produced hard small fruit that was quite inedible.

A grass tennis court to the side of the house, which my mother marked out with some kind of whitewash each May, faced the kitchen window. The net always sagged in the middle probably due to us children swinging over it as we chased one another . I still remember my mother and Dadda's brother, John, playing tennis in a most genteel fashion, serving underhand and never daring to attempt a volley.

My father did not exert himself. On a warm day, he would sit in the sun reading or snoozing. On a cold or wet day, he would be in the house reading and smoking his pipe by the open fire.

A Book Re-read is a Treasure Twice Enjoyed

My father was an avid reader. He read and re-read the same books over and over again and could recite passages from Dickens by heart. His favourite recitation was the description of the death of Nell in the *Old Curiosity Shop*. Tears came into his eyes as he finished speaking. Of course, he was a hopeless businessman, and my mother did all the practical things such as running the house, hiring and firing gardeners and handymen, handling the family finances and organising everything about the children from their clothes to their schooling.

She also enjoyed reading but, when it came to a real love of books, not just the stories in books but also the actual physical books themselves, my father was without peer. Although Dickens was his idol, Dadda loved many other authors too. Guy Boothby was among these. Who ever heard of him nowadays?. I can still see my father reading *A Lost Endeavour*, a rather uninspiring narrative, which I thought was great at the time. Willkie Collin's *The Moonstone*, John Buchan's *The 39 Steps* and yarns about sailing ships and shipwrecks were other favourites of his, but, like all of his generation, Conan Doyle's books were never far from his hands.

My mother, on the other hand, preferred historical novels and books of non-fiction. These included Butler's *Lives of the Saints* and a variety of adventure stories varying from Shackelton's voyages to Thor Heyerdahl's *Kon Tiki Expedition*. She was particularly fond of Axel Munthe and A.J. Cronin, and I must say that both *San Michele* and *Adventures in Two Worlds* by these respective authors influenced me greatly.

For light relief she read a variety of popular and classical novels. Among her favourite writers were the Bronte sisters and Baroness Orczy, originator of the *Scarlet Pimpernel*. I know that I was especially taken by books about the gallantries of Sir Percy Blakeney and thrilled to tales of aristocrats being snatched from *Madame la guillotine* under the nose of the odious Chauvelin.

As a child, before the age of 10, I literally 'gobbled up' books. I would lie for hours under a table or under my bed, getting lost in strange and thrilling tales of faraway countries, other times and daring heroes. Initially, I lived in the realm of Grimm's and Andersen's Fairy Tales, especially the former. By the age of 7, I was into hero worship. All my heroes were magnificent, wise, strong, generous and gallant, and usually fighting for the God, queen and country or else on behalf of the poor and exploited. Figures such as Robin Hood, Damien of Molokai and David Livingstone inspired me and planted a seed in me that never withered.

One of my favourite books was the *Lost World*, which seemed to combine most of the things I so admired: courage, honesty, adventure, discovery, truth and the triumph of right. Like most middle-class children, I shared the adventures of the *Four Feathers*, *Huckleberry Finn*, *The Swiss Family Robinson* and *Robinson Crusoe*. Of course, I soon discovered Agatha Christie and read each of her books. In particular, I loved Hercule Poirot and to this day enjoy the wonderful TV characterisation of the little Belgian sleuth by David Suchet. Cassel's *Book of Knowledge* (the 'poor mans' Encyclopaedia Britannica) became an unceasing source of delight for me. It was from this that I learned all about Napoleon, the Boer War and the Great War of 1914-1918.

Despite being generally aloof from his children, our father would sometimes read to us. He had a lovely speaking voice, steady and warm, although from time to time his false teeth would cause a clacking noise that was quite disconcerting for the listener. He also wrote with the copperplate script, slowly and deliberately, and he could tot pounds, shillings and pence accurately at a speed that amazed me. Above all, he had a twinkle in his eye and a sense of humour that always looked on the absurd side of things.

'The Flicks'

To a small boy, the movies – we called them the 'pictures' or 'the flicks' because the screen flickered as the film frames rolled on – held an overpowering attraction. Despite the fact that they were in black and white and had poor sound quality, they entranced us. We rode with the Lone Ranger, fenced with Errol Flynn and screamed at the indians who were showering the wagon train with arrows.

Remember that in those times, there were no mobile phones, no TVs, no fridges, no washing machines nor any of the electric conveniences we take for granted nowadays. The concept of computers, space travel, radio telemetry or even gates and doors that opened automatically were considered figments of the imagination. Orson Welles' *War of the Worlds* and Flash Gordon chasing evil men through the galaxies were regarded as Hollywood myths, invented to sate the unachievable dreams of the masses who slaved in factories and shops six days a week. We all needed to escape into fantasyland, even for a brief time, to make life bearable. Cinema with sound, the talkies – what will they think of next? – heralded the demise of the silent picture era. We laughed deliriously at the antics of Charlie Chaplain and were later regaled by Laurel and Hardy who in turn were replaced by the *Three Stooges* until finally Bud Abbot and Lou Costello took to the screen in the 1940s.

How we adored going to the cinema once a week on a Saturday afternoon. Waterford had three cinemas. The Savoy was on Baronstrand Street and lived up to its name by being the most luxurious cinema in town. The ground floor comprised of the reception and parterre and these contained the cheapest seats. The unfortunate occupants of these seats were frequently assailed by missiles thrown down from the more expensive balcony seats directly above. We would never do such a thing which we considered the height of vulgarity, only to be practised by 'corner-boys' and 'the lower classes'. No, generally we were brought by Mamma to the balcony where we sat demurely until collected about half past five. On occasions we would visit the café on the same level and there, say on a birthday, we would have lemonade and cake. It was in this café that I first saw, tasted and loved 'lady's finger cake'. This was a sponge cake, covered with cream and strawberries (or some fruit) and surrounded by 'lady finger' biscuits, which were thinly frosted with icing sugar and simply delicious to taste.

The Regal was a larger cinema situated down from Bally-bricken, not far from St Saviours Dominican Church on the Quay. We rarely went there unless there was a special film that Mamma thought we would like. I think that admittance was six pence. We believed that fleas could be picked up in the Regal and so made sure our coats were well tucked in around us.

The Coliseum was the third cinema, not far from Reginald's Tower and the present day Tower Hotel.

It was the cheapest of all three cinemas and definitely a flea-hazard. But they had great cowboy films (Westerns) which the adults called 'bang-bangs'. We kids shouted vociferously urging on 'the chap' (the good guy on a white horse), while he chased the bad guy (on a black horse). We did not mind that they raced around the same hill time and again, or that the chap seemed to have an inexhaustible supply of bullets in his six-shooter. We did not mind when the bad guy repeatedly fell for the old trick of shooting at a hat held up on a stick. We did not mind when the chap pretended to be dead and suddenly came to life at the crucial moment. We did not mind when he rode off into the sunset after cleaning out a gang of outlaws.

But we did mind when time was wasted with 'the chap' kissing the local saloon girl or schoolteacher, however pretty she looked. Then the talking in the cinema would rise to a crescendo and the more '*Shushes*' that were made, the greater the general din.

It was in this cinema that I first saw Elizabeth Taylor. She starred with Micky Rooney in *National Velvet* in 1944. She was 12 and I was 10. I thought she was lovely.

It was here too that my mother brought me to see *El Alamein*. It was so exciting and such a spectacle that Monty (Field Marshal Bernard Montgomery) became an instant hero for me. Nonetheless, like many others, I still preferred Erwin Rommel and, after seeing *The Desert Fox*, he stood head and shoulders – for me – above Monty. Although Tarzan, Charlie Chan and even the Lassie films enthralled us, we always preferred cartoons and Disney films such as *Snow White and the Seven Dwarfs* and *Alice in Wonderland*, although we pretended that they were too babyish for us by the time we were teenagers.

As for current affairs, we got the *Irish Independent* daily, and it is a sign of the innocence of those times that all of us followed its cartoon rhyming series, *Curly Wee and Gussie Goose*, with serious interest. I knew my parents also read the rest of the paper, including the column by Myles na gCapallín, but I confined myself to Curley Wee. The only other written media we bought – apart from religious magazines – was the *Dublin Opinion*. However, most of the jokes in that estimable journal were of a political nature, and they did not interest me.

After Charles E. Kelly was appointed editor, his cover-page cartoon was a regular feature. I mention this because later on his daughter, Mary Rose, entered pre-med with me in Dublin and was the first girl I ever 'dated'.

World War Two

The Second World War was an exciting interlude in our lives. I was too young to be aware of the lead up to the war, the gathering storm, as Churchill described those years. I was aware of the terrible war in Spain in which Franco emerged victor. As a staunch Roman Catholic family, we were fully on Franco's side, and failed to appreciate the menace of the fascist madness that was capturing the heartland of Europe. The rise of Benito Mussolini we greeted with mixed feelings. We were dismayed by his treatment of the Vatican and by his invasion of Abyssinia. But Dadda kept pointing out that the triumvirate of Hitler, Franco and Mussolini was a bulwark against the greater evil of Communism, which he saw as the greatest threat to humanity.

Besides, didn't Mussolini get the trains in Italy to run on time? Wasn't Hitler only seeking redress for the obvious injustice of the Treaty of Versailles? And hadn't Franco brought order to a chaotic country?

Our own fight for freedom and the subsequent Civil War had brought misery to thousands of Irish men and women. Economic ruin, unemployment, slave wages and mass emigration were the order of the day. The 'dirty thirties' held Ireland in a seemingly unbreakable grip. We all needed an '-ism' to hang on to.

From an early age, I was fascinated by the story of the assassination of Archduke Ferdinand in Sarajevo, the dramatic events in mother Russia with the murder of the last Czar and his family, and the rise in Communism. Lenin and Stalin became icons of evil. Leon Trotsky became an icon of good. Picasso, Kahlo, Monet, Matisse, Constable and so many other twentieth century painters seemed to me less attractive than those of the Renaissance during which I believed the architecture, sculpture and music surpassed anything in succeeding centuries. But back to the war – September 1939 and the 'phoney war'. Ireland remained neutral, much to the chagrin of both sides in the conflict, especially of Churchill, who derisively referred to the 26 counties as de Valera's 'cabbage patches' a phrase echoed tongue-in-cheek by Bernard Shaw in 1945 when he wrote of 'That powerless little cabbage garden called Ireland.... wins in the teeth of all the mighty powers'.

The coupling of Ireland with cabbage was not a new concept. The 'Battle of Widow McCormack's Cabbage Patch' had been used in 1848 to describe an incident when irish rebels ran in disarray from a handful of armed constables holed up in a small cottage. But in the dark days of the 1940s, Ireland's neutrality was a real and significant issue between Ireland and England, and nostalgia played no part in it. Dev remained obdurate despite a covert offer from Churchill that a united Ireland would be backed by Britain in exchange for the use of Irish ports. The famous radio exchange between Churchill and de Valera in 1945 remains to this day a remarkable example of passionate brilliance (Churchill) versus compelling statesmanship (Dev).

The war divided Mamma and Dadda. My mother was a Winston woman, totally against Hitler, a true devotee of the 'royal family', an absolute believer in British justice and fairness, and convinced of the impeccable behaviour of the good-humoured British Tommy. My father was the opposite. He admired Hitler and abhorred the injustice done to Germany in 1918 and thrilled in the efficiency of the Wehrmacht and Luftwaffe.

I do not think either knew anything about the way the Jews were being treated by the Nazis and equally they were unaware of the reluctance of the rest of the civilised world to help those being crushed by Hitler's thugs. The fledgling League of Nations itself was curiously inept and was even more toothless than the United Nations today.

Each day the *Irish Independent* published a map of how the war was going, indicating the advance or retreat of the Axis armies by black arrows and the movement of the Allies by white ones. I followed these maps keenly and they were, almost, but not quite, as important as our daily ration of 'Curly Wee and Gussie Goose', which I used to cut out and paste with glue into a cheap copybook.

The signs of war were few in neutral Ireland. Petrol was rationed and soon our car, a baby Ford, was up on blocks in the garage. Cycling or walking to town was probably good for us, but while it was downhill all the way from our house to the Mall and the Quay, coming home was not so easy. Often we would take Kennelly's bus (Billy's bus) back from the Clock Tower, still a prominent feature on the quays in Waterford. How we enjoyed those trips.

Occasionally, Thomas or Jim Magnier would be called. They were the first cousins of my mother on her mother's side. They were bachelor farmers living in a townland named Rathquague, about ten miles Southwest of Waterford city. Thomas was a big soft-spoken red-faced man whom my mother liked. He had two great qualities that appealed to her. He did not drink and he was generous (would bring us a bag of potatoes). On the debit side, he would hog the fire and we thought he would never leave, whatever hour he arrived.

On one visit, he showed us a pair of leather flying gloves he got from a German pilot who had ditched his plane near his farm. We were absolutely fascinated by them and kept putting them on and off. Thomas was in the local defence force (LDF, now called *An Fórsa Cosanta Aituil*, FCA) and had been with the party who apprehended the pilot. He told us the LDF party had guns that night (old Lee Enfields from the First World War) but no ammunition in them.

Thomas and Jim lived together. We preferred Thomas to Jim. Jim hardly said a word when we would meet him; Thomas never stopped talking. Jim I hardly remember at all.

They had two sisters, Helena and Peggy. All four were left orphaned when uncle Willie Magnier (Gran's brother) died. Gran took Peggy and Gran's sister, Lizzie, took Helena and reared them as if they were their own. Lizzie and her husband Tom Dempsey lived in 27 Daisy Tce, just down from Gran's residence, who lived in number 21. Tom and Lizzie had no children but were lovely to us and would listen to our prattle, something rare in times when children were 'seen and not heard'. Tom's brother was a Dominican priest who suffered much in China during the Communist revolution and who later died there.

Mamma always said Fr Dempsey was a saint. Gran minded Lizzie once she became a widow and my mother continued to mind her after Gran died. There was no need for an old folks' home in those days.

It is something of a misconception that people were much closer in 'the old days'. For apart from relations, few people came to visit us in Chatsfort. The Waterford I grew up in was quite reserved as far as visiting other people houses was concerned. There was no casual dropping in on neighbours as there was, for example, in the west of Ireland. This reserve may have had something to do with the strong influence English culture had on the east coast of Ireland as much as to the sort of people who lived in our area, Newtown, which was the most affluent part of the city.

Of course, our affluence was more imagined than real. We lived in a big house which we couldn't afford, we employed domestic and gardening staff which we couldn't afford and we kept up a show of money and of gentility which was a pretence.

Visitors

One of our few visitors was Fr Ralph Power, the curate in St Johns Church, Waterford. I liked Fr Ralph. He always saluted children and used to bring us a box of chocolates every Christmas. When visitors came, we were called down to say 'hello' and ushered out immediately afterwards to let the adults talk in peace. Our main hope was that the visitor would not eat too many biscuits or sandwiches so that we could scoff them later. On these occasions, the crusts were cut off the sandwiches and this gross waste made them an extra special treat for us.

Dr Myles Shelley was another friend who visited us time and again. In those days, GPs did 'rounds', but I think Dr Shelley sometimes just dropped in for a chat with Mamma. Each year we were trooped to his dispensary on the Mall and received a flu shot. These were delivered via glass syringes with blunt needles and were a dreaded ordeal. By common consent, we fixed our gaze on a picture of a 'drummer boy' who looked down on us impassively from the opposite wall. His very indifference seemed to steel us for the dreaded moment.

My Mother

Yes, a mother is special. She is surely the most special person in your early life. Certainly my mother influenced me not just in childhood but with an influence that continues to this day. The Jesuits say, 'Give me a child until the age of seven and I have him for life.' A mother might say, 'Give me a child for six months and I have him forever.'

My mother was a woman who was exceptional for her time. She genuinely thought 'outside the box', questioned all the 'holy cows' and had all the good features of today's feminist. She even favoured, well certainly did not dismiss out of hand, the notion of legalised prostitution – in the 1940s' Ireland!

Although a devout Roman Catholic, she would question many of the practices in our church ranging from the abuse of indulgences to mandatory celibacy and later to a woman's right to use contraception. She could see no rationalé for excluding women from the priesthood and decried the role of women in the church, which kept them subservient to men. She was keenly aware that many marriages were merely shams and kept intact for appearance sake.

She saw through many of the inconsistencies in the actual practice of the faith and spoke her mind freely to her family. She favoured divorce and re-marriage – in circumstances that fell short of the requirements for a church annulment. But she never favoured easy divorce.

On a practical level, as well as dealing with workmen, tradesmen, mechanics, overseeing the hiring and firing of servants, she did take care of Dadda's income tax and helped him sort out the process of election counts (Dadda was the returning officer for Waterford). She saw to the health, education and every other need of her children. If she erred, it was on the side of excessive worrying over trivia, a need to keep up appearances and perhaps in excessive expectations of her children.

She had an extremely practical and pragmatic view of life and of people. She could change a light bulb, fix a fuse, mend a switch or diagnose a fault in a motorcar (we started with a Rover, then a baby Ford and then a Ford Anglia – downward progression). Dadda could do none of these things. She could mow the lawn or trim a hedge – as good as any man – until she got sciatica. All in all she was a clever person, much cleverer than her brother uncle Michael who later became the professor of chemistry in Maynooth.

Like many a mother who carries responsibility for house, finances, children's upbringing and all domestic decisions, she tended to dominate her children's thinking and downgrade the father's role. Ultimately, this drove a wedge between her and some of her five offspring.

One story she told may give you some insights into how strict and puritanical she was in many ways.

She told how a guest at a dinner party noticed a slug in his cabbage. Not wishing to embarrass his hostess, he deliberately ate the slug not pretending to see it. My mother thoroughly approved.

My Father

My father, Thomas Andrew Colbert, was the youngest in a family of thirteen or fourteen children. His father, I believe, was in charge of the stables in Lord Waterford's estate. His mother died the night the *Titanic* sank and so my father always remembered April 14 with sadness. I was always under the impression that my uncle Paddy Colbert was lost in the *Titanic* that night, but my father never spoke about his family to us so I am not certain. Certainly, a Paddy Colbert was listed among those steerage passengers who were drowned that fateful night.

Dadda was the youngest member of the Colbert family who lived in Percy Terrace in Waterford city. I do not know about any formal education but he must have had enough because he secured a job as solicitor's clerk in *Dobbyn Tandy and McCoy* of Colbeck St, when still in his late teens. He aspired to higher things and ultimately graduated through his own efforts as a full solicitor, a most respected occupation then as now. This was no mean achievement in those days as it meant attending lectures in the Four Courts in Dublin and paying all fees.

Tom Colbert was a small dapper man who kept himself tidy and spruce. You never noticed his height for he always walked so upright that you thought he was tall man. He maintained this bearing until he died at 92 years of age.

Although essentially self-educated, he was well read and an excellent conversationalist – when he so desired.

He had a talent for music and played the piano by ear. My mother said that he always thumped the keyboard, but he was a good enough a performer to play in a local orchestra.

Socially he was often diffident and unassuming, but he was always charming, especially with women, and his office staff – all female – adored him. Indeed, we were well aware that Miss Maguire, the senior clerk, prepared all the office work so that Dadda merely rubber stamped every document that passed through her capable hands.

One of the less attractive features of his character was his tendency to project himself as a rich generous man – neither of which he was in reality. Thus, he tipped people, such as his barber, lavishly. He even gave sixpence, instead of two pence, for the fare when taking Kennelly's bus home from the Clock Tower to Chatsfort.

This 'big man' complex seriously annoyed my mother when we sold Chatsfort. He 'magnanimously' refused an offer of £3,000 from the Torries (the owners of the *L and N* grocery shops) and insisted on something in the region of £1,500 on the grounds that he only wanted as much as Chatsfort had originally cost!

This kind of false pride maddened my mother and with good cause. She had spent her life, saving every penny she could, fearing that she would be left destitute in her old age and recognising that, by the natural laws, Dadda would predecease her by many years.

It happened as she predicted, that is, my father died long before her. But by then she was secure financially and was cared for with extraordinary devotion by my sister Sibyl.

My father was almost 40 years of age when he married my mother who was barely 21. It was a mismatch in generation, in experience and in upbringing. He met my mother at her home when executing her parent's will. He probably dazzled her with his Colbert charm and his Rover motorcar. My mother's father, Patrick Casey, had little time for Tom Colbert. Hannah Casey, my grandmother, tolerated him until she came to live with us, when her toleration turned sour.

Grandad Casey gave the newlyweds a present of Chatsfort. But the good will stopped there. I do not think he spoke much to my father in the years that followed.

In time, my father was appointed county registrar. I think that he owed this post to the influence of Fr Tom Walsh OP who was a close friend of de Valera and had been chaplain to the 2nd Battalion, Dublin Brigade of the 'old' Irish Republican Army (IRA). The connection with Tom was via my mother's brother, uncle Michael, a fellow Dominican.

My Gran

Everyone should have a special gran. I had. We never called her Nana, although that is the usual term now. But Gran or Nana, it does not matter. Grandmothers are a special gift to all children, and I pity those who have none.

My own gran suffered from chronic bronchitis. She probably got this from standing long hours behind a counter in
Hearne's shop on the Quay, where she ultimately became a
'buyer' in the ladies section. Of course, like all employees in
those days, Gran worked six days a week for a pittance in a
cold drafty, gloomy environment. When Sibyl was about ten
years old, she wrote a poem about Gran's bronchitis. There
is no doubt in my mind that Sibyl was the most creative and
talented of us five children. For by 1940 we were five, our baby
sister Helen having joined us as an afterthought that year.

You could say that Gran was uneducated. Her formal
education finished in National School in Doneraile, where
Canon Sheehan wrote many of his novels.

But Gran was from a big family, impoverished after the
famine. Consequently, they could only afford to give their
children a basic education and then watched and grieved as
most of them emigrated to the United States or Australia.

Only four remained in Ireland, my gran, Hannah, aunt
Lizzie (Waterford), aunt Ellie (Glanworth, Co Cork) and uncle
Willie (Co Waterford). They did well whether they stayed or
left. All were exemplary people, highly principled and digni-
fied. But I think that my gran was the best of them all. She was
the one who held the family together, who saw that none 'went
in want', who made sure that when uncle Willie Magnier's wife
died the two boys (Thomas and Jim) stayed with him on the
farm and that the two girls would be reared by aunt Lizzie and
herself.

As I said earlier Lizzie reared Helena and Gran took in
Peggy. Poor Helena became virtually stone deaf from untreated
otitis media as a child, a disability that ultimately distorted her
life. She was said to be odd. But I liked her and her quiet ways.
Peggy, her sister, was outgoing and full of 'life', and was probably the more popular of the two. She became Mrs Mulcahy

when she married a Garda who I remember well because he had red hair and was very friendly and pleasant to us.

I often stayed in Gran's house when I was a child, sometimes alone, sometimes with Sibyl. There was a garden at the back in which I played, made pretending cities and had pretending wars between good and bad countries. We slept upstairs in a big bed and slept soundly. There was a bathroom off this room. This was the only bathroom and toilet in the house. Gran would wash my dirty legs – especially my grimy knees – every night. I hated my hair being washed. It was thick and curly and combing out the tangles was always an ordeal.

Worse still was the routine, whether at home or in Gran's, of using the 'fine comb' to clear nits. This was almost as bad as our weekly dose of cod liver oil or the black *Syrup of figs*, which was doled out religiously to keep our intestines moving.

Gran made apple tarts. They were fine, except that the crusts were thick and dry, and we all hated eating that part of the tart. This annoyed Gran who very justly scolded us for wasting good food.

Gran was proud and strict but very fair and generous to all. I would walk with her to 10 a.m. Mass in St Saviours Dominican Church on the Quay near the bridge each morning, and woe betide me if the seams of my socks were not straight. No wonder I dreamed of having long pants. This was the privilege of boys who were in secondary school and old enough to wear them. I had clothes for Sunday and clothes for the rest of the week. That was it.

After Mass, Gran would buy me a chocolate or an ice cream in Phelans in O'Connell St. They were very nice to me, but then, we children were invariably polite and only 'spoke when spoken to'.

My gran died on 9 September 1950. I was 15 years old and just back in boarding school in Newbridge. I returned home for the funeral and am ashamed to say that I was more excited about getting an unexpected break than in grieving for my grandmother.

Poor dear Gran. She died in our house, Glencove, in Tramore, and was buried in the O'Donnell grave in the most ungetatable hilltop graveyard near Glenanar, Co Cork. I visited her grave years later, and I still remember that fine lady every day of my life. I always picture her wearing a black dress with a black shawl and having a proud stately bearing. To 'steal a pin, it is a sin' was one of her sayings. It epitomises her innate integrity and unfailing sense of right and wrong.

Although she was strict, she was also generous and loving. I will meet her again and truly express how much I loved her but was unable to say so during life on this earth. It is certainly one of my failings that I seldom if ever tell anyone how close they are to me. It just makes me embarrassed. It is perhaps more a Casey than a Colbert trait, I do not know. Mind you I have no problem in telling a child that I love them.

First Time in Dublin

When my mother had to get her appendix out, she decided to bring me along to get my tonsils removed at the same time. So together with Gran, we set off to Dublin on the train. Now the train was a steam engine run on a burned timber, coke and coal. But during the war, it ran mostly on turf wet turf. This meant that it would take 4–5 hours to get to Dublin from Waterford if you were lucky.

The train had no heating, and no toilets, and there was no food or drink on board. But I thrilled to its *chug chug*, I loved its long whistles, I adored going through tunnels and was childishly proud of the green colour that all trains and buses were painted at that time.

We arrived tired, hungry and truly weary in Kingsbridge (now Heuston station) and took a taxi to Eccles Street. We only took taxis or hackney cabs on rare occasions, a habit that most of my generation shares to this day. On arrival at Eccles Street, we mounted the steps of Clerkins guesthouse. This was a gloomy cold Georgian building which looks much the same today as it did then, although it is now converted to rooms for consultants from the Mater hospital. It stood almost right across from the hospital and was to be our home during our stay in Dublin. But for me, an eight-year-old boy from the country, my thoughts were not on the guesthouse or the hospital or on Mamma's and Gran's worries, but about being in a *real city* for the first time.

It was worth coming to Dublin just to see the trams. They came like great beasts rattling along the tracks, sparks flying off their antler-like overhead antennae and flashes of incandescent light sparkling as their iron wheels screeched to a halt on the iron tracks. Trams had a special smell and even that made my heart jump. And then there was the tingling anticipation of waiting at a tram stop. First, you heard the distant faint clanking which grows louder and louder as the tram approached. Then a siren warned that the tram was very near. Finally, it came in view lurching forward like a giant green monster getting larger and larger by the second.

Now myriads of sparks scatter at all angles from the overhead wires and that adds more to the excitement.

Finally, the tram groans and creaks to a halt like an old sailing ship, and you wait impatiently for an elderly woman to get off, all the time fearing that it will start again without you. But you get on in time and it starts to lurch forward while you are still trying to get you balance and find a seat near the front with a good view. Upstairs if possible. How I loved those winding stairs to the top. And the ticket collector with his box of tickets hanging from a strap around his neck would take your penny or tuppence and, with a sharp ping, punch a small hole in your ticket to indicate what fare you had given. He had different coloured tickets. The cheapest were brown, and then there were red and blue ones presumably if you were going much further. Magic.

Gran would sit beside me, dressed up in her best black dress and coat with her shawl tightly tucked around her head to protect her from the wind. She even climbed upstairs after her grandson. Little did I know or care that old ladies might have arthritis. I was a thoughtless scamp.

But we were not in Dublin for tram rides.

Mr Eddie Doherty removed my tonsils. Little did either of us know at the time that I would study medicine with his son, Eddie junior, many years later in University College Dublin (UCD).

However, studying medicine was far from my mind as I was put in a gown and rolled into the theatre on a squeaky trolley.

I still vividly remember the white robed nurses looking like wraiths from another world and I remember seeing the white tiled walls, the ominous centre table and the big central light hanging from the ceiling. Most of all I remember the overpowering smell of carbolic or whatever they used in those days to disinfect the place.

I was asked to slide on to the table, and without ceremony, a black rubber mask was clamped down on my face completely covering my nose and mouth. I was too terrified to make a sound but when someone said 'Good boy…take deep breaths…count to a hundred…', I obeyed automatically.

I whirled down into sleep just like Alice falling down the hole into Wonderland. The looming outlines of the doctors and nurses faded into a haze, and then, suddenly, there was oblivion.

I awoke in a ward of four beds. The children's ward. My throat was very sore, but they gave me jelly to eat and hot milk to drink. That was okay. I remember a girl in the opposite bed. She was ten years old I think, much more advanced than me. She came from Cabra; No. 8 tram used to go there. She seemed to me so smart and knowledgeable that it made me feel inferior. I thought that she had very nice hair. It was long and brown and curly. She was like Shirley Temple. I do not remember her name.

Next day I was allowed to visit my mother who had her appendix removed the same day that I had my tonsillectomy. Charlie McCauley was her surgeon. Charlie McCauley used to smoke a lot. He used to go into the theatre with a lighted ciga-rette in his mouth. He said that the ash was sterile, so there was no need to worry! Perhaps he did not appreciate the inflamma-ble nature of the anaesthetics used in those days, in particular of ether and chloroform. Of course, nitrous oxide (laughing gas) was used widely then. It was the only non-flammable gas they used apart from carbon dioxide.

My mother's hospital room was typical of the old Geor-gian houses for which Dublin is famous. It had high ceilings, ornate coving, a centre 'rose', drafty wooden windows, heavy velvet curtains and a black grate fireplace, in which smoulder-ing damp turf produced an erratic warmth interspersed with clouds of white smoke, which billowed like a white parachute into the room and set us all coughing every time the door opened or the wind changed the direction.

My memories of this interlude in Dublin are very clear in some respects. I remember that my mother developed a wound haematoma, which needed draining. She was well aware that a haematoma would not have occurred had all bleeders been properly tied off. Dr Shelley, our local GP, afterwards called this 'sloppy surgery'. My mother was quite plump, well, fat really. I now know that it is very difficult to stop all bleeding when you cut through two inches of fat so I have some belated sympathy for surgeon McCauley.

I also remember slipping out of the hospital and taking No. 8 tram to the 'pillar'. In those days, Nelson stood atop a tall pillar in O'Connell St (erstwhile Sackville St), and it was only afterwards that, as a student, for 3d (3 pence) I actually climbed to the top. In 1966, it was blown up by the IRA, the fiftieth anniversary of the 1916 rising. Today its place is taken by 'the Spire', but most old timers still talk nostalgically of the 'Pillar' whatever their political allegiance.

In any event here I was, an eight-year-old boy, alone in the big city, totally ignorant of the doings of Horatio Nelson and taking my first ever tram ride on my own. I got off at the 'pillar' and went into a sweet shop close to the General Post Office. I think that I only looked and did not buy anything. I returned to the Mater a couple of hours later, also by tram, quite unaware that a search had been started for me.

I got severely scolded by my distraught mother and by Gran and by a fat nun. But they were so relieved to see me that I escaped the chastisement I deserved.

Nowadays, such an event would be taken very seriously indeed. In those times, no one accosted me or no one even noticed me. This feature of my character, this wandering off, was to remain with me all my life.

Are All Children Saints?

As a child, religion became part of my very being. I do not think that I was any different to most other children at the time nor do I think that I have grown up to be a fanatic. However, I revelled in the lives of the Saints and secretly wanted to become a martyr. I think that I was unconsciously wanting to copy Teresa of Avilla and her brother who as children set off from home to Christianise the world. In my mind, I relived the stories of Lourdes and Fatima and the deeds of holy men and women.

Damien the Leper was one of my favourite saints and the name Molokai conjured up for me all that was noble about the human spirit. Something of these childhood dreams echoed in my heart when I chanced on Damien the Leper's tomb in Louvain many years later.

I remember too that I sometimes squeezed the image of the cross, at the end of the rosary beads, so tightly into my palm, that I drew blood. That made me happy. To co-suffer with the Lord was an honour. None of this was special to me for I have no doubt that many children felt the same.

My early interest in Jesus, Mary and the Saints was fostered by my mother and by Gran. I suppose that I could be called fanatic since I wanted to talk to the Protestant minister who lived near us to explain that the 'Reformation' was a mistake. I liked that austere saintly old man and worried about his soul! My mother forbade me talk to him – with a good reason. I have no doubt that he would have received me kindly in any case.

Not Quite a Saint....
More a Bold Schoolboy

Of course, it is easier to die a (quick) martyr's death than live a saintly life in the gruelling day-to-day world where temptations of every kind surround you. I know that I was often, surly, uncommunicative and downright bold if I did not get my own way. One of my major weaknesses was the possession of a nasty temper which often got me into trouble.

One example is enough to show you what I mean. I was probably seven or eight years when I cycled to town from

Chatsfort, along the quays, across the bridge and on to Ferry-bank School, which was near the chapel of ease on the far side of the river, the Kilkenny side. I had revenge on my mind. Norbert, my brother, had told me that the boys from Ferrybank had thrown stones at the boys from Waterpark (his school). So this was retaliation. I would teach them a lesson!

I parked my bike against the low stone wall that bounded the school playground and watched for a few minutes as the children there played games, hopped and skipped around and generally created a din of screams and shouts and laughter.

There were some stones nearby which the road sweep-ers had piled into a large mound, waiting to be taken away I suppose. I picked one up and threw it into the middle of the yard. It hit someone on the back. I threw another and it hit someone else. Now a sea of angry faces turned towards me and one big lad started running in my direction. I felt a flurry of fear as he approached, but I had the advantage. I had a bike and he had to jump over the wall. I hopped up on the saddle and pumped my legs as fast as I could, all the time hearing, or thinking I could hear, an angry mob of schoolchildren shout-ing and threatening me with a fate worse than death.

The three miles home seemed interminable when at last I arrived, sweaty, exhausted and bone weary, but nonetheless triumphant.

Primary School, Waterpark College

I hardly attended primary school at all. Perhaps I was there for three months or so, but I do not think I learned anything there. However, I do remember that I had three special friends. They were Bill Davis and Gerald Griffin (GG) and Declan Power. We ganged a bit together and acted tough. I have no idea what happened to them in later life. I thought that GG's freckles were cool.

I remember just one teacher, a Mr Smith, mostly because he had us in a semicircle one day and, when one boy answered something incorrectly, he made us all put out our hands and went through the lot of us systematically lashing us with a leather strap.

I remember him in connection with something else too. At some time during my short sojourn in Waterpark, two big boys jumped on me and started twisting my arm. I think that I had been teasing them. I would not give in until the pain became intense and then I started to howl. They ran off. Luckily, Mr Smith happened to come by. Mr Smith was not known for his kindness. Indeed, there were few teachers more ready to use the strap than he. However, he saw my distress was genuine and told me to go to the Infirmary, about a mile across the town. I walked there holding my left arm as steady as I could all the while in severe pain.

The Infirmary in Waterford had been a leprosarium many years earlier, and it was a bleak inhospitable looking building situated at the base of John's Hill. You entered by a side door and immediately were assailed by the smell of a red carbolic soap. I sat on a long bench inside the door and waited patiently to be seen by someone. Eventually, a nurse came along who asked my name. She seemed to recognise the name Colbert (Dadda's home in Percy Terrace was off Johns Hill) and took pity on me. She got me to see a doctor who managed to have an X-ray done on my elbow.

I had broken my left humerus just above the elbow joint, a supracondylar fracture. Our GP, Dr Shelley 'set' it twice, but it never came right, even to this day. I remember the plaster cast becoming very tight and my fingers becoming blue, and I remember crying with pain. They say that you cannot remember pain. I am a proof that you can.

Luckily, they split the plaster in time. That saved the blood flow to my fingers. Otherwise, I am sure that I would have developed what is called *Volkmann's ischaemic contracture* – and perhaps lost a few fingers from gangrene.

My lost schooling, because of this fracture, was compounded by the fact that I got quite ill with scarlet fever about this time. In this condition, you get a severe 'strep' sore throat followed by an itchy desquamating red rash all over the body. I was kept in a room by myself in Chatsfort and a white sheet was hung over the door to keep out – or keep in – germs. All my meals were brought to me on a tray and a fire was kept going in the grate. After two weeks, I was still sick and remained sick for longer than expected. As a result, Dr Shelley examined me again and again, and ultimately believed that he could feel my spleen.

A similar illness had occurred in two of his other young patients, and one of them died of abortus fever. She was eleven I think.

Mattie Maugham, the public health doctor, was called in and blood was sent to Dublin for a Widal test. This was positive. It was either typhoid or abortus fever, and there was no treatment for either. Luckily, I got gradually better, but it took many months. During that time, I was treated with special care by my mother. I read and re-read books and listened to *Workers Playtime* from the BBC every day on the radio. *The Archers* (an everyday story of country folk) on BBC radio was very popular; my mother and I always associated that programme with Walter Gabriel and his deep Cornwall accent. Like the rest of the country, we listened to Joe Linnane and *Question Time* on Radio Eireann. This was an eagerly awaited programme that took place once a week and always followed the same format;

two two-mark, two four-mark and two six-mark questions. I also remember Lord Haw Haw and *Germany Calling*. He would sound a mournful bell for each allied ship the German U-boats sank that day, and he repeated this macabre performance day after day. There was something both fascinating and exciting about him.

My close association with Dr Shelley, my mother's intelligent interest in all things related to medical, and my reading of books such as A.J. Cronin's novels, all contributed to my desire to be a doctor some day. That desire never left me.

However, it was teeth that troubled us more than medical illness in those days. Teeth were always a problem. My mother was a great believer in taking teeth out once they caused pain. So one by one, we all lost teeth. As you know, conservative dentistry was only in its infancy in the forties and, unless you were very poor or idiosyncratic, all elderly people wore dentures. It was absolutely the norm.

Sibyl bled a lot after a particularly hard extraction, so much so that she had to stay in the Infirmary. I visited her once or twice at night walking by myself from Chatsfort, along Passage Road, then to Johns Hill and into her room, where I just sat and said nothing. I probably waited 5-10 min. Then I said goodbye and scampered down the hospital stairs rather than taking the awful cage of the lift that served all four floors. This was the only lift in Waterford.

My walks back to Chatsfort took place in complete darkness. I made it from the lamp post to lamp post, watching their shadows shorten and then lengthen as I moved on. And all the time, I felt uneasy until I came to the junction of Passage Road and Newtown Road and could see home.

I think that I even experienced mild panic on these excursions, a victim of my own imagination. There was a little jug at home with the inscription 'From ghosts and ghoulies may the good Lord deliver us.' I often thought that ghoulies – presumably worse than ghosts – must be something really terrifying. I was sure that they were ready to pounce on little boys walking alone at night along Passage Road.

Dangerous Play

I played a lot with my younger sister Helen and even made a house for the two of us in the woods. It was a sunny summer afternoon and suitable, I thought, for the two of us to leave home and take up residence in our forest home. After an hour or so siting on broken stools, we started to get cold and hungry, so I decided to light a fire and cook a few sausages that I had taken from the pantry (no fridges I those days). Very soon I had a good fire burning and a thick plume of smoke was wafting skywards through the warm afternoon air. How lucky it was that my mother was at the kitchen window watching everything. The fire was now beginning to spread alarmingly, but two buckets of water extinguished it completely. I cannot remember whether my mother was more angry than relieved. I do know that we never built a forest house again, ever.

Christmas

Ah Christmas! For a child, nothing can compare with Christmas. First of all, there was the lead up to the magical date of the 25th of December. In the kitchen, there was an extra air of urgency, an extra hustle and bustle. Raisins, sultanas, flour, brown sugar, almonds, castor sugar and many other necessary items were bought in Breens on the bridge, and stacked away in tins and boxes, until they would be used to make Christmas cakes and plum puddings.

My mother always bought a crate of lemonade bottles as a special treat for Christmas. These were divided up amongst us in as fair a way as possible. We were each allotted two bottles on Christmas day and two on St Stephens's day. That left just one bottle for each of us, which we could take whenever we wanted during the following days. And that was it. How we savoured the lemonade. We preferred it to the colourless lemon soda, which probably tasted exactly the same but lacked the rich red colour of lemonade.

Walking to Mass on the Christmas Eve was an exciting and joyful duty, and so was looking at the crib and wondering about the angels, the shepherds and, of course, the holy family. I am not sure I prayed much, but I was surely filled with wonder and excitement as I sat tired but starry-eyed in the cold pews of St Johns Church. Santa always came. Not in an impersonal way but to each of our beds, where he laid individual presents, which he managed to tailor to our dreams.

Do I Want My Parents to Separate?

I ask this from the child's point of view. Separation and divorce are focused on the needs and desires of adults, in particular of parents, and not about the needs and desires of children. That is not to say that there are some, yes, many marriages that should never have taken place or that become impossible to sustain or are even wrong for the children. On the other hand, no relationship is always perfect and always one has to forgive, reconcile, start again, and again and again.

So not everything was serene and happy in my parent's marriage nor was everything serene and happy in my childhood.

We were always made aware that money was scarce. Chatsfort was a huge house to maintain and paying the staff was a big drag on our finances. There was constant scrimping and saving, saving for 'the rainy day'. It caused much disharmony between my mother and father, but mostly the discord came from the disparity in ages and outlook and backgrounds.

The cost was a succession of rows, silences and bouts of palpable tension which seemed to get worse once my gran came to live with us. However, life for us children went on as normal, and we started to accept that things would never get better and hope that they would never get worse.

One incident, however, is indelibly imprinted on my mind. I was six years old and did not really understand the world of adults. I remember my mother waking me and telling me to get dressed quickly and that 'we were going to grans'. She spoke tersely and I obeyed mechanically not really understanding the implications of what she was saying. It was probably about 9 p.m. and, since it was dark, it must have been winter.

I came down the stairs to the hall to see Neville, Sibyl and Norbert, all fully dressed and wearing overcoats, just standing there silently. Mamma appeared after a few moments and tucked Helen, the baby, into the go-car. Then she shooed us all out the hall door. I can't remember any talk, even at this stage.

Dadda suddenly appeared on the top step and begged Mamma to stay, but she did not answer. We followed her, not understanding what was happening. My eldest brother, Neville, now turned 14, stayed with Dadda. The rest of us kept going, sensing that things were badly wrong.

Later, I was told that it was about Dadda drinking whiskey. Now, I am not sure, I still do not know the real cause.

In any event, my mother marched us all from Chatsfort to her mother's house in Daisy Terrace, a distance of about three miles. I clearly remember us trudging along Lombard Street, the Mall and the quays until we arrived at Daisy Terrace. The streetlights cast long shadows behind us and I can still feel the eerie excitement that any child feels when being mysteriously brought out for the first time into the night.

Gran's face, on opening her hall door, is etched on my memory. Her face physically fell as she saw us all there shivering in the cold. Separations were rare in those days, divorce impossible. A catholic wife stuck with her husband and was 'subject to him' no matter what. And yet this extraordinary event washed over me as almost an adventure or just 'another row' that would soon come to an end.

I think that we stayed away about two weeks, perhaps longer. Neville, stayed with Dadda all the time, but even that did not impinge on me then.

CHAPTER 2

NEWBRIDGE COLLEGE

Abandon Hope All Ye Who Enter Here

I was 9, going to be 10 in October, when I was sent to board with the Dominicans in Newbridge College, Co Kildare. I had spent only a few months in primary school and so was, in reality, beginning my formal education from scratch. It is true that I had been given private piano lessons by Bertie Downey in Manor Street, but they were discontinued early when my mother found out that he was rapping me repeatedly on the knuckles. This occurred when I played a wrong note and was probably due to the fact that I needed glasses to see the music sheet properly. I also went to Miss Deasey for Irish lessons. She was very nice, elderly and even grandmotherly. But every time she spoke, she emitted a spray of small spits. As a result, I gave most of my attention to ducking them rather than to learning Irish. Dadda gave me sums, but he only did so now and then, and there was no logic or method in his teaching and I learned little. Thus, boarding school remained the only option if I were to learn anything at all. My elder brothers Neville and Norbert were already boarders in Newbridge, and my sister Sibyl was a boarder in the Dominican convent in Wicklow. Although both Wicklow and Newbridge were fee-paying schools, life was tough for boarders and especially rigid in schools run by nuns.

In Newbridge, we slept on iron beds in large dormitories. We were given one hard pillow, two thin blankets, two white sheets (our own) and a cheap white bedspread. This was fine in the summer but icy cold in the winter. Before getting into bed, there was a mandatory washing of face and hands in cold water. Several of us shared each washbasin, so it was first come first served. After brief ablutions, we jumped into our beds and, for most of the year, cuddled up in the foetal position to keep ourselves warm.

Night prayers were said by the priest in charge. For Juniors and 'Ellers' (first years), the Vice Dean, Fr Tom Hegarty, used to say the prayers. He was normally a strict disciplinarian but showed a softer side at night when, before turning the lights out, he told stories about 'Blackshirt' to a hushed audience of 10-12 years old who lay quiet as mice between ice-cold sheets.

Blackshirt was a modern Zorro who performed daring feats in order to rescue kidnapped children or destroy diabolical devices which were in the hands of 'bad guys'. Even today, when I meet grown-up men who were at school with me, Fr Tom's stories remain an abiding happy memory and we talk of them with great nostalgia.

Rugby was an important part of my life in Newbridge. I put my heart into rugby just as I put my heart into studies, and I truly loved both. Most schoolboys dream of playing for Ireland and I was no exception.

There was one incident during a match that I will never forget. It was a home match, played on a pitch across the road from the college, and the day was fine. Our opponents were either Blackrock or Terenure College – I cannot remember which. In any event, I made an intercept as they were attacking close to our line. It was an easy intercept. The guy was obviously going to pass the ball to his out-half when I sprang forward, caught the ball, and ran like mad towards their goal. No one was near me.

I could hear the cheering from the sidelines and, as I neared the try line, I turned around to acknowledge the applause of my supporters. In my excitement, I never noticed that I was running straight towards the right hand upright. Bang, I smacked full tilt into it, so hard that I saw stars. I was concussed for a moment but recovered in time to realise that I had fallen on the ball and that everyone was still cheering me. I somehow managed to play on but have no memory of the rest of the game. As the preacher says, *'vanitas vanitarum et omnia est vanitas.'* So much for vanity.

By the time I was sixteen years old, I was playing with both the junior and senior cup teams. Although not really an outstanding player myself, I captained the only Newbridge team to ever win the Leinster Junior Cup and did so against a fancied Blackrock College team. As a result, Fr Hegarty and I became fairly close for he had trained the team almost like a father to the chosen fifteen.. This probably made me appear 'cocky' (a word we often used), although I was not conscious of being that way.

Being on the cup team meant special treatment. We got gruel every evening during 'cup time' and we loved it. No doubt, this contributed to the 'speed, sprightliness and stamina' that Fr Hegarty kept shouting at us during training sessions.

You see I had had a love-hate relationship with him depending on his moods on a particular day. I was too young to understand that adults have their own hidden problems and I was too selfish to care. I reckon now that putting a young man of 30 years of age in charge of a group of boys was not what any young priest wanted or expected on becoming a Dominican. I suspect that Tom Hegarty and his contemporaries almost certainly hoped to work in the missions, convert thousands and be 'out there' to help people in the real world. Newbridge must have frustrated many a priest who thought that he would have a different, more fulfilling prospect ahead of him when he entered religious life.

And so I now begin to understand the Fr Hegarty who put me down in no uncertain manner as the following incident shows.

Corporal Punishment, the Old-Fashioned Way

In my last year, I was made school vice-captain. This entailed sleeping in the Eller dormitory, where I was expected to maintain law and order among the boys after lights out. One evening, after winning a cup match in Dublin, I returned to Newbridge and distributed a bag of cheap sweets to the boys. They were absolutely delighted with such an unexpected treat and crowded around me hoping to get more good things from Mr Hero.

At that moment, Fr Hegarty barged in, all red-faced and obviously in a foul temper. 'Back to bed boys…NOW…', he bellowed.

They did not need a second warning. They scuttled back to their beds like frightened mice and I was left alone to face the music.

'Who do you think you are Colbert?' He stood there quivering in anger.

I made my first mistake.

'We won the match… I was only giving them a treat…', my voice sounded strained and hard and probably impertinent. I had not addressed him as Sir or Father. I really did not mean to be rude at that point. But then he spat out four words, unfair and unforgivable as far as I was concerned.

'Put out your hand'. There was venom in those words.

He had the power and both of us knew it. I stuck out my hand defiantly and eyeballed him. Another mistake.

He carefully pulled up the wide loose sleeve of his habit, flexed a long thin bamboo cane with both hands, and then lashed out at my upturned palm. After six lashes, and with searing pain in my fingers, I lowered my arm, but there was to be no respite. He beckoned that I put out my other hand and I did so, deliberately and defiantly, still eyeballing him. He proceeded to inflict another six.

I continued to stare at him, eye to eye, throughout the ordeal, ignoring the awful pain in my fingers. I just hated him at that moment. I was being humiliated before my charges by a sadist; yet when I turned my back on him and got into bed, I felt triumphant.

I hid my tears of shame and pain and anger as I silently massaged my throbbing purple fingers and prayed to Christ for strength.

It was a battle of wills and I had won. My coldness to Hegarty was palpable afterwards. In later life, I learned that it is better to shrug off past hurts than to let them simmer inside you like poison spreading in a pond.

Fr Hegarty was posted in later life to Tralee. I regret not having ever visited him in my adult life. My final verdict is that he was a good person, better that I would ever know.

I Loved School

I confess that was the only bad experience I had in Newbridge. Otherwise I loved the place. I was lucky in being consistently at the top of my class, in doing extremely well in my Intermediate and Leaving examinations and in excelling on the rugby pitch. I even got first place in Ireland in History in the Intermediate Certificate exam but was perversely disappointed that I had not achieved first place in science, which my uncle Michael taught.

Food, rugby and study were the three things that dominated school life.

School food was awful. Six boys sat at each table. But the vice-dean or dean (Fr Tom Hegarty or Fr Canice O'Riordan) ate separately on a raised dais at a separate table – adorned with a tablecloth. Their presence was essential to keep law and order, and we could not start before they said the 'grace'. They got far better food than us. We were always hungry.

The poor girl who came with the trays to each table could hardly stand up straight when six boys jumped to grab the biggest looking meal. I still remember with disgust the small yellow–green patties of margarine, one for each of us, which we spread sparingly on thin slices of bread. But I still remember with delight dinner on Thursdays which consisted of a small chop, a small overcooked sausage, mashed potatoes and veg all covered in brown gravy. On rare occasions, you might find a second sausage under the mash presumably there by mistake.

Sometimes the cold beat the hunger. For on many occasions, in those freezing dark windswept Kildare winters, I slipped a hot boiled potato into my trouser pocket after lunch so that I could keep my hands warm for a while afterwards.

But there were also good days in the 'ref'. Halloween saw barmbracks sent from home and guys shared these generously. Country lads might get a pound of real butter. This was divided among the lads at his table – with the birthday boy getting first go at it. If a boy's birthday was during term, there was bound to be a parcel with goodies. My brothers and I got few parcels from home and I was often ashamed of contributing so little to my table.

On the other hand, having uncle Michael a priest on the staff – although a mixed blessing – gave me privileges that other boys did not have. He often brought me to his room and gave me lemonade and fruitcake. And although kids normally detest fruitcake, I devoured anything he gave me. I also enjoyed the comfort of his warm cosy room, the glow of the fire in the grate and the soft leather chair that I sat in while he talked to me across a cluttered desk. I even tolerated the distinctive smell in his room which I now realise is common to all elderly men's rooms.

The priests' house was well heated, and entering its portals brought you into a whole new civilised world. My uncle was the science teacher in Newbridge and was well loved by the boys who nicknamed him 'Hiawatha'. He later transferred to Maynooth where he was appointed Professor of Chemistry.

Good Days

We all loved Allen Day. This was in the summer term when the days were long and sunny. The whole school trudged off to the Hill of Allen where we were told Fionn MacCumhaill and the Fianna, hunted and feasted long ago. However, all we did was drink tea and guzzle down as many big thick ham sandwiches as we could grab. It was just a super day out, and we were all happy.

Of course, we also had a 'tuck day' once a week, and the race to the tuck shop was worthy of an Olympic medal. The fleetest of foot got to the shop first and had the choice of a Kit Cat or a Crunchy or a Dairy Milk bar, while the slower ones were left with fruit gums.

Summer term was great. Long lazy days by the banks of the river Liffey, sneaking out of bounds to a little shop beyond the Pavilion, wearing our 'whites', playing tennis and finally taking part in Sports Day and maybe winning a medal or some boring book.

In reality, winter was good too. We had many rugby matches involving trips to Dublin to play Blackrock, Terenure, Belvedere and Kings Hos. Always there was a 'feed' after the match. A 'feed' usually consisted of rashers and sausages, lots of bread and big bottles of lemonade. All of which we consumed like little savages.

Teachers Do Matter, But Not Just for Their Teaching

There were many priests and teachers who made a life-long impression on me.

My uncle Michael is top of the list. He had been Assistant State Analyst before entering the Dominican Order, and it was natural that he was put in charge of the science labs when appointed to Newbridge College.

The science block was a separate building, at the side of the college, and so it was completely his demesne where he spent many hours with retorts, bunsen burners, test tubes and bell jars. These were his implements of trade and he used them for all kinds of experiments, most of which proved nothing.

But he was a brilliant teacher. His methods were innovative and always interesting. He made his own slides and projected them on a handmade projector long before this became common practice in schools. He sent out Charlie Callaghan, the College factotum, to find stray cats, which he anaesthetised and dissected in front of the senior classes in order to show the students a beating heart and squirming intestines. He would then give the cat a lethal dose of paraldehyde and bury the carcass in a patch of spare ground where it would 'contribute to the nutrition of the soil'. A classmate of mine, Seamus Collins, told me lately that Charlie once brought him a lovely white cat which my uncle duly dispatched for the class. Unfortunately, the cat was the pride possession of one of the older priests. Neither uncle Michael nor I were told the truth at the time.

He also had a passion for botany and brought in all kinds of wild flowers and weeds, and showed us how to identify and classify them into different families. I remember some to this day such as the *cruciferae* and *papilionaceae*.

However, chemistry was his real love. One of his experiments that buzzed among us boys was his attempt to analyse gases. The analysis that caught our imagination was his effort to discover if the type of food one ate changed the composition of subsequent flatus.

As part of this study, he found that methane gas increased considerably after eating leguminous plants such as peas and beans. Now methane, CH_4, is a flammable gas. Hiawatha was of the opinion that if you ate enough peas, your subsequent flatus would contain enough methane to explode if lighted. I am quite serious.

He picked a group of five volunteers, fed them peas and that evening during recreation gathered them in the Pavilion (the 'Pav'), where he proceeded to strike matches whenever one of the volunteers made a fart.

Onlookers could hardly contain their laughter. The volunteers did their best to oblige, but few could muster up enough wind to shake a feather. There was noise all right. Onlookers contributed their intellectual expertise by simulating rude noises (perhaps not all the noises were simulated) and in general there was bedlam.

The experiment was a total failure. All it did was prove that matches usually came alight when struck properly.

I was not personally present in the Pav that evening and merely repeated what I have been told by others.

But it must have been fun.

Hiawatha never physically chastised anybody but could lacerate you with words of scorn if you ruined an experiment or said something stupid in class.

However, many of us remember him as essentially a kind man with special kindness to anyone who was sick.

Although there was a school nurse, boys often got sick at night or on weekends, and then Hiawatha was the man to go to. He had some special black fluid he would put on an aching tooth and a special potion – I think it had Friars Balsam in it – which cleared sniffy noses instantly. He immersed swollen limbs in ice-cold water and had several immediate cures for warts and hiccoughs, most of which depended on giving the unfortunate a sudden fright. Then he would laugh hilariously.

Fr Tom Walsh was the headmaster during my early time in Newbridge. He was a close friend of Hiawatha. Although blustery and friendly, he was also a strict disciplinarian.

As a headmaster he had no teaching responsibilities despite being fluent in Irish. But he kept an eye on everything in the classroom. He came to my classroom one day while we were having a Greek lesson. The teacher asked me to translate some passage from *Medea*, which I duly did, and Fr Tom praised me in front of everybody. I was very pleased. We seldom got openly praised in those days.

The boys nicknamed Fr Tom 'misery'. I do not know the origin of the name for it hardly seemed to suit his outgoing bluff nature. But it was the name everyone called him and was used vociferously by the whole school when at church singing the hymn 'Sweet Sacrament Divine'. There is a line in the second verse that goes '... *we tell our tale of misery*'. We sang this hymn at least once a week at evening devotions, and, when we came to this line, everyone took in a deep breath and sang the word 'misery' as loudly as possible.

We would all look over to where the priests knelt to see Fr Tom's face, but it always remained expressionless. I have no doubt that he knew full well the reason for our apparent ardour.

He probably knew too that we would place bets on who would light the big candles that stood behind the altar the quickest. There were three of these candles on either side of the tabernacle and two altar servers would light them with long tapers. Each server had three candles to light. Tall guys had the advantage, but sometimes a little guy would have his three alight in the blink of an eyelid.

Then there was Fr Henry Flanagan who was even balder than Spike Nolan, our Irish teacher. Unlike Nolan, he had an aristocratic baldness that commanded immediate respect and even deference.

Fr Flanagan brought some sense of culture to our otherwise uncultured minds and instilled an appreciation of music, painting and sculpture into our untutored souls. He was himself a gifted artist, sculptor and musician, and many of his works can still be seen in Dominican churches.

He ran a gramophone club once a week and explained each piece of music before he played it. In this way, many of us were introduced for the first time to the wonders of Handel, Bach, Hayden, Beethoven and Mozart right up to Stravinsky, Ravel and Prokopiev.

He also produced the yearly 'opera', normally a Gilbert and Sullivan affair, which was staged in the college theatre at the end of the Michaelmas term. I was very proud of my brother Norbert who sang the leading role in *HMS Pinafore*. I did not even make the chorus.

As an ascetic, Fr Flanagan scorned athletic ability. On one occasion, he asked me – in front of my classmates – whether I thought being able to run the length of a field 'with a leather ball full of air and knocking down anyone in my path' signified that I was better than everyone else.

We had just won an important cup match and I was probably swaggering about, full of my own importance. I reckon

Fr Flanagan wanted to deflate my balloon of arrogance. He certainly succeeded.

I could not answer his question without losing face in front of my friends. So I meekly replied something to the effect that mere physical strength was no index of a man's worth.

'I'm glad you see that Colbert', he turned towards the class and sneered, 'otherwise we would all be bowing before elephants.' The class roared in approbation. All except me.

I think he did not get on well with my uncle Michael. Or perhaps my uncle did not get on well with him. There was a kind of intellectual rivalry, possibly jealousy, between the pair, with my uncle's love of science, on the one hand, and Fr Flanagan's love of the arts – the polar opposite – on the other.

For those reasons, I did not appreciate Fr Flanagan at the time, but later realised that he was a gifted and a good man, who was doing his best to season us with the music, poetry and art, things which would last and enrich us for life.

Years later, Fr John O'Reilly of the Claddagh, Galway, told me a story about Henry Flanagan. Apparently, one boy got such a bad report academically that his father wrote back to Newbridge complaining that his son had 'done his best'. Fr Flanagan wrote back politely, 'You are right. I am afraid your son *has done* his best.'

Among the lay teachers 'snotter Davis' had few peers. He instilled a love of English into all of us and in particular a love of the romantic poets and of Shakespeare. 'Spike' Nolan taught us Irish; he had a shiny bald head which fascinated us, especially when the sun shone through the classroom window and lit up his pate in a golden glow which was full of chalk particles which darted in every direction as his head bobbed up and down while he was scribbling on the blackboard.

We enjoyed the screech of the chalk cross the blackboard, which happened for time to time no matter who was using it. With Baldy Nolan, this was a constant occurrence.

Mr Kûypers taught music. He was a small tubby man like Hercule Poirot, and I think a Belgian too. He was alleged to have had a toe shot off during the war. We always stared rudely at his shoes wondering which foot was short of a toe. He wore small pointed, highly polished black leather shoes that made us wonder if he had any toes at all.

I did not do music in school. My mother was a practical woman who rightly announced that 'Serryth will never make a living playing the piano'. Any subject I was allowed to take had to have a practical objective for her. Even games were barely tolerated.

There were many other teachers who influenced my life in Newbridge, including 'Tubby' Leahy, Cyprian Candon, Bernard Casserly, Jim ONeill, 'Motha' (Canice) O' Riordan, Charlie Byrne and Fathers Mulligan and Valkenburg.

Neither space nor memory serves me well enough to write anecdotes about them. I leave that to others better qualified than I.

School Friends
All Flowers Wither Unless Watered

Sharing eases suffering and enhances joy. In the first case, we were all in the same boat in Newbridge. We all got exactly the same food, all got up at the same time, all endured the same cold and all got the same punishment according to the gravity of the offense.

There may well have been 'teachers pets', but I was not aware of them. There may well have been some boys constantly in trouble. But I was not aware of any injustice on the part of the priests. There were boys who ran away from school but we never enquired why they left nor did we question those who were sent back.

We were all subject to the same conditions and that made things easier to accept.

We all shared the same joys too. The thrill of a half-hour sleep-in to 7.30 a.m. on a Church feast day. The excitement of going to Dublin on the train, either to play rugby or to support our team. The excitement of the Christmas opera whether you were on the stage or not. The grabbing of the shuttlecock or billiard cues in the 'Pav' during free time, the soft summer days lounging by the riverbank.

These were just some of our common joys and sorrows and, through them, we gradually began to love Newbridge and become a family of boys. I cannot recall not liking anybody. I was lucky that way, just something in my nature, I suppose. I hung out with lots of guys, and if I had special friends, they were few.

Seamus Geraghty (Galway) was one. We were miles apart academically but often went for walks together. Seamus was known as Poteen and later became a psychiatrist practising in Sligo. Dhuring school holidays, I would stay with him in Galway and he would come to Tramore for a week. That was his first introduction to the South and my first introduction to the West. Little was I to know then that the West would become my home in later years. We drifted apart once we left school. Women are much better than men in keeping up old friendships.

I had another pal, Scorchy Maguire, from Lisdoonvara. He was a tough guy and a good rugby player. He went in to the hotel business afterwards, as did another friend of mine Michael Collins. Both are dead now. Michael and his brother Seamus were close to me, and I visited the home of their parents, Colonel and Mrs Collins, in the Curragh on more than one occasion. Seamus became a Dominican and served in Argentina most of his life. Doreen, my wife, and I stayed with him when he retired to Florida some years ago and he is now back in Newbridge. He has indifferent health and a dicky heart has curtailed his activities greatly.

I also liked the Berney brothers (Kilcullen), Fintan Buckley (Maynooth) and the Prendergasts – Kevin and Paddy – the horsemen! I was close to Tony Twomey (our team scrumhalf) and Brian Rigney – our team hooker – and also liked Brian's elder brother, Seamus. Brian died in 2014, but I see Seamus and his wife Mary from time to time.

In our last year of school, Seamus was the school captain and I was the vice-captain. Seamus was a very successful entrepreneur long before that word became fashionable.

There are many others. Off hand I remember, Jim Delahunty, Fabian Conway, Paul Hynes (became a Dominican and died some time ago) and Larry O'Hagan (also became a Dominican and is also deceased). Others were Tom Grace (played rugby for Ireland), Fergal Quinn (the Senator, a bit younger than me) and Diarmuid Clifford (later a Dominican, editor of *St Martins Magazine*). And then, there were the unforgettable O'Dwyer brothers from Kerry. Others will tell you more about these characters than I.

An Incident

All kinds of things go on in schools about which teachers know nothing. I think the following incident is one of them. There was a small lad in Newbridge in my time by the name of Jarlath Canning. He was from Bearna, Co Galway, and, by virtue of his small stature and 'culchie' accent, was being bullied by some seniors among whom Vinnie Morgan and his gang were prominent. I was outraged at such behaviour and challenged Vinnie and his gang to a fist fight. 'Take on someone of your own size' I shouted at them.

They shuffled menacingly towards me, ready to teach me a lesson. A small wiry guy called little Jim was the first in line. I hit him on the nose, which started to bleed, and he sat down. He had caught me on the ribs, which hurt a lot, but I pretended it was nothing.

I waited calmly for the next guy, goading him on with my fists waving threateningly. He was bigger than little Jim but I knew I could take him easily. He approached me a little tentatively. Before he could get within reach, I stepped forward and hit him hard in the stomach, and then slapped his face. He sat down, kind of crying. I turned to the rest and they just shuffled off.

Then Vinnie came forward. I braced myself. Vinnie was taller than me, lanky and awkward but had the advantage of a long reach and I knew this would be no easy matter.

Suddenly, he grinned and we both stretched out our hands at the same time. I said 'No hard feelings' and told him that little Jim had one hell of a punch and that my ribs knew it. We laughed and became fast friends for the rest of our schooldays. I tell this little story as I remember it, perhaps exaggerating my bravado in hindsight. But no one took me on after that incident. Now I realise what a wild and perhaps obnoxious animal I was when roused in those days.

Summer Holidays
Sun, Wind, Rain and Sea

The anticipation of summer holidays spread among the boys like a happy virus. The days and finally the hours were counted until we left the 'gates of misery' as we called the college gates. Charlie Callaghan would load all our cases on a dray and take them to the railway station. We would follow on foot along the miserable main street, turn right and file into the old-fashioned station. There we would wait for the train which came along puff-puffing before it stopped at the platform with a screech of metal wheels on metal tracks as if surprised that it had to stop at all.

We would then grab our suitcases and climb into the nearest second-class compartment. In some trains, the carriages were completely isolated from one another, whereas in others, there was a corridor which allowed people to stand or walk as they wished.

Each compartment had a window which was lowered or raised by pulling a leather strap which was punctured by holes so that you could fix it to a protruding hook on the lower sash and set the window at the desired level.

If you looked out and faced the engine, you were almost certainly going to get black soots and ash on your face. Often smoke entered the carriage anyway – if the window was open and the train moving and the wind in the right direction!

Mamma would meet the train in Waterford and there would be hugs and laughter and questions galore. On arrival home, whether Chatsfort, or later Swiss Cottage, Kingsmeadow, Caspesia, Brockenhurst or Thornycroft (we moved house six times), I would wallow in just being home. All the same old books, the familiar smell of Dadda's pipe and the special coffee cakes that Mamma made – all would reassure me that I was really back home.

The routine of home was restful and reassuring. I got along well with my sisters and brothers, and I do not think that we ever had more than the most trivial of disagreements. We all obeyed our parents and spent our days reading, walking and swimming either in Newtown Cove or in the Cove in Tramore.

Yet as the weeks passed, the euphoria waned and I thought more and more about Newbridge, the rugby and the 'lads'.

Uncle Michael Spends Summer with us

Uncle Michael normally used to spend the month of August with us and his presence dominated everything. He loved to take us walking and loved to examine wild flowers and plants which we would have to pick for him even if it meant climbing hedges and getting thorns in our fingers.

These walks would be long and tiresome, particularly when we had to push our way through brambles and jump ditches to pick purple loosestrife or meadowsweet which he would bring home much to the disgust of my mother who called them weeds.

One of the boys – usually me – had to serve his Mass in the local church in Tramore each morning, so I could never have a proper sleep-in. But it did not bother me or if it did, I did not complain.

Uncle Michael only listened to chamber music and plain chant. This meant that we could not get the 'Top Twenty' from Radio Luxemburg, which he considered thrash bordering on the devil's music. Worst of all, he was served the best piece of chicken, given a fry in the morning and got the first choice of any goodies that were on the table. He seemed to eat all the time. Nibbling at cheese, spooning sugar and always ready to buy ice creams for everyone (I now suspect mostly for himself).

To crown it all, he was never asked to wash a cup. The washing up was the children's' job.

He had little time for women except for enclosed orders of nuns and certain academic women. Nonetheless, my mother treated him with great understanding and consideration, although she challenged him about his views on many occasions.

Uncle Michael always favoured me above all his nieces and nephews. I suppose that this was because I was good academically and generally obeyed him without demur. We regularly went to stay with Aunt Ellie (Gran's sister) in Glenanar and spent our days cycling around the countryside to towns such as Kilfinane, Fermoy and Doneraile, always on a botanical hunt and almost always searching for lost relations.

Aunt Ellie lived in a traditional Irish farmhouse – complete with a front half-door – at the foot of the Ballyhoura hills in Co Cork. Rural electrification had not yet reached this corner of Ireland, and once darkness fell, the tilly lamps would be lighted and everyone would sit around the turf fire in a big open hearth telling stories, playing cards, reading the *Cork Examiner* or discussing politics, while aunt Ellie kept on knitting, turning the wheel of her old Singers Sewing Machine and putting in a word here and there. Neighbours would drop in regularly and discuss local issues. I am sure that there was many a piece of juicy gossip exchanged in these soirées, but I was always sent to bed after the rosary (and trimmings) and anyway I was ready to sleep by nine o'clock.

Aunt Ellie's husband, John, was a tall gaunt quiet man who hardly noticed me. When he spoke, he spoke with authority and everyone listened respectfully. When asked his opinion about anything, he considered the matter carefully and then gave his judgment in a very deliberate manner. Argument or discussion or debate was not his forté. His word was final and he had the final word.

He had long sensitive fingers, quite unlike the usual rough thick fingers one associates with those who work on the land. I am sure that he could have been a musician or a surgeon or an engineer had he got the chance.

Aunt Ellie was as small as he was tall. She had a wrinkled but animated face and her grey hair was tightly combed back into a bun, which made her look older than she probably was. She always wore a long coarse black dress and, apart from her white apron, the only colour you could see was the silver threading in her black shawl. A prayer was never far from her lips, and she must have said countless rosaries every day for her beads were always in her hands unless she was feeding the hens or washing clothes or peeling the spuds. She was exactly like the little old Irish mother in the film *Going My Way* when Father O'Malley (Bing Crosby) sent his parish priest Father Fitzgibbon (Barry Fitzgerald) home to Ireland to see his mother before she died.

Aunt Ellie was a small lady with a big heart.

I did not appreciate it at the time, but who else but her would provide a young scamp with a bottle of lemonade *every day* at dinnertime? And dinner was always the same. Home-cured bacon, cabbage and flowery potatoes smothered in loads of salty country butter made by 'herself'.

A black kettle simmered away over the smouldering turf fire and sides of home-cured bacon hung from metal hooks inserted into the wide black slate mantelpiece. The hearth was recessed into the gable wall and, as the house was one-storied, you could see the sky if you looked up the chimney.

There was a recess on either side of the fire in which you could sit. This must have been a lovely spot to be in if you were cold. Like most country houses, there was a fixed bellows to fan up the flames whenever the fire was low.

Lighting fires in those times was always a bit of a problem. In some cases, such as at home, my father would cover the dying embers with ashes and hope that he could keep the fire in a kind of hibernation until morning. However, if we had to start the fire from scratch, we twisted sheets of old newspaper into small sections, carefully placed a few twigs over them and judiciously added small pieces of turf so that the whole thing would take flame once ignited with a matchstick. If the turf was dry, you might build up a real fire in about 10-15 min. As a last resort, if the fire were clearly dying, you would hold up a sheet of newspaper against the entire fireplace.

This often worked, miraculously. By judiciously wafting the paper to and fro, you could fan young flames so that their yellow tongues would encircle the turf until a real fire began to sprout. Dare anyone enter the room during this procedure or smoke would billow forth and choke everyone in the room.

As a child, I never understood how 'fanning flames' actually works. But later my mother explained that by using newspaper as I have described, air, and hence oxygen, was drawn up through the turf, thus giving it the maximum chance of igniting. My mother had never done science in school. I think she was just a smart lady.

The art of starting a fire was refined to the stage where people became so adept that they could make a cold room warm and cosy within an hour.

Need I mention that the adults hogged the heat, while us children mostly lived in semi-cold outside the inner ring reserved for the grown-ups.

Soon I would have no more fires to light for I was now 16 years old and it was time to leave school and enter the real world. And that thought filled me with excitement and delight.

CHAPTER 3

UNIVERSITY DAYS

Going to university was my first taste of real freedom. I was now on my own, completely in command of my own life. It was up to me. Yet I was not really independent; I was always conscious that my parents were the ones supporting me and that they went without so that I could have.

While in school, I had somewhere seen a notice for an entrance scholarship to University College Dublin – UCD – open to everyone. Remember that in those days, unless you were means tested and found eligible for a County Council Scholarship and did an excellent Leaving Cert, you had to pay for third-level education. So off my own bat, I studied the curriculum for this open scholarship. This meant studying Macbeth as well as Hamlet – the one that was on the Leaving Cert course – and taking a different syllabus in Latin and Maths from what was taught in Newbridge. Despite managing all these on my own, I went to Dublin, and luckily got second place in the exam. This gave me a major remission of fees in UCD.

I was disappointed. I wanted to get first and secure complete remission of all fees. Even then, I was conscious that finances were not great at home.

Mamma feared that if Dadda died – he was so much older than she – then she would not be able to cope financially to educate the five of us. This fear was very real to her and was the basis of her pulling Sibyl out of pre-med and making her apply for a position in the Bank of Ireland instead. It was an unfounded fear but lasted all her life.

Initially, in my pre-med year, I stayed in the De La Salle Hall in Ely Place, known colloquially as 'Ding Dong'. The reason for this name was, and still is, unclear to me. I shared an upstairs attic room with Vivian Kelly from Westport, Co Mayo. He was also starting medicine in UCD and later became a well-known ENT surgeon in Dublin. We got on fine together and there was never any rivalry between us. During pre-med, I attended Earlsfort Terrace and the College of Science, which were later to become the National Concert Hall and the Department of an Taoiseach, respectively.

I had very little money, just a half crown (two shillings and six pence) a week, but it cost 1s and 3d – half my allowance – to go to the Saturday night film in 86 St Stephens Green, known simply as '86'. The rest went on coffee and the odd bun. '86' is located beside Cardinal Newman's University Church and was the hangout for most UCD students. It was always fun to go to a 'hop' there on a Saturday night.

A gang of us would occasionally go to the Yerrawaddies in the Olympic ballroom on Pleasant Street where the engineering students ran a weekly hop or to the one run by student teachers in the National Ballroom in Parnell Sq. On those nights, we met people from the real world and students who were doing things other than medicine.

A hop always had live music – quite unlike today's discos where there are flashing lights, canned music and colourful DJs. There were no DJs, no canned music and no drugs in my time.

It was always a treat to walk or bus it into town and go to a show in the Theatre Royal. This was the only place in Dublin – apart from occasional performances in the the Capitol cinema near the General Post Office – where the main film was preceded by a stage show, featuring comedians and acrobats and invariably – to everyone's delight – the Royalettes. The Royalettes were a troupe of dancers who kicked up their legs *a la* Moulin Rouge and wore skimpy skirts, colourful tights and satin knickers that riveted our eyes. In addition, anytime I was there, at some point, up would come Tommy Dando playing his organ. I mean *up*. He would ascend on some kind of lift in the front of the stage and play tunes and sing songs that we could all join in. The words were usually projected on the screen behind him so that everyone could sing along in the dark, in tune or out of tune, loud or soft as they wished, without caring what anyone else thought of their musical efforts. It was great!

There were lots of cinemas in Dublin. Among our favourites were the Green near the College of Surgeons, the Grafton on Grafton Street, the Metropole, the Savoy and the Carlton on O'Connell Street and the Capitol down a laneway beside the General Post Office. We always went to the cheapest seats and often sneaked in free, cleverly avoiding the usherette who checked our tickets as we pushed aside the heavy curtain that led into the darkened cinema. Our chance to sneak in would come when the usherette was away from her post, guiding people into empty seats. We frequently sat through the same film twice, just to pass the time and keep warm.

Walking in St Stephen's Green (the 'Green'), going to Cafollas for a 'Knickerbocker Glory', an occasional trip upstairs on a bus to Dun Laoire (carefully avoiding the ticket inspector) and attending daily Mass were all part of a very happy student time for me.

My best friends in those days were Jim Kelly, a law student from Templemore, and John Clery, the son of A.B. Clery (known as ABC), a surgeon who worked in the Richmond Hospital. I lost touch with both afterwards, but in those far-off halcyon days, we were great buddies often going for long walks together. Indeed, on one occasion, we heard Brendan Behan and Patrick Kavanagh shouting at each other in Mount St. They semed to us to be Philistines. We did not know who they were until long afterwards.

Girls were important but not all consuming. I did have a one and only 'date' with Mary Rose Kelly, but it was just coffee and a bun in the Carlton restaurant and the 'flicks' afterwards. I know I had a bad cold and no handkerchief and that I must have appeared raw and uncouth to Mary Rose. She was a natural blonde and very beautiful. I do not think I made much of an impression on her. She left medicine early and we have never met since, although I did ask her brother Frank for her address years later when he was doing a show in the Town Hall in Galway. I got Mary Rose's address from him, but never followed it up. Frank was the Frank who played the part of Fr Jack in the TV series *Fr Ted*. Mary Rose was his sister. Frank sadly passed away in 2016.

I studied hard, loved medicine and got first every year in all exams except in Third Med where I slipped to a H2 grade. It wasn't that I was brilliant; it was just that I studied with method and diligence. I can honestly say that academic achievements meant little to me. I just wanted to be a good doctor and I believed – and still believe – that the most important thing for me was to treat the patient as a person and not as a 'case'. I would sometimes daydream of becoming another Dr Schweitzer or Damien of Molokai. But then, I sometimes daydreamt that I was playing out half for Ireland and even playing better than Jack Kyle.

Bedside Teaching

In Dublin in those days, we attended undergraduate bedside teaching sessions in any hospital we liked. Dublin had been the first medical centre to introduce the practice of bedside teaching, a practice universally adopted later. We drifted from St Vincents to the Mater, to the Richmond, Mercers, Jervis St (Jervo) and Sir Patrick Dunnes Hospital depending on how we liked the consultant giving the session. Crowds frequented D.K. O'Donovan in Vincents and 'Flash' Freeman in the Mater simply because they would be examining in our final. 'Divine' John Cunningham was the professor of obstetrics in Holles St, but most of us preferred to go to either Arthur Barry or Kieran O'Driscoll. The latter was a superb teacher and gave us all a love for obstetrics. 'Narky' Walsh, a urologist in Jervo, was well favoured too. His sarcasm was famous, although often painful for the unfortunate student who was the butt of his tongue. Billy O'Dwyer's and T.J. Ryan's clinics in medicine were gentle affairs by comparison.

We looked on these consultants as little Gods, and we were constantly in awe of them. In our eyes, they could do nothing wrong. If a physician said 'Put your stethoscope here and you will hear a systolic heart murmur', the student would look up solemnly and say 'Yes sir. I hear it' whether he heard it or not. Or if a surgeon asked us to palpate an enlarged liver or spleen, we would have no hesitation in pretending that we could feel it too. The rest of the group of students would come along one after the other and all murmur the same thing, 'We hear the murmur, we feel the liver, we feel the spleen...' It was simply a case of the Emperor's new clothes except that we were young trainee doctors who should have been more honest.

Classmates

My main attachment was in the Mater where Tom Gregg was a medical tutor. He kept telling us that 'crows are commoner that swallows', meaning that we should think of the common causes of disease before diagnosing the rare ones. 'Common things commonly occur' summed him up. He later married Dorothea Coughlan from our class. Both are with their maker now.

Oh yes, I had a rival academically. He was Brian O'Connell of a very well-known medical family. He was a fine person and neither of us held anything but the highest regard for each other as far as I can tell. Brian later went to the United States, made a lot of money and gave up medicine to live on a large farm near New York.

The girls in the class always occupied the front seats and took the front places at clinics. This was a given. The nuns even got priority over the other girls, but the nuns in my class were really very good and very lovely people. Anne Ward and Deirdre Twomey were Medical Missionaries of Mary. Anne, whose father was a member of the first Dail Eireann, later became an obstetrician and worked in Anua, Nigeria. Anne's obituary appeared in the *Irish Times* in June 2016. But her legacy lives on. She was a pioneer in treating vesico-vaginal fistulae. In this condition, so prevalent in sub-Saharan Africa, prolonged labour causes erosion of the walls between the vagina and the bladder so that the woman is constantly dribbling urine. Anne simplified the operation to correct the defect and for this has earned herself an undying place in the annals of obstetrics. I worked with her later in Africa.

Deirdre Twomey worked afterwards as an obstetrician in Afikpo in Southeastern Nigeria for over 30 years. I got to know her well in later life and we have become fast friends since. She brought up in Manchester and never lost her attractive English accent.

However, probably one of the cleverest and wisest people I ever knew was another classmate, Carmel Garvey, a St Louis sister. Carmel was clever and wise at the same time – an unusual combination.

These were three nuns I worked with later and, perhaps, that is why I name them in a special way. There were other 'sisters' in my class, but mostly we were afraid to speak to them and they to us.

But even the nuns could not keep the foreigners out of the front rows. We had not many. There was 'Little Mo', an American who rented a flat in Mespil Road and who obviously had lots of money. She resembled the tennis star, Maureen Connolly, known as 'Little Mo', who shocked Wimbledon onlookers with her daring outfits. No doubt, we would consider her tennis skirts almost prudish today.

There was also Aziz Khayat. He seemed to have money to burn and was generous to boot. Aziz was a big burly guy who became an important figure in medicine in his own country almost immediately after he qualified. But Aziz was a nice guy and I liked him. I regret not having met him later when I travelled in the Middle East.

Other Classmates

It is wrong of me to mention specific classmates simply because I have forgotten the names of so many others. I know that we were just an ordinary group of young people who had neither the inclination nor the time to indulge in dislikes. I know that by the time we qualified and went our different ways, an unbreakable bond existed between all of us. Dermot McDonald and Jim Carr were responsible for the very occasional get together, the most memorable being our 50th. But time has so reduced our numbers that another reunion is most unlikely. From time to time, I meet Dan Kelly (Urologist, Dublin), Donal Keane (GP, Warrenpoint), John Taffe (Physician, Cavan) and Jimmy Ledwith (Psychiatrist, Limerick), 'Bee'Fahy (general practice) and Andy Heffernan (consultant physician in St Vincents,

Dublin) and of course Deirdre Twomey (mission doctor). We all comment on how well we look!

I did not mix much with the Irish girls in the class but was friendly with them all. Especially, with Mary Farrell (and her sister Jude, a radiographer student) and Helen Gavin (Ballina) whose brother Michael later married my sister Helen. There are many others whose faces I see before me but whose names elude me as I write this. You see my memory is not what it was for two reasons: first, from old age and second – perhaps more importantly – as a result of being in a coma in Switzerland in 1985, which I shall talk about later.

My First Earnings

It was unusual, indeed rare, for students to take paid work during their holidays, apart for working in the family business or helping on the family farm.

However, I did so in the two summers of my preclinical years and no one made any objections at home.

After First Med, I went with a few friends to London and worked in the 'Bachelors Peas' factory in Southall. My job was to stir a huge vat of the green fluid that went into every tin of peas. The vat sat on a large electric plate. My job was to switch on the electricity, wait until the green stuff began to boil, switch off the electricity and – most importantly – keep stirring the mixture all the time. Once everything cooled down, I was expected to open a valve in the bottom of the vat and let the contents drip feed into a conveyor belt of canned peas before a machine in another room would finally seal them. God knows what was in the mixture. That was not my affair.

Unfortunately, for at least two consecutive days on my watch, the final tins were rejected because they contained little white flecks, which were apparently insoluble and were tasteless and gritty. The supervisors came and examined the whole process in action and it took only a few moments to see that the steam from my vat was causing particles of ceiling paint to shower down into the mixture almost continuously. I was of course mixing everything up assiduously without noticing the white flecks because the whole place was steamed up.

I was fired immediately. I must have cost the company quite a bit. Yet they gave me an extra week's salary and were probably glad to see the end of me. I was happy enough. I had enough money – and spare – to go home.

The next year, I went with a fellow student, I think it was Pat Byrne (Ennis), to the Isle of Man. We called in to every place on the promenade in Douglas, and, at last, I got hired as the assistant night chef in *Butlins Holiday Camp*, at the end of the promenade. Pat got working in a pub.

On the first night, I was told to prepare omelettes for the residents. I was given 50 dozen eggs which I had to break into a big pot and discard the shells into another pot, the 'shell-pot'. I got very fast at this, breaking two eggs, one in each hand, at the same time. Unfortunately, I must have lost my rhythm because in the morning many of the guests complained that their scrambled eggs were full of eggshell. I must have discarded lots of good eggs into the shell-pot while at the same time casting the shells into the egg-pot. I was fired after my first night. Misery me.

I trampled the prom again and got a job as a waiter in a lounge bar that faced the sea and was full of holidaymakers. Maybe the owners took me in out of sympathy, I do not know, but after two nights, I was told my services were no longer required. I had very little money and nowhere to sleep so I walked outside the town, lay down in a field under the protection of a hedge and slept soundly until morning when I was awakened by the curious sensation of having a cow breath directly on my face. Not being sure if this was a cow or a bull I made a hasty retreat and eventually reached the ferry terminal.

However, on the way, I spotted a white summer frock with red roses in a shop window and decided to buy it for my elder sister Sibyl, I think it was of 17 shillings. Not all my money, but almost all. Arriving in Dun Laoire, I hitched all the way to Tramore and presented Sibyl with the dress. I think she liked it.

So, in truth, my efforts to earn money as a student failed abysmally, but now I treasure the memories of those far off days. They were a special interlude in my life.

CHAPTER 4

LOURDES

A Place of Wonders

I am not now sure whether it was before or after the Second Med that uncle Michael, Mamma and I made a pilgrimage to Lourdes. This was the first for all three of us. We went with the Kildare and Loughlin pilgrimage. Uncle Michael, still based in Newbridge, must have been the moving force in this choice. The fare was or £27 for each of us – all-inclusive. I know that I was thrilled about the prospect of going. Most Irish people had never set foot outside Ireland except as emigrants.

We travelled by rail to Dublin, boat to Holyhead, train to London, train to Dover, train from Calais to Paris and train from the Gare du Nord to Lourdes!

On our overnight in Paris, we were put up in a small no star hotel. The hotel and breakfast were atrocious but that did not bother me. On the contrary, I found everything absolutely exciting. I had never been 'on the continent' before.

I gazed in wonder as we were coached to and from the hotel, totally fascinated by the shop signs: Tabac, Boulangerie and Patisserie – all in French. We saw the Eiffel Tower close up, the stunning Champs-Élysées and crossed Seine via the beautiful Pont de la Concorde and then circled the Arch de Triumph. The whole experience breathed magnificence.

I was equally excited at the prospect of our train journey down through the heart of France next day. In reality, the journey was long, boring and featureless.

The train seemed to rattle on forever, the countryside was unremarkable and it was only as we approached the hill country near Lourdes that I became excited once more.

However, we were all tired and weary when we arrived in Lourdes. Here we were met by a bus and brought to the Hotel Myosotis which was to be our home for the next week. The hotel was a drab affair, but somewhat better than the one in Paris, so we were delighted.

The chief wonder in our room was a white porcelain washbasin beside the WC. None of our batch – including us – had seen a *bidet* before and all assumed it was a footbath. There was many a giggle when someone who had been to Lourdes previously disclosed its real purpose.

It was my first time staying in a real hotel, and while the rest lay down for an hour, I wandered around the explored every inch of the building and even went outside.

Lourdes itself was fabulous. Just meeting people from so many lands, taking part in the ceremonies, the spectacle of the rosary procession at night, the grotto, the baths, the infirmary, the bustling colourful gift shops, the babble of different languages, the trip to Gavarnie in the Pyrenees, the delicious French coffee – the list goes on.

I worked as a *brancardier* most of the time and became especially attached to a girl in a wheel chair whom I used to push to the blessing of the sick each day. Her name was Mary Brady and she was from Errith, somewhere near Castlerea. She looked like a twelve years old but was actually 32 years of age. This was very old as far as I was concerned.

My attachment was totally platonic and essentially one of pity, and I prayed really hard that she would be cured.

On our return trip, we stopped a while in London and visited some catholic church, perhaps Westminster Cathedral, I did not know exactly where. While in the church, which was quite dark – even in early July – I prayed intensely for Mary Brady as only a young person can pray. I seemed to see a light radiating around the tabernacle, which my mother put down to tiredness and over anxiety. Now I wonder if it was not my astigmatism.

About ten days after arriving home, we received a letter from Mary Brady stating that on arrival home she had got up from her wheelchair and walked, the first time in fifteen years. I understood later that this was on the same day and at roughly the same time, 3.30 p.m., that I had been praying for her recovery in London. She had flown home by air with all the invalids and so arrived home two days before those of us who travelled overland.

This is a true story but, as with all youth, it was for me just a normal thing for our lady to do. What was the big deal?

Mary Brady was apparently born with a congenital heart defect so never developed physically as a normal girl. Her cure was either a miracle or not. It must have been one or the other.

I do not believe that I have talked about this to anyone since that day including my own family.

Now I was in the Third Med and my own life was to change as dramatically as that of Mary Brady when I met my future wife.

CHAPTER 5

DOREEN

I was in the emergency room in the Jervis St Hospital doing whatever medical students do when suddenly I saw this tall attractive student nurse and became instantly smitten. I simply had to see her again. This had never happened to me before and I could not explain it to myself. I was not obsessed with her; yet she dominated my waking moments. I was so pleased and excited when she came to the pictures with me, and the more I got to know her, the more I found her company easy, happy and non-demanding. I believe that I wanted to marry her from the first moment I saw her. Certainly, that was my intention from very early on in our relationship.

We spent every moment we could together and quickly became young lovers hand in hand. Being apart was difficult, which only long phone calls, full of listening to each other's chit chat, made bearable. We were both strict Catholics and there was never the remotest hint of any sexual impropriety between us, although we embraced each other as often as we got the chance.

Such a love is rare but not unique. Doreen changed my life but only for the better.

Our walks on cold winter evenings, coffee and a bun in the Carlton, an ice cream in Cafollas (money permitting), our bus rides on No. 16 to the McCann family in 86 Rathgar Rd, our going together to the odd 'dress dance', these were the things we enjoyed most, in what seems a very naive courtship compared to what happens today.

It took two years for me to actually 'pop the question'. I asked Doreen to marry me in the back of a car after some sort of a 'do' in Powers Hotel in Kildare St. She did not say yes, and she did not say no. But I would persist.

That 'do' in Powers Hotel involved her sister Mary, just back for Nigeria with her engineer husband Jim, and some of the Gleesons of Galway, notably Paddy and Michael, who both got a little tipsy. The Gleesons were a well-known Galway city family. Mary, a physiotherapy student in the Mater, was two years younger than me. She later went on to marry Joe Costello, an anaesthetist from Galway, and they lived eventually as our neighbours in Taylors Hill. Sal, her older sister, ran the family business, Gleeson's drapery shop, in Shop St opposite Lynch's castle. Sal was widowed early on; Mary, the younger sister, died shortly after her husband Joe had succumbed to lung cancer. He never smoked or drank alcohol in his life. Life plays unfair tricks on all of us.

My Doreen was originally Doreen Hoade, one of four children born in Annagh House, Ballygluinin, Co Galway. Her father died when she was an infant and so her mother, Delia, had to run a big house and very large farm on her own. It was the 'dirty thirties', emigration was rife, there was no social service, there was little local help available and everything had to be paid for in hard cash, including running the farm, hiring labour and keeping abreast of the mortgage. Her father, James Hoade, had borrowed a lot of money to buy Annagh and all that money had to be repaid.

Annagh itself was the former residence of the Bodkins, a 'gentry family' and well-known landlords.

Unfortunately, like many of the great Irish houses of the day, it was unsustainable after independence. Despite being straddled with Annagh and her late husband's debts for stocking the farm and buying machinery, Delia sent her children to a boarding school.

The girls followed her own footsteps and did nursing, Mary in Galway and Doreen in Jervis St. hospital , Dublin, where you paid for the privilege of being trained as a nurse.

Joseph, the eldest boy, did an agriculture degree in Dublin. Anthony, destined for the 'foreign missions', entered St Kierans seminary in Kilkenny.

The farm kept losing money and so. reluctantly, Delia moved her family to Galway city where she hoped her expenses would be less. Property there was expensive, scarce and usually of poor quality. But she was desperate and finally bought the Bridge House on the canal near St Joseph's Church.

The Bridge House had three small bedrooms, and an indoor toilet – not that common in central Galway on those days. Importantly, it had a self-contained shop as part of the ground floor and Delia saw this as a necessary source of income.

For the rest of her life, she eked out an existence always putting a little away to pay the rates, always putting a little away to pay for the children's schooling and always helping those who had less than herself.

It is a terrible thing to lose your property and come down in life. Only those who have had to do so understand this. She died in 1965 of coronary thrombosis, quite suddenly and without much pain. The only one of my children who remembers her is the eldest, Mary. She used to sleep occasionally in the same bed as 'Mudna' who would tell her stories and totally spoil her. I think this gave more pleasure to Mudna than anything any of us could do or say.

When it came to Doreen and I, she was wise enough to accept that we would have to make our own mistakes. I clearly remember her shaking her head and saying 'there is no good giving you two advice... you will do whatever you want anyway.' As young people have always done.

That was true. Doreen and I were intent on spending the rest of our lives together and, although we knew this meant facing lean years, working day and night and even emigrating, we were prepared to do so as long as we were together.

Doreen's brother Joseph died in a single car accident in 1979 leaving behind Rita, his wife, and four children. Many farmers in County Galway have warm memories of Joseph who was working among them as an agricultural instructor at the time of his death. I liked Joseph very much.

Anthony had been posted to Australia where he was highly regarded, not just locally by his parishioners, but also nationally. After his death in 2008, a memorial to him was erected outside Government Buildings in Canberra. He was a man of action always helping people, building churches and schools and playing golf. He was good at that, and played with his friend Greg Norman, a famous Auzzie golfer.

In those days, there were few families in Ireland that did not have a son or a daughter a priest or a nun. Maybe Irish mothers were responsible for this, for I am sure that many a boy and girl felt obliged to enter religious life not from their own choice but rather to please their mothers.

As for Doreen and me, we were to spend the next 60 years together. Lucky us.

CHAPTER 6

THE REAL WORLD

Bittersweet

My childhood dreams came true when I qualified as a medical doctor from UCD in June 1957. I was 22 years old at the time and ready to take on the world. However, I was only one of many young men and women who were on the threshold of a new and exciting life. And I am sure that they all felt the same as I. There was not one of us who did medicine for the money, and there was not one of us who expected an easy life ahead.

We all knew that for the first few years, the pay would be less than that of a cleaner, and we all knew that most of us would have to emigrate in order to survive. On the other hand, there was no great competition to get into medicine, there was no Health Professions Admission Test to be passed and no requirement other than passing the leaving or matriculation examinations, although passing in Latin was mandatory. So in June 1957, as we clutched our scrolls and marched out of the Aula Max in Earlsfort Terrace, we faced a new life full of hope but also tempered with realism.

In my case, I had everything. I had the woman I adored, I had achieved first place in my final medicine exam, had amassed lots of medals and absolutely loved medicine.

Both Doreen and I had health, youth, dreams and a deep love that we were convinced would endure. Our certainty of each other made us determined to get married and be together to face life, whatever it might bring.

My family disapproved that entirely.

My mother must have cried bitter tears to see her darling son rushing off into the arms of the first woman he met, presumably trapped into marriage, probably driven by lust. My uncle Michael wrote damming letters and tried to intervene with the Archbishop of Dublin to stop the marriage, but to no avail. We were determined that nothing would keep us apart.

On the first of July – in the middle of all this controversy – I climbed the steps of the Mater Hospital in Dublin, the same steps I had climbed as an eight year old when I was getting my tonsils out. This time I was a qualified doctor and was now starting my career as an intern under 'Flash' Freeman, the professor of medicine.

My salary was £5 per week plus board. Since I would be paid at the end of the month this, meant that I had no money to spend at all. I had £150 in the Bank of Ireland in Waterford. This was mine. I had earned it from bits and pieces of poetry published in minor magazines.

My parents refused to release it, although they did so at a later stage.

Strangely enough, I was not resentful. I was happy with my bride-to-be and with my career. Had I been asked to defer marriage for a year, I would have done so, but the storm at home was so intense that this idea was not even floated. My brothers and sisters remained silent; how could they have done other than comfort my mother.

At least, with the exception of Norbert, none of them openly condemned Doreen and I to our faces.

Marriage

And so, on 2 September 1957, we got married in Rialto Church in Dublin.

Fr Denny Bergin, a young curate, presided. He was a friend of Doreen's brother Anthony. Both had been ordained priests together in St Kieran's College, Kilkenny. In later years, we drifted apart from Denny for reasons that were unclear to me. We called to see him many years later in Dublin but got an indifferent reception. Doreen's mother was at the wedding, but needless to say, there was no one from my side. We had just four other guests.

One was Joan Crowley, a close friend of Doreen's. They had nursed together, first in Cork St Fever Hospital and later in Cherry Orchard Hospital, where Joan was a ward sister. She eventually married Jimmy Burke, a Fine Gael TD, and went to live in Tulsk Co Roscommon. Jimmy's sister Maureen 'came with the house'.

Maureen had polio when she was younger and used a wheel chair. Mentally, she was a powerful lady with a mind of her own and perhaps she resented the new bride becoming mistress of what she regarded as her home. It was not such an easy place for Joan, especially after Jimmy died.

However, Joan went on to take her late husband's seat in the Dail and was a serving TD (teachta dála, member of parliament) for many years. Originally, from Bandon, Co Cork, Joan never lost her lilting Cork accent nor did we ever lose our life-long friendship with her.

The other three guests were Emma and James MacCann and Mrs O'Connell.

The MacCanns lived in 86, Rathgar Rd, and had befriended us for many years by letting us into their home whenever we had nowhere to go and by giving us meals when we were hungry and shelter when it was raining. We got to know them through Mary, one of their daughters, who was nursing with Doreen but who could not come to the wedding because she was on duty that day. Both Emma and James acted like surrogate parents to us and we have never forgotten them.

Mrs O'Connell was a widow who lived in Griffith Avenue, and her daughter Bernie, who acted as our bridesmaid, was also a student nurse along with Doreen.

Bernie would bring us occasionally to her home and there we would have tea and 'Fuller's cake' with her mother who was a big buxom woman generous and warm-hearted, the typical Irish mother.

Pat Curry, our best man, was my friend. He qualified as a doctor the year after me and sadly I lost touch with him completely afterwards. I know he was a descendant of one of the visionaries at Knock Shrine in 1879 but that meant little to us at the time.

The Wedding

I clearly remember travelling upstairs in a double-decker bus along the South Circular Rd to the church in Rialto. As the bus pulled to a stop near the church, I looked out the window and saw my best man alight from a taxi. Strangely, I was not a bit embarrassed. Pat always seemed to have money to spare. I would only take a taxi *in extremis*. Pat would take a taxi without giving it a thought.

We met at the church door and took our places in the front pew. There were just a few stragglers in the church who must have been surprised to see such a small wedding party. And that was it. No music, no confetti, no rice, no carnations and definitely no dress suits. No wedding reception as such: just breakfast – rashers, sausages and fried eggs – in the priests house. 'Lucky' Morris, a friend of Fr Dennys, took a few photos. We went to the pictures in the afternoon and took the mail boat to Holyhead at 8 p.m. along with many others who were seeking work in England at a time when things were bad at home.

We travelled by train, third class, to London. I remember the stop at Crewe where we ate sandwiches that we had wisely brought with us. I think that they were ham and cheese. They tasted good and kept us going until we arrived in the big city.

Denny had recommended a small guesthouse somewhere in Ealing where the lady of the house ushered us into a small room in the garret – but only after we had produced our marriage certificate. The wedding ring was not enough.

The few days of our honeymoon are a blur. We walked a lot, took the tubes – what a thrill – and window-shopped. One night we decided to splurge on a posh place. We spotted this basement café called the *Trocadero* on a side street, which looked quite romantic. It was dark inside and the tables were grouped around a central space, presumably a dance floor.

We were hardly seated when a trio of seedy looking musicians appeared and began to play current hits. Half way through the first tune, a small troupe of middle aged rather bored looking topless ladies came out, and after a few twists, turns and provocative gestures the self-same ladies came to take our drink orders. We ordered a jug of orange juice from the lady who came to our table, which she duly brought and planked down unceremoniously, with a disdainful shrug of her shoulders. We were getting uneasy at this stage and ordered the minimum to eat, some kind of a starter I think. We got up to go as quickly as we could but not before the waiter had handed me a bill for £3.0 for food and eighteen shillings for 'drinks'. As we rose to go he kept saying 'Sir, there is no service charge', but we did not know what he meant. He followed us out to the door and when we made to move away, he hurled abuse at us but we just kept on going. If he had said there was no tip included, we might have known what he meant. That was the first and last of our excursions to posh eating places.

We showed how naïve we were on another occasion too. We were walking somewhere in the West End when we spotted a crowd of people at a corner listening intently to a fellow in a yellow jumper standing on a chair and waving around coloured boxes which he was auctioning.

'What am I bid for this?', he asked the crowd, holding up a small box for all to see. 'It is guaranteed to be worth more than a tenner…that goes for everything here….' After a slight pause, someone shouted 'two bob….' No one else said anything, but all turned their heads to take a good look at the bidder.

'Aw common' yellow jumper replied 'You got to be kidding mate….' He looked expectantly at the rest of us but we were silent, wondering what he would do.

After a moment, obviously realising that no one else was going to bid, he turned away, bent down, and conferred with someone behind him. He then straightened up and said 'OK Guv… I have to sell everything even if I lose a packet…But can I show everyone what you just bought for two bob?'

The buyer nodded 'Yeah… Go right ahead mate ….'

The crowd were now quite interested and a murmur went around as yellow jumper produced a brand new omega watch. 'Blimey you're in luck Guv…', he said as he handed the box and watch over. 'But don't worry friends. There are lots of valuable items to be had in these boxes and I cannot bring them back today. I must get rid of everything or the boss will fire me.'

And true enough several expensive items went for a song after that until people were now bidding fivers and tenners for boxes and still getting great bargains.

I got caught up in the excitement and was delighted when I got a box for only £5. We could hardly wait to open the box but held our curiosity in check until we were in a quiet spot well away from the crowd. When we opened the box, there was nothing inside but a cheap comb and hairbrush.

We knew then that we had been conned. We hotfooted it back to the corner but everyone was gone and there was no sign of yellow jumper. I even complained to the police who listened politely and were kind enough not to laugh in my face.

Once home, Doreen went off to Galway and I continued in the Mater. Wives were not allowed in the 'Res' and it was absolutely taboo for them to spend the night with their husbands. But we did not mind. We spent whatever free time we had together and I went to Galway whenever I could.

My impoverished fellow students presented me with a set of suitcases and about £50. The prime mover in this was Dermot McDonald, later to become Master of the National Maternity Hospital on Holles Street. I have never forgotten him for this.

Later I understood that many of them thought that Doreen was pregnant, and that was the reason for such a rushed wedding. Nothing could have been further from the truth.

But the cases and the money were perfect gifts for us at the time, and we are still grateful to the class of '57 for being so generous to us in our hour of need.

The Art of Giving a Blood Transfusion

My internship in the Mater was uneventful. It was during this time that I learned that an intern is the lowest form of life in the hospital. The only ones who respected us were the patients who presumed (wrongly) that wearing a white coat and having a stethoscope wrapped around our necks conferred magical powers on us. Staff nurses knew better. I learned this painfully the first time I attempted to set up a blood transfusion on a patient.

Before I could start the procedure, the staff nurse covered the floor around the bed with old newspapers and then put more papers under the patient's outstretched arm.

'Is this the usual thing..., I mean putting papers everywhere...?', I asked. 'You know John here is not a bleeder...', my voice trailed off. I was beginning to suspect that the papers might have something to do with me.

'Oh, just a precaution...' She grinned knowingly, 'It's your first time isn't it?'

I admitted – in a whisper – that it was. But I knew that confidence is half the battle and I did not want to show any weakness in front of the patient and especially in front of her. I proceeded as nonchalantly as I could.

I started by tying a tourniquet, a piece of red rubber tubing, around the upper arm so that the forearm veins would fill up and stand out. But I put it on too tightly and should have waited until everything else was ready – *first mistake*.

I assured John that there would be no pain – *second mistake*. There always is some pain, often quite a lot of pain if you cannot get the needle in first time. In those days, needles were big and often blunt.

I then took too long cleaning the area in front of the elbow and in unnecessarily draping the intended field of action. I suppose that I was playing for time – *third mistake*.

A quick rub with an alcohol swab is sufficient and there is no need to drape the area as if you were doing a major operation.

Now I was about to make my *fourth mistake*. A huge vein stood up invitingly almost asking to be pierced. But I was slow in piercing the skin and, when I did, no blood came back. I

THE REAL WORLD | 83

had gone too superficially. I poked again, three times, until finally John's blood poured out as if I had hit a geyser. I had stopped saying 'sorry for hurting you' to John. Things were gone beyond such civilities at this point.

Yet now I had the needle in, and all I had to do was connect it with the blood bottle, which was hanging forlornly on the drip stand – *fifth mistake.*

I had not let all the air out of the tubing and so had to let the blood run all the way down the rubber tubing and out on to the floor before I could connect it with the needle in John's vein. Meanwhile, he was being exsanguinated.

Eventually, I got everything connected but now the blood would not run into John. The nurse disdainfully released my tourniquet and bit-by-bit the red fluid (what was left of it) started to course into John's veins.

As the nurse turned away, she hissed 'Put the newspapers into the waste paper bin in the corridor' and then left without another word.

I picked up the sodden papers, feeling quite small in front of John. I certainly lost his respect that day. I think we lost more blood than he received and I think he knew it.

My only consolation was that the ward sister was not present. Even the consultants were afraid of ward sisters.

After leaving the Mater, I went to Holles St where I spent the next six months doing obstetrics in the National Maternity Hospital. Here I worked alongside two classmates. One was Mick McCabe who later went into general practice in Dunboyne, Co Meath. Mick had been in school with me and we were very close. Sadly, he died in his forties. The other was John Taffe, who later became County physician in Cavan. I saw John recently and he has not changed much since our time together as young interns. They were both easy to get along with and we never had any disagreement.

It was while doing my six months in Holles St that Doreen and I began to live together at last. We took a bed-sit in 21a Upper Leeson St for two guineas a week. We paid for electricity by putting either sixpence or a shilling into a slot. We shared the little kitchen and toilet and washroom with two other bed-sits and paid our rent in cash to the landlady every Saturday.

When we complained that we had no wardrobe and no place to put our shoes, she informed us that we should get some shoe boxes and stack them on top of one another. 'That will give you plenty of room for your things', she told us, and then walked away.

Doreen helped eke out our existence by doing some stand-in nursing in St Kevin's Hospital (now St James) as well as an occasional private case in people's homes. They all seemed to want enemas. However, one of the boons of her work was being presented with an occasional box of chocolates. One old man was very fond of her and gave her the biggest box of chocolates I ever saw. It lasted us over a week.

It was shortly after the last sweet had been eaten and towards the end of the month that we stopped one evening to gaze into the window of a small greengrocers on the corner of Leeson St, near the bridge. Among the items displayed, two caught our attention. One was a plate of large green apples, and the other several assorted bars of Cadbury's chocolate. We only had six pence with us. We chose the chocolate.

We Go to Northern Ireland

It was now 1958. By April, I became acutely aware that we had to get a paying job, especially as Doreen was pregnant. First, I tried psychiatry in London. They paid my travel expenses and obviously wanted me, but when I saw the hospital with its turn of the century façade, dark dreary corridors, listless blank-faced patients and grim-looking nurse attendants (more like prison wardens than nurses), I knew I could not cope with that kind of life.

I left the panel who interviewed me in no doubt about my feelings and I am sure that they were privately annoyed at this Irishman so highly recommended by Dr Malone, a colleague of theirs in Dublin.

However, I had to get a job. There were no structured careers in medicine at the time and no one gave a damn what you did or where you went.

I sat in St Stephens Green on a late spring morning reading the jobs page of the *Irish Independent*. I saw that they needed a senior house officer in general surgery in Larne, Co Antrim. The salary was a staggering £650 a year.

I decided to apply. Surprisingly, I got the job – without any interview – and set off to Larne, my first foray into the 'black' North as many Southerners called that part of Ireland.

The hospital in Larne was a dreary place. Almost work-house in design, with long wards, drafty corridors and peeling flakes of grey where there was once white paint. I was assigned to Mr Hugh Wilson who later became an Alliance MP for the area. He was a genial fellow of the old school of surgery, all cut and little thought. I worked hard and put in long hours for him and was always loyal. He even told me that I was the best houseman he ever had. Yet, when I left, he gave me an insipid non-descript reference, which seemed to 'damn with faint praise'. However, it did teach me that many a smile cloaks a hostile heart. I now suspect that it was religious bigotry that made him down me.

In Larne, at the time, there was vicious hatred between Catholics and Protestants. Doreen and I were completely unaware of this until we were warned against going to Protestant shops. We stepped out of line further by becoming friendly with Protestants, despite remaining absolutely Roman Catholic in our beliefs and practices. Nonetheless, ultimately , most of our friends were Catholics.

We found a place to stay on 59a Main St Larne over an electrical shop. You had to climb up steep stairs to get to our flat and this was no easy thing for a pregnant woman. However, we loved our little place and it was only five minutes walk from the hospital if you crossed the road and made your way up the hill along small lanes and alleyways.

Our landlady was Kay Hanratty, a ward sister, and – you guessed it – a Catholic. Kay moved to Dundalk in later years and we used to visit her there. Her kindness to anyone in need gave her life a meaning beyond price. I think that she was a rabid nationalist at the time but mellowed considerably as she got older.

But there was nothing mellow about the religious bigotry in Larne in those days, a bigotry that even extended to my professional life. On one occasion, I was called to attend a dying woman and distinctly overheard her say to the nurse 'Don't let a Papist doctor near me.' When I went to her bedside, she asked me if I was a Papist! My accent had betrayed my Southern origin. She was dying. I managed to avoid telling her the truth by saying something like 'Do you think I'd be attending you if I were a Papist.' She died in peace.

Our First Baby

On 22 December 1958, Doreen delivered a baby girl. Dr Rutherford was in attendance. It was a tough delivery and a tough pregnancy. But we were overwhelmed with happiness at our first-born. Our joy was complete. In January, we went on the train to Belfast and bought a little red 'tansad' pram. It was the latest in baby carriages and also the cheapest. You could detach the carriage part and use it as baby's cot. This pram was to be of great service later, even after I repaired rips in the plastic lining with sellotape.

Our precious bundle was christened Mary Dolores in the spring of 1959 in Rialto, Dublin, by Fr Denny with Mick McCabe and my mother standing as sponsors for Doreen's brother Joseph and my sister Sibyl, respectively. Babies heal so many hurts. What normal person can resist the innocence of a baby. It was the first time I had seen my mother since before my marriage.

A Year in Cork

A cademia, the Refuge of the Ineffectual?

I always loved Physiology. I even gave grinds in it to First Meds while I was a Second Med in Dublin. So when I saw a chance to do an honours BSc in Physiology in University College Cork (UCC) – allied to teaching medical students – I jumped at the chance. I bought our first car, a fourth-hand VW Beetle, CIK 53, and proudly drove it to Galway. I paid £230 and borrowed £100 from my brother Norbert and £100 from Doreen's brother Joseph. I repaid these loans within six months. That's the way Doreen and I were all our lives.

Baby Mary's carrycot fitted in snugly behind the back seat and off we would go with smoke streaming from the exhaust. There was no radio, no heater, no air bags, no seat belts, no *sat nav* and the weak 6 V headlights made night driving a nightmare. But we were as proud of our little car as if it had been a Bentley.

So now we are in Cork. We have found the cheapest place we can, two small rooms in a bungalow in the Commons Rd. Doreen keeps up a smiling face and buckles down to hard living and tough budgeting without complaint. I start doing my BSc in college under Jack Sheehan, a rather stodgy Corkonian with little imagination but a tireless plodder and an honest man. He and his English wife had spent two years in Zambia where he doctored in the copper belt before returning to Cork as a Professor of Physiology. I got to know and appreciate Jack much better when we examined together in the Primary Fellowship in Surgery many years later.

But the student-teacher relationship never disappeared completely and I always called him 'Professor' while he called me 'Dom'.

The lab assistant in Physiology was nicknamed Sandy because of the colour of his hair. His real name was Bernard Allen and he later became a Fine Gael TD for Cork much to the pride of Professor Jack.

During my year in Cork, I studied very hard, first in biochemistry, because I had to do a pass BSc in that subject, and then in Physiology for my honours BSc. I also studied at night for my Primary Fellowship and this meant that, after a dreary day in the house, Doreen had to put up with a husband who spent every evening poring over books. Yet we were very happy in Cork and the car gave us a freedom we had never experienced before.

Our major treat in Cork was to go once a week to *Thompsons* in Patrick St and have coffee or tea and a French fancy. *Thompsons* was to Cork what *Fullers* and *Bewleys* were to Dublin, *The Greenbank* to Waterford and *The Dane* to Limerick. All sold gorgeous pastries.

Perhaps it is old age or perhaps it is the use of synthetic cream and the addition of all kinds of 'e's that has robbed food today of its erstwhile flavour. Or perhaps, it is the huge variety of cakes and pastries available to us on a daily basis, but nothing tastes as good as it did long ago.

A second treat was to visit our parents. We went once a month to Galway to see Doreen's mother. She always made us welcome and we spent many a happy day in her house. We also visited my parents in Waterford, in Tramore to be precise. Here, we were received, perhaps tentatively at first, but warmly as time went by. It actually did not take much time for Mamma to like Doreen, and finally become proud of her.

Babies break down all barriers and Mamma was soon very excited about rolling little Mary out in the pram and showing her off to her friends who cooed and made silly noises as they bent down over the pram. Doreen learned to play bridge while on these trips, and often played in the local club or at house bridge, always partnering my mother. This pleased both of them enormously and bound them together in a special way. Dadda would sit puffing his pipe and also got to like Doreen. And she him.

Our friends in Cork were few but important. One was Liz Condon, the other BSc candidate. Her dad was an ophthalmologist in Waterford and they lived in Kilsheelan Castle on the banks of the river Suir not far from Waterford city. Both Doreen and I were very fond of Liz but, as has happened with so many other friends, we lost contact after a few years.

While in Cork we also became friendly with Dan and Una Carey. Dan worked in the Munster and Leinster Bank (later to become the Allied irish Bank) on the Mall, but moved to several different places afterwards before ending up in Galway. Dan was born in the village of Muillinahone of which he was very proud. In later life, he used to repeat the poem about the glories of that place loudly repeating the following lines:

'The man who hasn't travelled to Muillinahone
Hasn't travelled at all'

These lines always strike me as comical simply because few people ever heard of Mullinahone and fewer have been there.

Dan's wife Una was one of the Canavans of Nun's Island in Galway. I liked Una from the start and count both Dan and herself true friends to this day.

We were to meet up with them again many years afterwards in Galway and renew our friendship. I meet their son Cormac and his wife Mary when I go for my early morning swim in Blackrock, and think nostalgically of those days in Cork when I gave little Cormac his MMR vaccine. Cormac is now a tall, distinguished man not far from retirement age who has worked all his life with Glaxo Smith Kline.

About half way through my year in Cork, a lectureship in Anatomy became vacant in Galway University. I had always been good at Anatomy and felt that I would be well able for the job. So I applied. As was the custom, I visited members of the Senate of the National University of Ireland (NUI) to lobby their support. Doing the rounds of those on the Senate was a *sine qua non* for anyone aspiring for a lectureship in the NUI in those days. It was a demeaning and difficult exercise and thoroughly unfair. Despite being received cordially by most, I failed to get the job.

The incumbent Professor Stephen Shea had his eye on Jim Doyle who was a family friend and much older than me. It was no surprise that Jim got the job. Jim was a son of Professor Joe Doyle (Botany, UCD) and had a brother Stephen who later became the professor of medicine in UCD. Helen their sister had a high administrative post in Earlsfort Terrace. Altogether a well-got family.

In fairness, I must admit that Jim was a better choice than me. He was older, more experienced and an excellent teacher. Indeed, I liked him very much as a person.

My life would have changed radically had I been appointed to that post. As it happened, not getting it was a blessing for me in that I could now pursue the kind of missionary life I had dreamt about as a child.

For Jim it was a mixed blessing. He had hoped to succeed Steve Shea in the Chair of Anatomy in Galway but, when it became empty, it went to Turlough Fitzgerald, an outsider at the time. This was probably the reason for Jim emigrating to Canada and spending the rest of his life there.

So life had surprises in store for both Jim and I.

CHAPTER 7

THE ARMCHAIR TRAVELLER

There Are No Boundaries to the Imagination

There was little opportunity for a young doctor in Ireland in 1960. Money was scarce and, since I had failed to get an academic appointment, it would prove difficult to support Doreen and myself and baby Mary on what I earned drifting from one GP locum to the next. Emigration seemed the right option. But where would I go? I could go to America, like many of my friends, and that was an attractive thought. Or I could go to England. What I had seen of England had not enticed me to live there, nor had working for the NHS (national health service) in Larne enarmoured me with working in that system. And then there was the chance to go to Africa, where they really needed doctors.

The chance to do this, and earn enough to keep my family in reasonable comfort, came when I saw that University College Hospital (UCH), Ibadan, in Nigeria, needed a junior registrar in surgery. Up to now I had been an armchair traveller.

It was from reading Somerset Maugham's collected short stories that I first learned the term 'armchair traveller'. Not the most athletic of men, he was clearly referring to his own predilection for travelling through the pages of someone else's accounts of journeys to exotic places, rather having to undertake such laborious travels himself.

He explained that armchair travelling is by far the most comfortable, least dangerous and least expensive way to see the world. I would add that it also gives the 'traveller' a chance to learn something about the history of different places and the cultures of different peoples.

When the advertisement appeared in the *British Medical Journal* (BMJ), I had just finished reading *The White Nile* and *The Blue Nile* by the Australian war journalist Alan Moorhead.

These books would fire the imagination of the most lugubrious person and they certainly fired mine. Never mind that the Nile was thousands of miles from Nigeria. They were both in the same continent. That was enough for me.

My decision was easily made.

CHAPTER 8
NIGERIA, 1960

The Bight of Benin, the Bight of Benin, Few Come Out, Though Many Go In

By September 1960, Doreen and I were three years married. We had a two-year-old daughter, an old VW Beetle, about £66 in the bank and the clothes on our backs. And although we were very happy, we were also at a crossroads in our lives – and very poor.

I had got a first honours in my BSc in Cork and my external examiner, Professor Verney, of antidiuretic hormone fame, had invited me to work with him in Cambridge. I hesitated. Something inside me was uneasy at the prospect of a career in Physiology no matter how attractive the thought of working in Verney's renowned laboratories. I did not really want to spend my whole life in teaching or in doing full-time research. I was first and foremost a service doctor, wanting *to practise* medicine. And – quite truthfully – I wrestled with the problem of how and where I could I do the most good and yet support my family.

Many of my classmates had gone to the United States and were already making a lot of money. But that was not for me.

Thus, when that junior registrar post in general surgery was advertised by UCH, Ibadan, I immediately applied and, after going to London for an interview, I was delighted to receive a letter informing me that I was accepted. I believed that I could now work where doctors were scarce and at the same time earn enough to keep the three of us in reasonable comfort.

Doreen would have preferred to go to almost anywhere than Africa. But we were young and healthy and very much in love, and she soon got caught up in the excitement of travelling to a new life and to seeing new places.

The one mitigating factor for her was that her sister Mary was also living in Ibadan, where her husband Jim was working as an engineer with the Crown Agents.

We left Galway by the 3.30 p.m. train to Dublin on 29 November 1960, a cold clear lovely winter day. Having arrived in Dublin, we visited our friends the McCanns in 86 Rathgar Rd, and then stayed the night in the North Star Hotel in Amiens St. Next day we took a taxi to Collinstown (now Dublin Airport) where we caught an Aer Lingus plane to London. That was exciting. Air travel was luxury in those days and we enjoyed being pampered by smart air hostesses. All cabin attendants were female, and it was obvious that youth and good looks were important prerequisites for the job.

At Heathrow, we caught a British Overseas Airway Corporation flight to Lagos. Our plane was a Britannia 'Comet', then the latest thing in the jet planes. Of course, smoking was allowed on board, but that did not bother us. We were too excited to either sleep or care.

We stopped briefly in Frankfurt at 6 p.m. and a few hours later landed and refuelled in Rome. Here a motley group of voluble Italians boarded. They talked, smoked and gesticulated non-stop, none of which bothered us. However, those in the rows directly behind and in front of us took off their shoes and the resultant smell of feet laced with tobacco smoke and garlic created a nauseous smell that I still recall with a shudder. Strange how one remembers such trivia after all these years.

The plane droned on and on and, despite the constant babble from the Italians, we slept fitfully. It was still dark when we were aroused for a 'full English breakfast', after which there was the usual stampede to the toilets. One of our fellow passengers must have either fallen asleep or been engrossed in Tolstoy or Dickens, for he spent for ever in the toilet, so much so that the Italian man next in line started to bang at the door shouting something that must have meant 'hurry up... or...I'll come in', because the occupant emerged flustered and red-faced within seconds.

We were now well into our journey and landed in Kano at 6 a.m. on 2 December 1960 for another refuel.

Coming down, just around dawn, was a memorable experience.

Africa looked barren and brown and inhospitable. Yet it emanated an air of mystery which thrilled me. As the plane descended, we could see a line of camels moving parallel to the airstrip. The riders were all dressed in the now familiar Arab garb called a thobe or *jalabiyah* or *khamis* depending on where you live. But at that time, they were the first living Arabs we had ever seen and, we began to realise, that yes, indeed, we were coming to a different world.

Almost as the plane was taxing to a halt, a muezzin called the locals to prayer. Again a first for us. Doreen began to cry.

By now the African sun had started to peel its way up through the hazy Eastern horizon. No matter how often I see sunrise near the equator, I get a tingle up my spine. Perhaps it is the obvious insignificance and transience of man compared to the power and constancy of nature that makes us feel this way. Or perhaps it is the beauty and sheer majesty of this King of the heavenly bodies that humbles us. As the psalmist says 'What is man that you should keep him in mind, mortal man that you should care for him.'

That's the way you feel when faced with the magic of dawn in the tropics.

But more to the actual moment. We were confronted for the first time by lots of Africans hurrying to the plane. They all wore navy shorts and white shirts. Some dragged long hoses and connected them to the under-wing fuelling points; others pushed steps to the front of the aircraft and helped passengers disembark. So many black people! There was only one black person in Galway at that time. Her name was Grace. She was a lovely lady, married to Roy Cazabon, a doctor friend of ours. So you can understand how we gawked ungraciously at the many black people who busied themselves around the plane that morning.

The first thing that greets you when the door of the plane is opened in a tropical climate is a blast of hot air. We arrived in Kano in December leaving an Ireland in the grip of winter. The temperature in Kano, even at that early hour, was already probably in the mid twenties. So we got our first taste of what was to come.

Once in the transit lounge, Doreen stopped crying, but then the baby started to cry, so altogether that morning in Kano airport is one I wish to forget. There was nothing in the transit lounge except hard wooden benches and people kept standing up, shuffling around and sitting down again all without any discernible purpose. We just kept sitting.

At noon, we took off for Lagos, then the capital of Nigeria and, as present, the largest city in the land. Lagos airport is located in Ikeja, which was at that time the most affluent, safe and quiet suburb of Lagos.

But the airport was chaotic. There were queues everywhere, anxious travellers holding documents between their teeth, filling forms and forming queues at all kinds of desks, many unmanned.

So it was a pleasant surprise to find that that someone from UCH was waiting for us with our names on a large placard inside the area normally out of bounds to the general public. He led us deftly through customs and immigration, neither looking to left nor right, and only once left our sides and that was to get our passports stamped after he strode officiously to the head of a queue of grumbling people.

On leaving the airport, we were accosted on all sides by crowds of bustling, haggling, aggressive 'porters' and 'taximen', all claiming to give the best price and many trying to pull our suitcases from us. However, our Nigerian guide had little difficulty in driving them away with obvious threats to their personal integrity should they continue harassing us.

Mary Kenny, Doreen's sister, was waiting in a white Peugeot 404 outside with UCH Ibadan printed boldly on the bonnet. Mary was an old hand in managing such things and shouted at those who besieged us in a way only old coasters can. Most unladylike but most effective.

In a short time, we loaded the hospital car and headed under a glaring white sun towards the city. The drive from the airport to the city is like a drive through life itself. They say you see more people on that drive than you would see during a two-year tour in East Africa. It is a confusing compendium of raucous shouting, tooting horns, near misses and chasing children – gaping at our white wan faces in undisguised fascination.

Progress was slow and beggars crowded around the car. You saw all kinds of people, including lepers, cripples, paralytics, albinos and those with huge goitres, all thrusting their hands at you, all hoping for a *naira* (a penny), all with pleading eyes and harassed expressions.

The streets were unpaved, just plain red sandy laterite, or murram as it is called in other African countries. Open drains were present on each side, which our driver, a local Ibadan man called Jackson, carefully and expertly avoided. This was the dry season, so the drains merely stank with rotting food and the excrement of people and dogs. In the wet season, the drains turn into foul flowing rivers of filth. Why everyone did not contract cholera is a mystery.

Of course, there were no sidewalks until one approached the city centre. But even there, the concrete was broken and people picked their way through scattered debris, bits of iron bars, discarded prams, broken bikes and every imaginable thing, dare I say, 'from a needle to an anchor'.

Sometimes you see such scenes in a James Bond movie when you are sitting in a comfortable seat at home or in a cinema. It is altogether different in real life.

The Yoruba people live in this part of Nigeria. They are loud, noisy and colourful. The men dress in long voluminous flowing robes and the women wear wonderfully patterned, full-length, wrap around dresses with multi-coloured turban-like headdresses. Some women wear an *abetiaja cap* on their heads; this is believed to have been worn by their ancestors over 1,000 years ago in the ancient Yoruba Kingdom.

All walk gracefully and without any self-consciousness, quite unlike the walk of the average European. Both men and women – and indeed children – carry loads on their heads. These loads can be of an enormous size and weight, and are balanced so carefully that you often see people running across the road, zig-zagging between cars, crossing drains or merely stooping to adjust their footwear (if they have any) without mishap.

Babies and little children are called *peckins*. They are wrapped securely in the woman's clothes and are always carried on the mother's back. This again is a sensible way to carry a baby, far more ergonomic than the Western way.

However, we often said later that Nigerian babies were very prone to develop bowlegs, not just from vitamin D deficiency, but also from being carried with their legs, one on each side, firmly clasping their mothers' backs.

We took little in on this first drive in Africa. It was just a blur of colour at the time, and the passage of years has blurred my memories further. Later I learned that the drive to Ibadan took us through what had once been the tropical rain forest, but was now scrubland spotted with native huts, acacia trees and banana groves. We passed through many villages, which were always a hive of activity. People were sitting outside their houses, or gathered in bunches talking, laughing, playing and always dressed properly, although few had shoes.

Typically, men wore long trousers and tee shirts or ordinary shirts often under ill-fitting jackets. However most women stuck to Yoruba dress. One wondered how everyone looked so clean and smart considering there was no running water, no sewage system and no electricity in most of the country.

A feature of Nigeria – and still a feature of Central and East Africa – is the ubiquitous presence of pick-up trucks, land rovers, taxis and mini buses. All the taxis were black Morris minors, probably the best-selling car in the world outside the United States in 1960. Although taxis were inexpensive, most people travelled from place to place in 'mammy wagons'. Indeed, this was the mode of transport for any long distance journey. A mammy wagon was simply a wooden over-structure erected on the chassis of an old-fashioned lorry. It was designed so that could be packed high with goods and people and, when it moved, it was almost like a huge chest of drawers on wheels. Sadly these jam-packed wagons were often unstable and horrific accidents occurred every day. To make matters worse, they were always hopelessly overcrowded with people, animals (dogs, goats and sheep), goods of all sorts and local produce such as plantain, rice, and yam and cassava tubers. Much of the *Garri* and *fufu* (both come from cassava), the staple diet in West Africa, was transported in this way.

Bad driving, bad roads, bad signage, bad weather and badly maintained vehicles contribute to horrific road accidents in developing countries, and Nigeria is no exception. Little heed is paid to safety and overcrowded vehicles are looked on as normal. We regularly saw 'passengers' hanging on for dear life to the back of mammy wagons or perched precariously on the roof.

Mammy wagons were so called because they were the means by which colourful market women (mammies) travelled to work with their chickens, yams, tomatoes, peppers and babies. Nowadays the mammies travel in small Japanese buses and the traditional mammy wagon is only allowed to transport goods. At least, that is the theory.

Ordinary cars often carried more than ten people and once I saw a man on a bicycle on which there were two people sitting on the crossbar, two children in the front basket and three others behind on the 'back seat'. Eight in all! Later, in hospital, I was to see the result of the carnage that was inevitable.

On the lighter side, all the lorries, trucks and mammy wagons we saw had gaily painted slogans such as *In God we trust, No devil here, San Francisco kid, The Lord is my shepherd, Life is transient* and many others which proclaimed the importance or the philosophy of the owner. These slogans never failed to intrigue and amuse us, not only for their ingenuity but also for the genuine artistry that went into many of them.

Most larger villages had rather suspect 'hotels', again with vicarious slogans and names such as *La Paradiso, Heavenly Stop, Gods Resting Place* and many others. Eating-places were frequent but we were in no mood to stop, and anyway we felt that it was better to avoid the local bacteria as far as possible. Every town and village also boasted numerous brands of Christian Churches, too numerous to name. But all proclaimed that they had the message of salvation and most warned of Hell for the wicked, with *The wages of sin is death* being a favourite slogan. We even passed an eighth-day Adventist Church. Obviously, this was better than a seventh-day one.

I would be remiss to omit the odd mosque. Islam is very strong in Northern Nigeria but had made little impression on the South and East in 1960. Yet the mosque and its minaret are so distinctive that it was hard to miss even one as we passed through town after town.

Spirituality

The theme of the supernatural seemed to run through many such public expressions. And this spirituality, this belief in a 'Power' beyond us, is evident throughout Africa up to present times. Nowhere does one see it more than when working in hospitals, where death is accepted as an *inevitable and normal* continuation of life. Not an ending of life.

This does not stop one expressing grief when someone dies. Such grief is as real as anywhere else in the world. Indeed, at the death of a loved one, especially of an infant, grief is expressed far more volubly than in our society.

This was brought home to me recently, while working in the University Teaching Hospital of Lusaka. I was lecturing in the Department of Surgery when we all hushed as the heart-rending screams of a woman who had lost a child in the nearby Obstetric Department split the air. A real African *banshee.*

There was nothing I could do, so, after a moment's hesitation, I continued my talk.

However, it brought back memories of similar scenes in Monze (Zambia), Turkana (Kenya), Abakaliki (Nigeria), Khartoum (Sudan) and Benghazi (Libya). It is as universal as motherhood.

But I digress. We were now approaching Ibadan, the largest 'black' city in Africa. It was an amazing sight. Thousands and thousands of corrugated tin roofs spread below us as we descended from the Western side.

Everything shimmered in a heat haze. Those who were out and about walked or cycled very slowly. Even the odd scrawny dog moved lethargically.

In the midst of the countless shacks and mud houses, stood a handful of concrete buildings, marking the centre of the city.

The long tentacles of Western commerce had reached the heart of this great African conurbation. Bata (shoes), Kingsway (groceries), CFAO (cars, typewriters, technical) and Barclays Bank stood out as reminders of an outside civilisation. All taxis – as in Lagos – were black Morris minors, Britain's answer to Hitler's Volkswagen. However, there was a sprinkling of 'Beetles' and Peugeot 404s, but not one Japanese car was to be seen. All manner of trucks and pick-ups and landrovers and mammy wagons filled the streets. Most of these were proof that miracles do happen in that they actually moved on atrocious roads, with spluttering engines and threadbare tyres.

Skirting the northern rim of the city was the Queen Elizabeth Highway. This was a proper tarmacadam road named after the Queen of England, Elizabeth 11, who had visited Ibadan a few weeks earlier on the occasion of Nigerian independence. Just off this road was our destination, UCH, gleaming white, in the glare of a merciless sun. It stood proudly, a monument to the end of the Colonial rule, the centrepiece of a little town of staff bungalows, apartments, workshops, maintenance buildings and even a small outdoor swimming pool.

The campus of the university lay north of UCH. We later enjoyed walking through this gracious compound. It was beautifully laid out, with halls of residence, lecture theatres and staff quarters, all set in parkland and manicured lawns.

In the succeeding months, we would visit the university campus many times. Sometimes, we were invited to visit consultants who were housed there, and sometimes we went to work in the animal house of the Pharmacology Department as part of my MD thesis. Often, on a Sunday afternoon, we would park the car near the entrance of the campus and stroll through flower-banked avenues or secluded pathways, which were shaded by leafy trees on both sides.

We always went to Sunday Mass in the university chapel. Fr Foley was the resident chaplain. He genuinely loved Nigeria and the Nigerians. Like many an old coaster, he regarded us as belonging to a new breed of traveller – out for the money, out for a life of luxury and adventure and caring little for the Africans. Of course, he was wrong on all counts. But he never saw that.

The Society of African Missionaries (SMA) was the Catholic Church in this part of Nigeria. Fr Foley was an SMA man, as was the local bishop, Richard Finn. Richard Finn, a Mayo man, was the last foreigner to hold this office, and it is a tribute to him that he passed on a vibrant church to his Nigerian successor. He was a man of integrity. Simple, holy, down-to-earth and quite unlike the pompous Bishop Michael Brown who held sway in our hometown, Galway.

We really liked Bishop Finn and used to visit him in Knock in later years where he had retired to a small bungalow near the basilica. We also saw him the day before he died of a heart attack in the Regional Hospital Galway.

He appeared to have had a lonely end to his life lying on a small bed in a small room, but in reality, he was already in heaven before he left this earth, and we could sense that, like a physical force, on entering his room. It was good to have known him.

Initially, we were housed upstairs in a staff apartment block. This necessitated carrying baby up and down several flights of bare concrete steps. We complained about this and somehow got on the right side of Ron, the Chief Maintenance Officer, who offered us a house, No. 21, which had just become vacant.

It was a typical dun coloured colonial bungalow. Two steps led to a small front veranda from which you entered the main living space. Off this was a largish bedroom on one side and a small bedroom and bathroom on the other. A tiny kitchen – with a washbasin and noisy kerosene fridge – led to the back garden. All cooking was done on a wood stove out the back, but water could be boiled inside using an old brown electric kettle, when there was electricity. Unfortunately, the plug was missing and the wall socket was so loose that we were afraid to use it.

Although we had running water, we were warned not to drink it under *any circumstances* unless it was boiled and filtered. We learned quickly to do this as a matter of course and I am sure that it was the single most important health precaution we could have taken.

The furniture was sparse but adequate. The living room had four high-backed wooden chairs and a central table at which we could take our meals. There was also a low settee pushed against one wall flanked by two small tables which were stained with the marks of glasses, spilled tea and cigarette burns. A tall dresser with a motley assortment of crockery stood against the opposite wall and its drawers contained an incomplete set of stainless steel cutlery, a can opener, an old-fashioned corkscrew and a ball of twine. The walls were an off shade of brown and were bare except for one picture of a black woman with a calabash on her head.

There were wooden beds in the bedrooms. They had lumpy mattresses and were overhung by mosquito nets, which had once been white and useful, but were now an off grey colour, torn in many places and completely useless.

All the furniture was standard-issue solid mahogany.

And we were delighted. Everything was wonderful. It was our first house, our very own (for the moment), and we were in no position to criticise anything.

The place was secluded and had a small private front and back garden. A little two-roomed brick house was tucked into the corner of the back garden, close to the main house. This was the servants' quarters. We were lucky in hiring Ogon as our cook/cleaner, and he seemed very pleased to get a position with us and have living quarters for himself and wife and child in our back garden.

Apart from cooking, his duties included washing and ironing clothes (using a solid iron heated on a fire), cleaning the house, gardening, washing the car and doing anything that the 'master' or 'mistress' asked – without question. We paid him slightly above the going rate, for which he worked six days a week with afternoons off. In many houses, servants were treated like slaves and had no time off at all. Hiring and firing occurred at a moment's notice and servants often lost their jobs for no reason other than the whim of the employer. Most treated their staff harshly and told us that the only way to treat servants was with 'the carrot and the stick'.

Some expatriate wives would hit their 'help' across the face, often for trivial offences like breaking a plate or failing to turn down the beds to the satisfaction of the mistress.

Despite this, most preferred to work for expats rather than for fellow Nigerians, who treated their staff even worse, and paid them less. Yes, it was far preferable to work for a mzungu.

The locals called us 'misungi' or 'mzungu' or 'musungu'. This is a generic term used in many African countries irrespective of the native language. Most of us believed that this was a word for a 'stranger' or a 'white man', but it meant more than that. It also implied someone not really wanted, someone out of place or someone lost.

In fact, mzungu is a somewhat derisory term and always brings a smile to the faces of locals when they hear whites calling each other by that name.

I think that Doreen and I had a social conscience even then. For we regarded any ill-treatment of servants as disgraceful. To us, everyone warranted respect no matter who they were, how well educated they were or what job they did.

Indeed, we not only respected but eventually got to love Ogon very much and from the start took care of his wife and child when they were sick. He in turn respected us but was not obsequious, nor did we want it so.

Ogon was not a Yoruba. He was an Ẹdo from Benin city and named after Prince Ogon, the famous fifteenth century Oba (King) of Benin.

Our Ogon's turn of phrase was both original and amusing. For example, he would refer to a bra as a 'knicker for upper' and underpants as 'knicker for lower' and would announce solemnly 'I go for piss Madam or I go shit Madam' without blinking an eyelid. He referred to foeces as 'cú-ca', a term which has since become part of our own vocabulary.

We had a sad parting when we finally left for home.

Doreen settled in well despite the heat, the recurrent bouts of tummy palaver (diarrhoea), the erratic electricity, the 'terrible tiny eggs' (her words) and the expense of anything imported. She loved bargaining with the travelling Hausa men who laid out their wares on the porch. They too loved to haggle. She had one favourite trader who called himself 'Quality'. When 'Quality' was approaching, the house would keep chanting 'Quality coming...Quality coming....' As he left – usually without a sale, despite spending over an hour displaying his wares – he would call out in his sing song way 'Quality going...Quality going....'

Bargaining with Quality always took at least an hour and I think that he enjoyed it as much as we did.

Doreen also made many friends. I suppose that Dorothy Wokoma was her closest one. Dorothy was a blonde nurse, from Belfast, who fell in love with a Nigerian medical student, Charles Wokoma, who was studying medicine in Queens University at the time.

It was a real love match and Dorothy, an only daughter, insisted on marrying Charles and going to live in Nigeria with him. Her family looked on askance but love had its way, and there was no stopping Dorothy.

However, once she arrived in Nigeria, she began to wake up to the realities of being snubbed and sneered at by the women she met, both Nigerian and expatriate.

Local women were annoyed that a 'catch' such as Charles had been trapped by a mzungu. Many of Charles' Nigerian male friends assumed that she must have been a lady of easy virtue and constantly propositioned her and groped her. Add to this the cool reception she received from her husband's immediate family and her own reluctance to fall into Nigerian ways and you can see the marriage was on a disaster course.

The white ladies were no better. They excluded her from their company as much as possible and rarely invited her to their homes.

What a shame.

I liked Charles as a friend and admired him as a professional. But as time passed, I realised that he was easy prey for attractive women and that sooner or later he would leave Dorothy. The inevitable happened. Dorothy fled to Ireland and Charles stayed in Nigeria.

We have long lost touch with either of them, but I was told later that Charles died in the tribal killings that accompanied the Biafran war.

This was our first experience of a mixed marriage and brought home to us the inherent difficulties of marriages between people of different cultures, races, religions and social or educational class.

The day will surely come when such differences will not be important but that day is not yet.

Money was still very scarce despite my salary of £975 per annum. I had many expenses that I had not anticipated. Apart from paying Ogon, buying food and paying rent for our bungalow, I realised that I had to have a car, if only to get to the hospital when on call. This meant getting an advance on my salary. I needed the whole cost of a car and so was advanced £424 which got me a lovely green second hand VW Beetle, LE 6288. It was the pride of our lives and ran without a problem for the next eighteen months.

I still remember the day we sold it. It was a Saturday afternoon. The buyer, a local Muslim, came into our living room swishing his robes imperiously. He sat down and asked how much I wanted for the car. He did not look at Doreen at all or acknowledge her presence in any way. I told him £480 expecting that he would begin to bargain down and that I might get £400. I am useless at buying and selling. I always seem to pay top price when buying and lose heavily when selling. But much to our amazement he agreed there and then without demur.

He produced a chequebook with a great flourish and then a pen – an ink pen – a 'fountain pen'. It would not write. Either it had no ink or the ink would not flow to the nib. I waited anxiously. Surely, the deal would not collapse now. He pointed the pen at the floor and shook it vigorously. At last, the ink came through splashing the mat at his feet. I took the cheque, we shook hands, I gave him the keys and we parted wordlessly.

He had two silent companions waiting outside. The three of them got into the car and drove off without looking back.

What a relief. Then I began to have doubts. Would he stop the cheque before the bank opened on Monday? Was there enough money in his account? I did not know his name or his address or where he worked or where I might find him. What an idiot I was. Doreen was upset but said nothing.

When my sister-in-law heard what I had done, she was furious and was sure that the cheque was worthless, so were any friends, both expats and Nigerians, whom I met that evening. They all agreed that I should have only taken cash. But they all wished me well – as if that would help.

Sunday passed slowly and Doreen and I barely spoke to each other.

I awoke even earlier than usual on Monday morning and suffered in silence watching the clock until it was time to take a taxi and go downtown to Barclays Bank.

I was too early but I was first at the head of a growing queue. I wondered if those behind me were also trying to cash cheques about which they were uncertain.

At last, I heard a rattle from inside and the sound of a heavy bolt being drawn back. The door opened and I made a beeline for the cashier. He was a tall black fellow, beautifully dressed with white shirt and green tie and smartly creased black pants. I pushed the cheque across to him along with my passport as ID.

'Can I have cash please?' I asked. Tremulously.

He looked at me, then at the cheque and then back at me again.

'It is a large amount, Sir… I will have to ask the manager… can you hold on a minute please.'

All very polite and all normal I suppose but all making me more agitated inside.

I waited. It seemed for ever, but was probably only a few minutes. The manager himself came out with the cashier. Both seemed unperturbed.

The manager smiled 'Ah, I see you sold your car…was it giving trouble? … Do you want a loan for another?'

'No…No… trouble…No …I just want to cash the cheque …Please.'

'Of course, doctor. Just a moment.' He turned to the cashier and nodded at him, and then left with a good-bye smile.

The cashier counted out my money and then suggested I do the same before leaving the bank. But I had seen him do it and unless he was a conjurer it was correct. My relief must have been visible. It was certainly palpable.

This was the first and only time I ever made money on a deal.

Having a servant, having lots of time on her hands and knowing our need for extra cash, Doreen decided to work in the local mission hospital at Oke-Offa, which was run by Our Lady of the Apostle Sisters (the OLAs) from Ireland. She worked there for a few weeks, but it was very tiring, very hard work and very poorly paid. She left after one month, and received £25. Small as it seems, nonetheless, this was not to be ignored.

But she had bigger ideas. She would open a crèche in our house to take care of sure-to-pay children from the nearby 'government' district. She did this bravely and started with one child on the first day. After a week or so, other children began to trickle in and finally she cared for 13-14 children from 7 a.m. to 2 p.m. – government working hours.

Our Mary became quite jealous of the attention her mother gave to these children, in particular to one little baby, the daughter of Victor and Clara Ngu. Imagine our distress when we found that our two-year-old Mary had scratched the Ngu baby's face when Doreen was not looking. We were too upset to tell the truth, which was a mistake. Instead, we said something about an insect bite, which was not at all plausible, but was the best lie we could think of. The Ngus continued to use the crèche and even presented us with a memento book before we left Nigeria. But I am sure that they never believed our explanation for their baby's scratches.

Despite working in Oke-Offa, despite running a crèche and despite my salary, we never seemed to have any spare money. I was reading recently through patchy notes Doreen made in an old copybook at the time and which has somehow survived down the years. It illustrates what I say clearly.

On 20 November 1961, she wrote 'I have only one shilling left until the end of the month…how we will manage I do not know.' We had one shilling to live on for ten days.

But we did manage.

My own work in the hospital was initially with Richard Batten, a trauma surgeon (a humble Englishman), then with Peter Konstam, a general surgeon (an arrogant Englishman), then with Hugh Jackson (a gentle Englishman), who was more suited to playing bowls on the village green than to surgery.

Finally, I worked under the Professor of Surgery Will Davey. He was a Northern Ireland man, a meticulous surgeon and a committed outspoken member of Moral Rearmament. His lifestyle mirrored his religious beliefs. He neither drank alcohol nor smoked cigarettes (a rare combination in those days); indeed, he did nothing that was not as perfect as he could make it. It was my first time being close to a truly committed fundamentalist and I found much to admire in him apart from his genuinely held view that the rest of us were of second class in the eyes of the Lord.

The obstetricians in UCH were both burly Englishmen. I remember Professor J.B. Lawson in particular. He was genial and friendly to all and we went to a party he gave, about which I remember nothing except that everyone was laughing loudly and pretending to have a great time. In the lab, E.J. Watson-Williams was outstanding. He was involved in describing haemoglobin D-Ibadan, a variant haemoglobin, often associated with the sickling-type Hemoglobin S. In 1960, the knowledge of sickle cell disease was in its infancy and UCH played a major role in elucidating the condition.

Herb Gilles

The expatriate doctor I knew best and admired most in Ibadan was Herb Gilles, an Egyptian by birth but a Maltese by adoption. Herb was a brilliant malariologist and later became renowned worldwide for his knowledge of parasitic worms. Like all real brilliant men, he was modest, genial and at ease with people from every class of society. He was a small round little man with sallow Mediterranean skin and a big head that contained a remarkable brain.

The death of his first wife Wilhelmina, in a car accident in 1972, came as a crushing blow to him but he recovered and went on to have an outstanding career in medicine. He received honours from many countries and heads of state, including one from Queen Elizabeth 11 of England. He once showed me the scroll, citing the most exotic honour he ever received. It was that making him a Companion of the Most

Exalted Order of the White Elephant presented by the king of Thailand in 2008!

Herb was much in demand as a lecturer and I got to know him well many years later, when we taught tropical medicine together, in the Royal College of Surgeons in Dublin (RCSI).

We both used to stay in the Hibernian Club on St Stephens Green, a rambling old Georgian building, full of nooks and crannies with creaking stairs, gurgling plumbing and freezing bedrooms. Yet we both loved the place because of its air of facilitated neglect – and of its nearness to the RCSI.

Herb was an outstanding scientist, a keen sportsman and no mean a musician. But it is as a warm, generous 'ordinary' personality that I remember this extraordinary man.

His second wife Merja died in 2009 and Herb joined both her and Wilhelmina two years later.

Nigerian Colleagues

In truth, I felt much closer to and was much fonder of my Nigerian friends and colleagues. Felix Udeh was junior to me in rank but an excellent surgeon with a quiet gentle way about him. I loved working with Felix whose natural talent and modest demeanour marked out a great future for him. I do not know for certain what happened to him, but I have been told that brigands murdered him later. A similar fate awaited Ralph Erucharlu (Eruch), my immediate senior.

He was a small guy, very dark, with twinkling eyes and a warm personality that put you at ease immediately. He spoke in a loud voice and with a distinct British accent acquired during his days of training in London. Socially, he was very easy company and professionally very understanding of the problems each of us faced every day in theatre and in the wards.

Poor Eruch would later die, I think in Enugu, during the Biafran war. I was really sad to hear of his death. Caroline, his wife, was full of life, always laughing and always ready to see the funny side of things. She came to stay with us for a while in Ireland after her husband died before going back to live with relatives in the United Kingdom. I am sorry we lost contact with her.

Then there was the aforementioned Victor Ngu, who had entrusted his child to Doreen's crèche. I only knew Clara, his wife, slightly, but understood that she was an outstanding artist. I knew Victor quite well. Victor was a soft-spoken Cameroonian who later became professor of surgery in Ibadan, and was widely admired, not just for his surgical skill, but also for the courtesy with which he treated everyone.

His subsequent career was studded with awards and honours both in Africa and overseas.

He died in 2011 and – with no disrespect to today's African doctors – he left a legacy in the field of cancer surgery that is a jewel in the crown of what I believe was a golden age for medicine in Africa as practised by Africans.

Research

The cause and cure of disease have always fascinated me and so, besides meeting all the challenges of tropical surgery, I embarked on my own little bit of medical research. I was wondering how the human kidney responded to intravenous saline and whether it was different in lower animals, and whether the pituitary gland controlled the response.

I picked on the rat, the most accessible animal I could find. And I decided to use two groups of rats: a normal control group and a group from which I had removed the pituitary gland. Each group would be given the same amount of saline intravenously and the volume and composition of subsequent urine would be estimated during the next week.

My target group consisted of twelve hypophysectomised rats, that is rats from which I had removed the pituitary gland.

I had only two people to do parallel human experiments on, Doreen and myself. We would represent the whole human race! Needless to say, neither of us were about to lose our pituitary glands. I shudder when I look back at the whole thing now.

Doreen was not only my human 'guinea pig' but my laboratory assistant in this work and, as such, accompanied me to the experimental laboratories in the university at night where I had permission from Professor Schneider, Head of Pharmacology, to operate on as many rats as I wished.

Most of the unfortunate animals died painlessly under the anaesthetic, but I was able to complete my studies on twelve that survived.

The human side was easier. Doreen and I set up infusions on each other while we lay on the settee in our living room. We must have looked an extraordinary sight lying there side by side with our drips running and both of us probably smoking a cigarette. Ogon must have thought that we were the strangest mzungus he ever worked with. Perhaps we were.

Unfortunately, I do not think that my research was of any great benefit to mankind. It certainly was of no benefit to the rats. However, it did contribute to my being awarded an MD a few years later.

Settling Down to Ordinary Life

Much of our time in Ibadan, as recorded by Doreen in her makeshift diary, is probably of interest only to our children. It recounts a time of hard work, ambitions, trials and tribulations as well as of happiness and fun. It was a good time for us.

We were happy together, worked together and thought that life was never ending.

It was also a time when we developed new tastes in food and were able to enjoy magnificent tropical fruits such as pineapple, oranges, lemons, avocado, paw-paw, mangoes, passion fruit and bananas, fresh and sweet as nature intended. Pulled straight up from the ground or plucked straight off the tree.

We lived very frugally, but well. Ogon made lovely yam cakes, baked pineapple pie desserts, cooked up a super ground-nut stew and occasionally presented us with a ten-man curry. It is not that it takes ten men to eat it or make it. The name refers to the fact that there are at least ten different sauces, spices, condiments and types of nuts and fruits already placed on the table, which you add to your steaming hot rice and curried meat according to your taste.

It was a stock Sunday lunch in many mission houses after which everyone, except the unfortunates who did the wash up in the kitchen, fell asleep.

But only Doreen could make a special glazed American cake that everyone loved, colourfully called the devil's food cake. It was a combination of *baked Alaska*, chocolate cake and a *soufflé*, all smothered in white frosted icing decorated with smarties or sparkling 'hundreds and thousands'. It was everyone's delight, including the ever-present 'sugar' ants.

These little creatures even entered the fridge to feast on it.

I am sure that not only us but also our friends ate many a slice of Doreen's special cake blissfully unaware of the fact that dozens of sugar ants were deeply embedded in it!.

Anyone who has lived in the tropics knows that an afternoon siesta is an essential part of life. Newcomers like myself could never get into this habit, which we considered indolence at its highest. But old-timers knew that it was necessary to avoid the heat of the day if they were to survive and that breaking up the day with a siesta gave them renewed energy to face the evening and night.

Many called the afternoon siesta the 'holy hour', during which they were not to be disturbed for any reason other than imminent calamity. I now realise that an afternoon nap fits in nicely with our circadian rhythm and makes a lot more sense than driving ourselves at a time when our bodies need rest. It is probably for this reason that 8 a.m. to 2 p.m. is considered a normal working day in the tropics and virtually all official businesses cease from 2 p.m. onwards. However, in the commercial world, shops re-open around 5 p.m. and stay open until 10 p.m. Air conditioning has made little impact on a practice so long established.

Mostly life was routine and breaks were few and far between. We did not drink alcohol, but there were many who did and I expect many of these drank too much. We still recall with laughter the visit from a Holy Ghost priest who was no acquaintance of ours and who decided to give the local Irish doctor a visit. We offered him a whiskey, which Ogon duly brought on a small tray. He then offered our guest a tumbler into which he poured, what seemed to me, a generous amount of *uisge beatha* (lit. water of life).

He asked 'Fadder' if he wanted some water with his drink. The priest shooed him off with a wave of his hand.

'Water spoil the drink… Fadder needs proper drink.'

Ogon smiled and went to leave taking the bottle with him.

But before he could reach the door, our visitor called after him in a sharp voice:

'Boy… Leave the bottle boy… NEVER take away the bottle when serving a Fadder….'

Ogon did as told and left the bottle down on the ground beside Fadder's chair. He immediately lifted it up and filled his glass to the brim.

This shocked our puritanical minds. But we were to learn in time that alcohol was the means by which many expats, including priests, managed to survive. It was often the only solace for those who were far from home, in a land where it took up to three weeks for an airmail letter to come, in a place where you had to go to the nearest big town to book a phone call and in a climate where the monotony of the seasons was mirrored in the monotony of life. Where loneliness is the norm.

Ado-Ekiti

On a rare occasion, when we took a trip, we visited Carmel Garvey, a classmate of mine from my days in UCD. Carmel was one of the St Louis sisters, a French order of sisters, founded in response to the wave of atheism that spread in Europe as a result of the French Revolution of 1789.

The Irish branch ran a well-known school for girls in Monaghan, but their remit went far beyond teaching once they spread to countries where medial facilities were poor or non-existent.

Thus, when they came to Nigeria in 1948, they opened hospitals as well as schools. My classmate Carmel was posted to Ado-Ekiti, a modest-sized town 125 miles east of Ibadan, where she was the only doctor in a busy mission hospital.

Ado-Ekiti or Ado, as it is known, is now a large city, capital of the state of Ekiti, and it boasts all the amenities of a thriving metropolis with its own airport, university and medical school.

The Ekiti area has been inhabited by proud and warring tribes for thousands of years but unfortunately most its history is lost in the fog of antiquity. Yet folk memories persist, and today's administration is making every effort to promote its unique cultural heritage. However, there was little of the 'city' about Ado when Doreen, baby Mary and I made the trip there from Ibadan one Sunday early in 1961.

We approached the hospital about 11 a.m., happy to see a faded 'H' sign hanging at an angle from a rusty roadside pole and happier still to see the hospital itself. We pulled up at a low-set white-washed building, obviously the convent, with large flower-filled calabashes on either side of the front door. The watchman had waved us through the gates of the hospital compound as we were obviously expected. As I turned off the engine of my VW Beetle, the covent door opened and Carmel came out, all smiles and hugs for both of us.

Carmel was closely followed by her community who were almost as effusive but that was nothing to the joy they showed when fussing about our little girl who had been hanging back shyly tugging at her mother's skirt.

Her shyness soon evaporated when they put a plate of jelly and ice cream in front of her assuring us that the ice cream was homemade.

After the excitement died down, Carmel said that she would show us the hospital while one of the sisters led Mary off by the hand – without protest – to explore the convent and the back garden.

Carmel was a typical example of a dedicated missionary doctor who put her patients welfare above all else. She worked seven days a week, twenty-four hours a day and grabbed what sleep when and where she could. She told me that there was little time for prayer and that she often slept during communal prayers such as Matins and Lauds.

She was greeted warmly in every ward by staff and patients alike, and there was no doubt that everyone loved this pale white Mamma.

However, we were taken aback when we saw hens walking about in the operating theatre. But Carmel only laughed and shooed the hens out saying this was an everyday occurrence when the theatre door was left open.

The theatre was little more than an ordinary room with a table in the centre. Yet it was here that Carmel delivered babies by section, it was here she resected gangrenous bowel and it was here that she saved the lives of many a bread winner, many a mother and many a child. Years later, we reminded Carmel of the hens when visiting her in the St Louis Convent in Rathmines in Dublin. She retired there until becoming a victim of dementia in 2016.

Carmel was a clever doctor and, more remarkably, a brilliant thinker who could articulate her views clearly and simply. She and I became even friendlier in later years when both of us served together on the executive board of *Medicus Mundi*, an organisation dedicated to promoting health issues in the developing world.

Mission Hospitals

Mission hospitals were far better than the government ones. They were much cleaner and the staff was more caring and compassionate than in any government-run institution. Treatment was far better; it was given independent of means. No bribes were allowed and no '*dashes*' were asked or expected. Medicine was of a good quality, operating equipment was sterile and the doctors were not only brilliant professionals but worked day and night irrespective of tiredness, salary or conditions.

And yet everything was basic. Gloves were re-used, gowns patched and needles were re-sterilised again and again, until they became as blunt as crochet needles.

Ado-Ekiti – Matters Arising

I think that it was our visit to Ado-Ekiti, and seeing the work done there, that finally made me face up to a call I had always felt, that someday I would work in a mission hospital. The second great influence was the work of my four childhood heroes: Fr Damien in Molokai, Dr Albert Schweitzer in Gabon, Mother Mary Martin in Nigeria and that redoubtable mill-hand from Aberdeen, Mary Slessor in Calibar.

The great explorers of Africa, such as Mungo Park, Henry Morton Stanley and David Livingstone, inspired the less altruistic desire of seeing and discovering exotic places for myself.

Night Terror

After that, digression let me get back to our humdrum lives in Ibadan.

It seemed just an ordinary night. Although I was on duty, things were quiet, and with the baby settled down in her cot, we both turned in at eleven o'clock.

It must have been around 1 am in the morning when the phone woke me up. Any doctor who has done 'on-call' will tell you that you are instantly awake at the first ring of the phone. Indeed, I have often dreamt that I could hear the phone ring, even on nights off! And I would be so relieved to wake up and realise that I could turn over and go back to sleep again.

However, this was a real call, but nothing that necessitated me leaving my house. I sat on the edge of the bed, phone to my ear, telling the nurse at the other end what to do. I was in fact half out of the bed with legs dangling on the floor. As I spoke, I could feel my feet itching, and by the time, I finished the call, the itch had crept up to my knees. I switched on the bedside light and pulled up the legs of my pyjamas.

Both my legs were covered in big dark red ants that were rapidly climbing upwards and biting like mad as they ascended. I beat them off, slapping myself wildly and, when I looked at the floor, I could see that it was covered in a dark swirling mass of ants – something you might see two decades later in an Indiana Jones movie. Doreen was wakened by the hullabaloo and together we started stamping on the floor trying to kill as many ants as we could. With all the lights on it became clear that there were millions of ants everywhere and that all we were doing was disrupting their march and causing them to panic and scatter everywhere.

By now we realised that they had invaded not only the bedroom but also the whole house. We raced to make sure the baby was safe and were relieved to see that she was still fast asleep. Nonetheless, we decided to take no chances and carried the cot into the living room where we put it on the centre table. Baby still slept soundly.

We next tried to sweep the ants out the door with brooms, but to no avail. Their numbers seemed infinite. Finally, in desperation, I poured methylated spirit all over the floor and set it on fire. This was stupid and dangerous, but luckily the flames died down quickly before any real damage was done.

The ant attack lasted till morning and by dawn the numbers of ants passing through was less. For that was what they were doing, just passing through. They were on the march and saw no reason why a house should cause them to deviate from their path.

The hospital maintenance men came shortly after dawn and smoked the remaining ants out of the house. We learned a lesson that night. Never disturb soldier ants when they are on the march. Let them pass. Live and let live.

We had been warned about the dangers of mosquitoes, scorpions and snakes coming into the house. Geckos and cockroaches and different sorts of lizards could be ignored. But no one told us about the possibility of an invasion of ants.

Ron, the genial beer-bellied maintenance officer, explained later that Nigerian soldier ants only march at night and were commonly seen on the move around Ibadan. He told us too that there would not be a living thing left in our house once they had passed through. He was right. We were free of cockroaches, ants, spiders, geckos and lizards for months afterwards. Ron, a good humoured 'tommie', always saw the bright side of things.

Dining Out

People eat out nowadays without giving it a second thought. It was not so in my time when eating out was reserved for special occasions like a funeral or a wedding. So in our year and a half in Nigeria, we only ate out once, and that was because Doreen's sister Mary and her husband Jim Kenny invited us to dinner one evening, explaining that a Lebanese couple had invited them, and by extension us, to dinner in their city centre restaurant. We did not know our hosts but Jim had done some plans for enlarging their premises and this was their way of saying thanks.

I do not remember the meal exactly but thought it rather insipid. Neither Doreen nor I drank alcohol at the time and so were perfectly sober leaving at about 10 p.m. Ibadan had no city lights and since it was a cloudy night, there was little to go by except the weak headlights of our VW Beetle. I was picking my way slowly in the half dark, not sure of the way, when turning a corner, I misjudged the closeness of the roadside drain and suddenly felt that the car was tilting to the left. I braked and we came to halt with the front and back wheels on my side spinning in the air. The car was now leaning at an angle so that

I was looking down on Doreen who was sitting speechless in the passenger seat. There are times when things happen so fast that one is dumbfounded, paralysed and completely unable to think clearly. That's the way we were.

We were not afraid that we might be assaulted by locals, although we could have been. We were not worried about the car, although we should have been. We were not even concerned about our child, alone in the house with a foreign babysitter, although we would have been – if we thought at all. It was only afterwards that these thoughts entered our minds, and when they did, we felt as if a sledgehammer had hit us.

What happened was sudden and unexpected. We both climbed out gingerly and terrified that the car would tip over completely. But it stayed there, swaying slightly but steady enough. There was no way that I could push it up out of the drain. There was no way that our combined strengths could shift it. We stood silent for a moment gazing at the car. Silent and blank. And then, as if by magic, a group of men came out of the shadows like moving silhouettes, coalescing into human shapes against the dark background.

For a moment, I was afraid but I soon realised that they had come to help. 'You need help Massa?…Na so?' one asked.

'Oh yes…please. We need to get home to our peckins… I am a dokita….helping your people…' I was pulling all the tricks I knew. 'I see you in hopikal' one of them replied and grinned happily at me 'You give me injection for power?' I knew what this meant and I nodded vigorously 'Sure, no problem, You come to me anytime… But help us first, please.'

An injection for 'power' meant an injection to increase his virility. Today he might look for Viagra. I would have given him anything at that moment.

In no time at all, they heaved the car up and back on the road. We sat in again, gratefully, and Doreen dispersed whatever change we had as I revved up the engine and took off with a screech of tyres, this time keeping strictly to the centre of the road. That was to be our first and last night out in Ibadan outside the Hospital complex apart from our trip to Ado-Ekiti.

Our rescuers were the ordinary people of Ibadan. Probably none of them had a regular job. Probably none of them were literate. Probably all of them lived from hand to mouth eking out a living by selling bits and pieces in the market. No comment.

We travelled home on the *MV Auriol*, the flagship of the Elder Dempster lines. Our journey from Lagos to Liverpool took almost fourteen days and included stops at Takoradi (Ghana), Freetown (Sierra Leone) and Las Palmas (Canary Islands). We bought souvenirs at every stop. In Takoradi, we bought a beautiful mahogany table held up by a carved elephant. It cost one English pound. In Freetown, we bought some small African carvings for a few shillings and in Las Palmas we bought a colourful dressing gown for three pounds, which Doreen still had – as new – almost 60 years later.

For us the voyage was an experience we would never forget. We were served the best of food and treated with the old world courtesy that still exists on the high seas. The boat was small and intimate but even so we lived in our own little world and did not mix with the other passengers. The only times we mingled were when we had to attend the Captains party and when we were invited to dine at the Captains table. We got a table just for the two of us in the dining room and probably looked like a pair of honeymoners to the seasoned eyes of the other passengers who all seemed to be middle-aged colonials with loud voices and empty heads.

Bit by bit the weather grew colder. This was very welcome at first, but by the time we got to Liverpool and found ourselves facing a cold March wind, we began to miss the warm sun of

Nigeria. For all that, we were absolutely delighted when we set foot on Irish soil again.

Even the cold, rain and wind of Galway could not dampen our spirits. We were home.

It would be three full years before I was to step on African soil again.

CHAPTER 9

LIBERIA, 1965

The Call of the Coast

This time I travelled to Africa on my own, drawn back once more to the West Coast. There was nothing altruistic about it. We had a very poor salary at home and absolutely no savings nor any hope of gathering enough money ever to buy a place of our own. Furthermore, I wanted to go someplace where I could do some clinical research and so advance my career.

An ideal opportunity came up when I saw an ad in the BMJ for a temporary post as a medical officer in the Liberian Institute for Tropical Medicine (LITM). I applied successfully and was contracted to do a locum for Dr Earl Reber. The locum was to last three months and the pay was in US dollars.

And so, in June 1965, I set off for Liberia as an 'economic migrant' knowing little or nothing about where I was going or what duties I would have. And although I was torn at the thought of leaving my family, I was excited at the prospect of working in Africa again.

I was given a prepaid air ticket which specified that I must overnight in either Madrid or Lisbon. I chose Lisbon on the outward leg and Madrid coming back. I had never been to either city and so this was to be an added bonus for me. As happened I saw little of either city. In both cases, a taxi ferried me to my hotel and back to the airport next morning so that my hopes of sightseeing were limited to peering out a car window. Still I could always say that I had visited these cities and duly impress my friends.

The flight out was uneventful. I flew from Dublin to Lisbon using Transportes Aéreos Portugueses (TAP) popularly called 'Take Another Plane' because of its reputation for delays. Next morning, I caught a Pan American Airways (PAA) flight to Liberia. Nowadays air travel is cheaper, faster, more efficient and safer than before, but the service and attention paid to the traveller have deteriorated greatly unless one travels in first class and pays an enormous fare. The important thing is to arrive safely at your destination and that I did when the big PAA jet taxied slowly to a halt in Robertsfield, an hour drive from Monrovia.

Robertsfield International Airport belied its grandiose title in 1965. The terminal building consisted of a run-down arrivals-cum-departure hall, a few rooms where staff and aircrews worked or rested, and an elevated tower for the air traffic controller. However, it did have radar and its tarmacked runway was long enough to take the largest jet planes at the time.

Two red and white tenders stood outside the terminal building on the steps of which several soldiers stood carrying Kalashnikovs carelessly under their arms. Others lounged or dozed in the shade nearby. The atmosphere was hot and sticky and – if an atmosphere can be described as such – it was indolent.

Dr Reber met me. He was an evangelical American from the Deep South, overtly committed to his beliefs, who liked to be seen primarily as a missionary and secondly as a doctor. It was the first time I had met a southern Baptist and the first time I had heard a southern drawl in real life, although it was instantly recognisable from having seen *Gone with the Wind* many years before.

It was a hot humid June afternoon when I alighted from the plane. The good doctor was waiting just inside the terminal building and recognised me immediately. He was obviously delighted to see me as he clasped my hand with a sweaty palm and I think that he would have embraced me continental style had I not unconsciously stiffened.

He was small, chubby and perspiring heavily. Indeed, I was to discover later that he was constantly perspiring and constantly wiping his brow with a large white handkerchief. He reminded me of a smaller edition of Robert Morley in the 'African Queen', a film I had recently seen in Dublin. Of course, his accent was different, but his passion for the Bible was similar and his self-righteousness in all subjects was very similar.

Nonetheless, it was a warm welcome and a good start. We went together to the immigration counter where my passport was duly stamped with a red and black imprint worthy of a Picasso. After that, we waited for my luggage to arrive. It came more quickly than I expected and I easily identified my tattered suitcase among the smart ones which were stacked on a trolley pulled by an officious looking porter.

All the while, we were making conversation about my trip, the weather and the dreadful state of the world.

Our next call was to a bored looking custom man who marked my case with chalk and then we were through.

In those times, it was normal to meet passengers once they entered the arrivals hall or even on the tarmac as the plane rolled to a halt. That is unheard of nowadays unless you are meeting a Head of State or a special VIP.

A big black American Ford was waiting outside with a uniformed driver at the wheel. We both settled in the back seat and waited while the driver took my case and put it into the boot. Then we were off, driving through a plantation of tall well-manicured rubber trees. Dr Reber explained that the Firestone Corporation managed thousands of acres here producing rubber for their tyres. He described Firestone as a benign giant that took care of all the little people that worked for it. 'They even have their own hospital, they have a school for the locals, they allocate nice houses to their employees.... without Firestone this place would be lost, there would be no money, it would be back to barbarism.' I paraphrase, of course, but there was no doubt that he was sincere.

I wondered if my chubby friend knew anything of the history of this land or did he think that civilisation only came with the white man.

In a short time, we passed through the village of Harbel. This was a cluster of native huts where the general workers, cleaners and clinic attendants lived. Just beyond it was a group of nicely built brick houses, each with its own garden. Dr Reber told me that, except for one, all these were occupied by 'expats'.

We stopped here.

One of these houses would be mine 'The smallest... since I was living alone.'

The clinic where I would work was about 200 metres further on. It was somewhat bigger than a house but nonetheless only a small one-storied red brick building with a corrugated iron roof and a rather gloomy appearance.

'This is where you will see patients and although there are two beds for in-patients you should send anyone who is really sick to Monrovia.'

He explained that most routine tests and investigations could be carried out in Firestone hospital, but since one had to pay an economic fee there, it was mostly used by whites. He left me in the care of John Baum, the maintenance man at LITM, who was really a *fac totem* for the institution.

John was a German, had fought in the Second World War and made little secret of his Nazi past or of his Nazi sympathies. He had a wife Ruth and a twelve-year-old daughter Anita neither of whom spoke much although I am sure they had plenty to say when alone.

John was competent at his job and always reliable. He often talked about using the 'stick and the carrot' to get the 'natives' to work, and I have no doubt that he regarded the native people and probably me as somehow inferior beings.

However, as LITM was funded by the United States, he owed Uncle Sam for his livelihood, and he constantly talked about his hopes to emigrate and settle finally in the United States.

I became very friendly with one expat family, the Lafontaines, from Valleyfield, Quebec. Yvon and Ruth Lafontaine obviously pitied the lone Irishman and frequently had me to dinner in their house. I enjoyed their company – and their food – very much. It was with them that I first tasted *fondue*, a dish virtually unknown in Ireland in those days. It was with them too that I got my first taste of *Nasi Goreng*, an Indonesian dish. They told me that even better *Nasi Goreng* was served in the Bali restaurant in Amsterdam. I had the chance to vindicate this claim a few years later when Doreen and I visited Amsterdam.

My friendship with Ruth and Yvon was more than the usual transient friendship one strikes up with fellow travellers abroad. We kept it up for a long time, and Doreen and I even stayed with them some years later when visiting Quebec.

I filled my time in Liberia as best I could. I quickly realised that there was little work to be done apart from the morning clinic. Here I treated the usual tropical illnesses as best I could with chloroquin for malaria and mebendazole for roundworms. There were of course the usual chest infections, coughs (sometimes TB), skin rashes (usually as much a mystery to me as to the patients) and various cuts, bruises and simple fractures. Often I would see 60 or more patients at a clinic session.

I Become a Vet

I know that I made myself unpopular with the expat population by insisting that expats who wanted to see me must queue up like any other patient.

This was brought to a head one morning when a white couple pushed their way to the top of the queue and insisted on seeing me immediately – even as I was examining a local child. Imagine my amazement and then anger when I saw, in the man's arms, a small dog who was presented to me as an 'emergency'.

'We think he has broken his leg' the wife explained 'and he is in pain.'

'Ma'am' – I really was stern – 'Please go to the vet and keep this dog out of my clinic.'

'The nearest vet is in Monrovia', she wailed, ignoring my rising anger.

And yet I relented. That's typical of me. I can suddenly get very angry, and just as suddenly, my anger melts away. They both clearly loved this dog and later I learned that they always had a place set at table for him so that the three of them would eat together. So I said more kindly

'Well, wait until I have seen all the patients and then I will look at your dog.'

They had then no alternative but to wait until after1 p.m. A two-hour wait. The dog's leg was fine, no obvious break. I think that I wrapped a bandage around it and charged them ten dollars, which I gave to my attendant. So the story ended well for everyone.

Clearly, someone thought it strange that I should be living alone much less leading a celibate life. I presume people thought it unnatural. That probably explains why an elderly man knocked on my door one evening and asked me outright whether I would like to take one of his daughters, a virgin he stressed, presumably to provide for my every need.

I declined politely, wishing to give no offense, saying I would be going home to my wife in Ireland in a couple of months. But this did not seem to deter him. He repeated his offer once more and this time I was much firmer in refusing. He shook his head sadly and looked at me presumably wondering what kind of man I was and then turned on his heel and went away quietly, without a word, into the darkness. I never saw him or got another offer again.

I now realise that he was showing me a great kindness and mark of respect, and that my refusal was quite unexpected and even rude. This was to be only one of many lessons in transcultural differences that I learned in my long career overseas.

I have always loved both dawn and dusk in the tropics. As the new day starts, the sun ascends majestically above the horizon like a living ball of fire emerging from some hidden furnace. Everything is suffused in a golden glow while tentacles of probing light pencil the distant hills and make the dew glow on the trees.

Soon, quickly, inexorably, the gold turns to yellow and the individual shapes of trees, shrubs and houses come into focus. The animal world is awakening too. Songbirds begin their dawn chorus, loud, often discordant, but always vibrant. There is a stirring in the ponds and the undergrowth as the night creatures find shelter in deep pools and in crevices and caves. Shortly, day will take over and the sun will become a blinding molten white disk and glare down from a clear blue sky with an all seeing eye.

Dusk is gentler. It too comes almost without warning and night follows swiftly. At first, you are conscious of a softening of the sunlight as if a dimmer switch were being slowly turned. With this, a slight breeze arises which ruffles the grass and causes leaves to tremble. Little ripples disturb the calm surface of ponds, rivers and lakes, and clouds of winged insects rise up from the surrounding rushes and reeds.

Quite suddenly, there is a conscious deadening of the day's heat in step with the failing light. Songbirds thrill the air once more, not with the raucous, impetuous, dissonant cacophony of daybreak, but rather with sweet melodic tunes and with plaintive evening calls as mother birds bid their young to come home and father birds signal it is now a time for rest. All except the fruit bats and flying foxes who swirl out from their daytime roosts and blot out the moon as they sweep across the darkening sky and search for food.

It is time to end another day in peace and harmony.

The Hum of Night

Once it is night and the shadows have stretched full-length, loud-mouthed frogs, raucous male African crickets and little winged insects such as mosquitoes, gnats, midges and cicadas take centre stage. Together they create a rhythmic night symphony that fills the evening air with an obsessive hum. The most intrusive players in this night orchestra are the bullfrogs that try to drown out the rest by sheer volume and who seem to ignore any semblance of recognizable musical order.

Now it is full night. You are alone under a velvet sky embossed with a thousand stars. It is still dark, still warm, noisy, humid and absolutely delightful. You and the world are at peace.

I wrote a poem to dusk in Liberia in 1965. Does this sound strange? I only came upon it the other day (50 years later) as I was clearing out the immense amount of rubbish, old letters, lecture notes, unwanted photos and *bric a brac* accumulated over a life time.

This poem, an amateur dirge without literary value, comes from those days. Skip it if you wish. I always skip long poems in the *Lord of the Rings*!

Dusk (1965, Liberia)
The mood of dusk can turn the cup,
The cup that we call life
Into a frightful fearful thing
That dreads approaching night

And as each minute slowly turns
And beckons darkness on
A night bird pauses in the still
To sing a mournful song

For with each note the gathering mist
Envelops sky and land
Phantasmogoric things appear
And flit on either hand

At length as darkness drapes the scene
To hush up every sound
Shy moonbeams pierce the darkened sphere
And creep along the ground

The images that dusk begets
To haunt the ebbing day
Make all things still, as still as death
That stalks unknowing prey

My little house was a lonely spot but I read a lot at night using a bush lamp. Sometimes I would use a candle but I know that using a candle is a stupid thing to do. Candlelight is weak and it flickers. This puts a strain on your eyes. But worse, candles are dangerous. You may fall asleep but the candle does not, and so you can set your house alight in a moment.

Worse still, if you take the candle inside the mosquito net, your whole world can go up in flames in a few seconds. I have used candles many times under my mosquito net, even as recently as 2013 when I was in Malawi. It is both a stupid and dangerous thing to do.

I did not take afternoon siesta like most others. Instead, in order to pass the time, I spent most afternoons in the clinic where I measured the albumin and urea levels in the plasma of native Liberians and compared it to that of expatriate blood. Of course, this was totally unethical and done without asking anyone's permission. I published my findings later in the *Irish Medical Journal* showing that the levels of albumin and urea in native Liberians were significantly lower than in expats. I reckoned this was either because of the lack of protein in the local diet or else the lesser ability of the Negro kidney to retain protein. This work passed unnoticed and undoubtedly is crude by today's standards.

There was little recreation as such. There was no club to go to, no sports to watch, no television, no radio and I could not speak the local language. Sometimes I would walk from the clinic down a path to a small lake where the weaverbirds congregated on a large tree that stood close to the edge of the water. They were so busy bringing twigs and leaves to the tree that I could almost touch them without interrupting their work. There were thousands of these little birds and it was fascinating to watch them at work.

I suppose that the locals thought that I was just another eccentric or slightly 'touched' expatiate and perhaps they were right. Many expats are eccentric and are slightly 'touched'.

Many expats cannot survive back in their own country. Many expats feel themselves 'big men' when lording it over the 'natives' in a developing one. At least that was the way I saw things.

Independence Day

July 26 is Independence Day in Liberia, you could say William Tubman's day, for he was the father of the modern nation. Historically, independence was declared in 1847, a year that marked the height of the famine in Ireland and that presaged the rash of revolutions in Europe in 1848.

Independence Day in Liberia in 1965 turned out to be fine and sunny despite occurring in the middle of the rainy season. Since I was the only doctor in the area, I was invited to the celebrations in Marshall City, an hour's drive towards the coast. This was probably the original 'city' in Liberia where the Paramount Chief lived in the old days. It was named, as so many places are in Liberia, after an American, in this case Chief Justice John Marshall, who had strongly supported the repatriation of emancipated slaves to West Africa in the 1800s.

In 1965, Marshall City was a derelict half-shanty, half mud-hut, bedraggled place, scattered somewhat haphazardly on the banks of the Farmington River. This is a wide crocodile infested river with many sandbanks and treacherous stretches, but sprinkled with many lovely little islands. The most famous of these is Chimpanzee Island, which has become a major tourist attraction in recent times.

Being a foreigner, and a guest, I got special attention and was ushered politely into a dug-out canoe just wide enough for one person. Four strong boatmen, two in front and two behind, paddled me safely first upward and then across to the other side of the river. Well not quite to the other side because we suddenly beached in shallow water about three metres from our destination.

I was prepared to wade ashore but, without a moment's hesitation, my four paddlers pounced on me and carried me bodily to dry land. This embarrassed me enormously as I did not know whether they were doing this because I was a white man or because I was a doctor or because they thought that I was an old man. In any case, I was deposited on the dry ground amid much laughter and grinning.

Five minutes later, I found myself in the town square which consisted of an open space surrounded by low buildings. This was clearly the focal point of the town where the market was situated and in which all public celebrations and meetings took place. We crossed the square to the largest and most imposing building on view, the 'Superintendent's House', where I was given a seat second next to the chief on the front veranda.

From here, we had an unimpeded view of the square. Lest I give the impression that the 'Superintendent's House' was an imposing affair, I hasten to add that it was a single storey building, made of mud bricks and had one small front opening with a window on either side. There was no glass in the windows, and no discernible front door. There was only a heavy drape over the entrance, which was pulled aside, revealing a dark interior.

Our seats were slatted garden chairs placed so that we were in the shade. This made a welcome change from the glaring sun that beat down on us when crossing the river. There were a few low tables beside the chairs on which there was a box of cigars, dishes of roasted peanuts and several bottles of Fanta Orange. There were also several crates of beer on the ground immediately below the veranda and within easy reach of the dignitaries.

These dignitaries included the Chief, the Liberian Ambassador to Senegal, the Secretary for Information and Cultural Affairs, the Mayoress and a local, addressed as General Marshall. Yvon Lafontaine (who had arrived separately) took a seat beside these and we were very conscious that we were the sole white men in the whole assembly.

We all greeted one another politely and then waited, sipping our beer and wondering what was going to happen next.

We had not long to wait. For above all the din, there came – gently at first-, the sound of music, obviously from a live band. It grew louder and louder and then, as we craned forward, we caught sight a flamboyantly dressed brass band appearing between the houses across the square.

They were playing a rousing Souza march worthy of a passing out ceremony in Westpoint. Although there were only about ten members in the band – none with music sheets – they played magnificently, and their music sent a wave of excitement through everyone.

Like all bands, they were followed by lots of youngsters. These laughed, danced and skipped around and their obvious happiness transmitted itself to all the adults present – even to the Chief and his sombre little entourage. It seemed that the whole population of Marshall City was gathering together to make a fiesta.

The band stopped smartly in front of the Chief and saluted him and each of the dignitaries in turn. Then they turned their backs to us, sat down unceremoniously on the ground in front of the veranda and faced the crowd all the time playing away – except when gulping beer.

At this point, dishes of chicken, rice and cassava were served and once again those on the veranda were singled out by getting the first choice of everything after the Chief. Cutlery was scarce, but I managed to corner a knife and fork. Most of the rest had to make do with their fingers.

A silence fell as the Chief raised his hand and a young Liberian girl came forward. She recited the Liberian Constitution without a break for fifteen minutes.

This was followed by a series of rambling speeches accompanied by much nodding in my direction and then lots of clapping.

Now the best part of the entertainment began. Masked dancers appeared in front of us gyrating, swinging and moving with quick bird-like movements. Mostly the masks were ghoulish and frightening. All the dancers had their bodies decorated with splotches of red henna and stripes of white paint so that they looked like Halloween ghosts. They danced for over an hour whipping themselves up into a frenzy. Periodically a dancer would stop and quaff local brew from one of the many large calabashes that the onlookers proffered. However, as it approached 4:30, I began to get uneasy thinking of the journey home to my little house that now seemed so snug and secure.

I informed the Chief of my concerns. 'It will be dark soon and you understand that I have to tend the sick in the morning' I ventured. He made a polite effort to detain me. I am sure he was happier to be left alone with his people than having to entertain this white man, for I was now the only outsider in the whole gathering. Yvon had somehow escaped earlier, unnoticed by me. And so, with many signs of thanks and much shaking of hands I left, escorted by my rowers, to retrace my steps.

The current was much stronger now and the water higher so that my rowers pulled the boat to the river bank. This saved me the embarrassment of being carried again for which I was grateful. But now, everyone was a little drunk, certainly tipsy, and they started to row the canoe in a reckless fashion almost tipping it over on several occasions.

This caused them much hilarity, but I was scared as I could clearly see crocs following us and I think the more scared I became the more the rowers enjoyed seeing my distress.

The river here was lined with dense mangrove trees whose sprawling roots stretched out several feet into the main steam. How we avoided being capsized, I shall never know. It was a combination of the rowers' skill, my prayers and luck. Mainly the latter.

I had taken photos of much of the proceedings that day but my camera was drenched in river water and by the time I reached dry land those pictures were lost forever.

Apart from this trip to Marshall city, and, of course, several trips to Monrovia for shopping and the odd meal in *Heinz and Marias* – allegedly run by an SS Colonel on the run – I had few breaks during my three months in Liberia.

Voinjama

However, there was one week, which I will never forget when I went with Dr Hseih (pronounced 'Shay'), a visiting WHO doctor, to a town called Voinjama, on the border with Guinea. Dr Hseih, who was Chinese, was assigned to Liberia to study the incidence and type of different enterohelminths in the human population. Worms in other words!

He had invented a special microscope for examining specimens of stool that he called a Hseihscope ('shayscope'). I never understood exactly how it worked, but he was very proud of it. He and I became fast friends; yet, like so many others, we meet in life, after the first few letters, we gradually drifted apart.

From him I learned to look at things from other people's perspective and so became, I think, more tolerant of diverse opinions and more understanding of human behaviour whether or not I condoned it. He was the one who taught me that when in disagreement with anyone, we should always 'put ourselves in the other person's shoes'.

Our plan was to stay in a guest house in Voinjama and from there go to the surrounding villages where he would do his work on as many stools as he could find. In the meantime, I would hold clinics for the local population, who had no medical assistance apart from witch doctors.

Voinjama was a drive of about 163 miles from Monrovia and was a very isolated place, cut off from the outside world during most of the rainy season. When I went there, it was just about accessible by road and dirt track. Nowadays, I hear that one can fly from Monrovia to Voinjama. How things have changed.

In 1965, the people in Voinjama and the surrounding villages lived as their forefathers did and believed firmly in the spirit world, a world inhabited by good and evil. It was always necessary to placate the evil spirits and many spells, incantations and rituals were used to ward them off. The villages were similar to those in many parts of Africa in that they consisted of a group of round mud and thatch huts (roundels) encircled by a sturdy fence made of intertwining branches which protected the village from thieves and wild animals. At sundown, the children of the house would round up any animals their father owned and herd them inside this barrier, which was then closed for the night. In this way, both humans and animals were kept safe from intruders.

The Huts

The huts were circular and had a place for a wood fire in the centre from which the smoke was supposed to escape through the open top of the conical roof. The walls of many were made of a mixture of mud and red clay or consisted of bamboo canes held together by firmly plaited dried banana leaves. The roofs were a mixture of leaves and branches of trees carefully cut to the correct lengths. The concept of building with bricks had not yet reached rural Liberia. As in other parts of sub-Saharan Africa, it was the women who built these huts.

It was dark inside the huts. But essentially they were only used for sleeping at night or for cooking during the rainy season.

The floors consisted of dried animal dung, and if you inspected the floor carefully, you could see myriads of little insects crawling around merrily. I was to see the same thing later when working with the Maasai in Kenya, but it was quite a shock when I first came across it in Liberia.

One of the most annoying and irritating things about these huts was the constant presence of smoke. The central hole in the conical roof never cleared the atmosphere. As a result, one breathed smoke all night from the smouldering embers of a dying fire, but this probably reduced the number of night biting mosquitoes that descended in masses on the unprotected sleepers. Unfortunately, even one bite from one infected mosquito can give you malaria and you can take it from me that everyone got bitten many times every night.

'Fever' raged through the population all year long. Many died, especially children and old people. No one was overweight much less obese. And yet they showed no sign of the misery and hardships of their lives. On the contrary, they were among the happiest people I have ever met.

I wrote these words in my diary at the time: 'Up here the natives are shy and nice and pleasant – such a difference from Monrovia.'

I imagine not too many white men have stayed in a natural native hut as I have. But this is no boast. I cannot say I ever enjoyed the experience. My main concern was that snakes might fall from their perches inside the roof on top of me. This was a real fear based on what the locals told me and I believed them.

On Sunday, 22 August 1965, while lying on a raised plank in one of the huts, I have just described, I made another entry to my diary. I wrote this after spending two nights alone in an outlying village that was only accessible by foot.

> *There is no electricity, phone, radio, transport, post or any means of communication with the outside world in Voinjama. We are surrounded on all sides by virgin jungle. Incidentally snakes are all over the place.*

Keeping Evil Out

While in the villages, I noticed that just before dusk the local witch doctor invariably appeared in full regalia. He proceeded to tie a rope between the trees that stood on either side of the path leading from the jungle to the village. This was in addition to the 'gate' with which the children sealed the actual entrance each night. He then proceeded to tie coloured ribbons randomly on several of the larger trees at the sides and back of the village.

On enquiry, I learned that this was to keep evil spirits away during darkness. These evil spirits might otherwise enter and grab your soul. Not a nice thought.

The Village Chief

I became friendly with the chief of a local village. He was a young articulate man, handsome and well-built. He was also the local witch doctor and told me, through my driver Henry – who acted as interpreter – that he treated cases of broken bones, joint dislocations, burns and fevers. In addition to this, he treated people who had returned from the clinic in Voinjama, but who were far from cured. He had six wives so was kept busy by all his jobs.

He was delighted with my visit and gratefully accepted a large stock of paracetamol and chloroquin. He led me to the 'woman-hut' where his senior wife was ill, because he wanted my opinion. I quote from my diary again.

> *I entered the woman-hut where all six wives plus many more women and lots of children lived in a heap. How can I describe it otherwise? Everyone is naked and only the adult women are covered from the waist down. The women sit around in the dirt with babies sucking at their breasts and there is a big wood fire burning in the centre of the hut filling the whole place with smoke, so that it is difficult to see clearly let alone breath normally.*

At the time, this whole scene shocked me, but I failed to appreciate that all these women were happy, just to be protected by the Chief, to have a baby at the breast and to have enough food to survive on. I also wrote that the Chief was drinking beer and palm wine all the time and was probably surprised – perhaps insulted – when I refused to take any.

Hollywood is quite wrong to depict chiefs as dissolute corrupt despots. In my experience, they are almost all intelligent, wise and just rulers. Joseph Shanahan, who spent 30 years in Southern Nigeria, should know. He wrote 'to be a chief demands superlative qualities of body and mind.' I agree.

There was a Catholic church and school in the town of Voinjama itself. A Fr Fergus from County Galway lived in a small annex. He was a good man, but isolated and lonely. Later, I made a point of visiting Bishop Maloney in Monrovia to complain that to leave an expatriate priest alone in a remote area was both unfair to him and to his flock. He listened politely.

I brought my friend Dr Hseih to Mass one Sunday morning. It was the usual wonderful African Mass with beating drums, crying children, spontaneous singing and a sermon that seemed interminable. It was his first encounter with a Christian ritual; indeed, the first time, he had ever crossed the threshold of a Christian church.

He was very attentive and respectful, but I am not sure that he had any idea of what it was all about.

I Get Capped for Liberia

Before I finish my Liberian escapade, I must boast a little about my (short) appearance as an international rugby player. I had met a Welsh chap called Jones one day in early July, and casually we talked of rugby. Wales were top dogs in Rugby at that time with Garrett Edwards and Co. storming the five nations, as it was in those days. So it was a bit of a shock, but not a complete surprise, when the local bank manager, Rick Grant, called to my house one Saturday morning begging me to stand in as outside centre that afternoon. Liberia was to play Sierra Leone and Liberia was one man short.

Foolishly, I accepted and off we went in his car towards Monrovia. After a short while, we came across an open space where there were several cars and jeeps and a lone bus standing. They were all facing a roughly marked out rugby pitch complete with goal posts and crossbar at both ends. There were about 50 people lining the sidelines and a number of children milling about, but there were no turnstiles and nobody was asked to pay.

It was a hot afternoon, even so the pitch was soft after the rain of the previous day. I had not played rugby for fourteen years, so my apprehension turned to something like panic, when I saw the big muscular Sierra Leone guys getting out of the bus and start throwing not one but two rugby balls to one another as they raced on to the playing field. They were already togged out in clean shorts and bright jerseys.

In contrast, the Liberian team were shoddily dressed with shorts of varying shades of white from cream to light yellow. And our jerseys – admittedly all of the same faded green hue with a white star on the back – were hopelessly ill fitting. They were too small for some and too big for others. Mine fitted reasonably well.

We had forgotten to bring a ball. I suppose that we assumed the referee would have one, so we stood in rather hapless small groups watching our opponents go through their paces.

The match started at a furious pace with Sierra Leone scoring three tries in the first fifteen minutes. None were converted; they even missed a 'sitter' in front of the posts.

The pace dropped dramatically after that. I think that our opponents got fed up with us and decided to take it easy. Luckily, the referee was on our side and we were awarded several penalties, most of which we missed, but all of which gave us a chance to rest and get our breath back.

The most exciting moment in the match came when play stopped to allow the removal of a large snake that was found crawling across our goal area.

Both teams stood around mesmerised by the skill with which our outhalf (a local) curled the snake around a long stick and deposited it in the bush.

The game resumed as if nothing untoward had occurred.

It was after the snake incident that I hurt my shoulder and had to retire. It occurred when I tackled the big Sierra Leone centre who was at racing towards our line.

My shoulder hurt for several weeks afterwards and when it gives me pain now I well recall that mindless tackle.

Where Am I?

Wherever I travel, I like to learn something about the history of the place. I think this makes my visit much more interesting and makes things, often ordinary things, come to life. I expect, like most people, I forget 90 per cent of this newly acquired information but something always sticks.

So forgive me if I only say a few words about the history of Liberia.

For centuries the land was divided into many tribal areas with strict boundaries. This was not altered by the temporary appearance of Portuguese and Dutch coastal trading posts which had been established from as early as the fourteen hundreds. But they did not stick. Liberia remained unconquered and its interior remained unknown to the world at large. In fact, Liberia was unique in Africa in that it was never colonised and never became a protectorate.

People point to Ethiopia (Abyssinia) as an example of an African country that was never colonised. But this is untrue. The Italians ruled Ethiopia for many years and Victor Emmanuel even added the words 'Emperor of Ethiopia' to his many other titles. The positive legacy of Italian rule remains to this day, chiefly in the form of roads and infrastructure, but Italian atrocities, in particular those of Mussolini, have also left an imprint that will take a long time to erase.

Liberia was thankfully spared such foreign interference. Any interference that did occur was from the United States and was mostly good. The very name Liberia ('*freedom*' in Latin) was coined by the American Colonization Society (ACS) whose aim was to repatriate emancipated African slaves. US

President James Monroe so strongly supported the ACS that the city of Monrovia was called after him.

In post-Tubman times, Liberia has been subjected to vicious internal squabbles and almost constant political turmoil and gross corruption. These things have held back the advance of what should be one of the richest and most tranquil states in West Africa. Today it is recovering slowly from the worst Ebola epidemic in history and one wonders what the future holds for this lovely troubled land.

1. Dom with Doreen 2015, a year before her death

2. Honoured in Addis Ababa 2012

126 Moylagh Rd
Beragh
Co. Tyrone
23/7/90

Dear Dr. Dom,

I saw your letter in the paper it was interesting.

My daughter Collette 8½ yrs. died 24th May with cancer she wants her money send to hungry children!

So this is her money I'm sending to this great charity.

God Bless
Yours truly
Philomena
Mrs. (Gallagher)

3. A random letter! 1990

4. Goretti Hanrahan (21) my VSA student died in air crash en route to Sierra Leone 1983

5. The Colbert Medal. Travel Med Soc Ireland

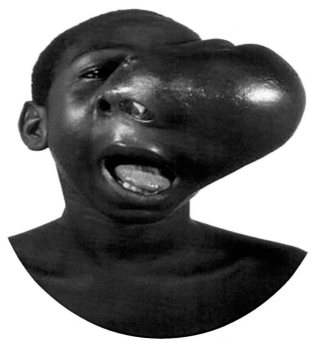

6. Burkitts Lyphoma Nigeria 1960 (with permission)

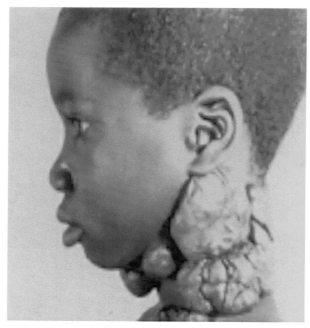

7. Keloids after minor surgery, Ibadan 1960 (with permission)

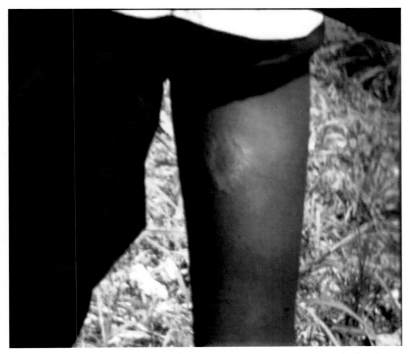

8. Acute Leprosy Nigeria 1969

9. Pére Joussemet St Lucia 1968

10. Voinjama, Liberia 1965

11. Little boy lost Turkana 1984

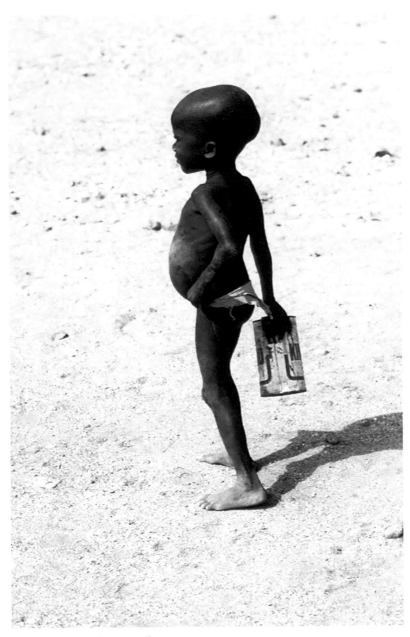

12. Little boy lost Turkana 1984

13. Doling out rice, Kenya 1984

14. Sr Evangelist MMM, 'Mary' and me. Kakuma 1984

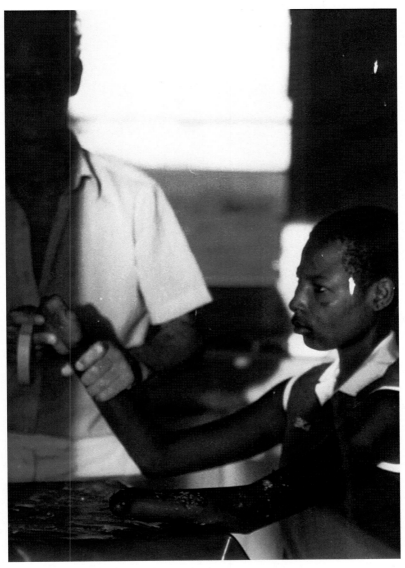

15. Taking cast for new hands Kakuma 1984

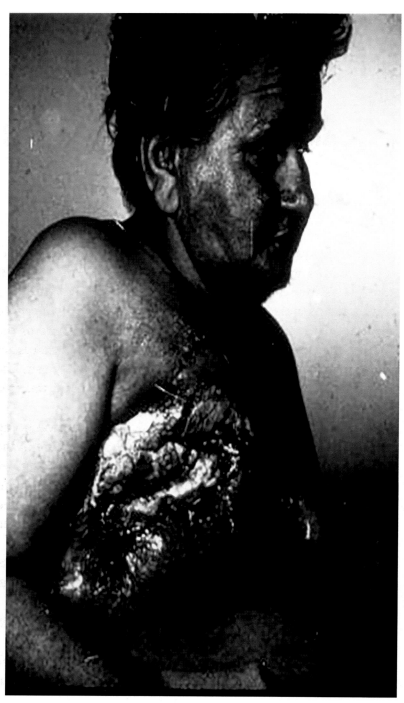

16. Cancer of breast Sudan 1971

CHAPTER 10

A Caribbean 'Holiday', 1968

First Sight of the USA

Doreen always understood my desire to serve the people wherever doctors were scarce irrespective of money or comfort. So in 1968, we decided to spend three months working in a mission hospital – somewhere, anywhere. We managed to connect with an American group of nuns, the Sisters of the Sorrowful Mother, who had opened a hospital two years earlier in St Lucia, one of the windward islands in the Caribbean. The hospital, St Judes, served the south of the island and was free of charge to all. Just perfect.

They needed a doctor urgently as the incumbent was going on leave, and they promised to provide accommodation in the hospital plus a stipend of 480 British West Indian dollars per month. This was the equivalent of £100 sterling and would amount to £300 after three months. The flights for Doreen and me and our eldest cost £420 so I was only out £120. We would carry the two youngest on our laps and get them free!

Our plan was to fly from Shannon to New York, stay there with Sr Sarah, Doreen's cousin, for a week, and then fly to Miami. From there, we would take a plane to St Lucia.

All this was arranged by letter. There was no e-mail in those days and phoning was far too expensive.

I must tell you a little about Sr Sarah. She was born Sarah Joyce in Bearnadearg, a small village in Co Galway, and was the eldest of a large family. Bearnadearg was backward in those days and there was not much money in the Joyce household. Hard work and eking out a living from a small acreage on poor soil was their lot. However, like many others, they were the salt of the earth.

The children were sent to primary school where they received a good grounding in the three 'Rs' –Reading, Riting and Rithmathic. But secondary school was expensive and so most Irish people at the time finished formal education while still very young.

Many of the local boys went to work on their fathers' farm or in their fathers' businesses. Others joined the army or emigrated or entered seminaries. If the girls did not marry, they 'entered service', emigrated or 'took the veil' (entered convents).

Only the well-off could afford secondary school and only the *very well-off* went on to university. Free education for all eventually came when the Minister of Education, Donagh O'Malley, introduced it – against much opposition – in 1967. That was after Sarah's time. Her calling was to join the Sisters of St Joseph of Newark with whom she spent the rest of her life in the 'States' – apart from a year of two in Newry, in an offshoot convent.

Her life was dedicated to helping disadvantaged, difficult and orphaned children and, like Christine Noble, she was brilliant at managing children whether they were disabled or not. Her main gift with adults was her constant good humour and her innate sense of simple fun, which lifted the spirits of everyone she met. Other equally important gifts were her generosity, her child-like innocence, and her untiring efforts to help others, in particular to help her family and friends.

This was the lady who was to meet us on our first visit to the United States. Like all firsts, it was memorable in every way.

On arrival at John F. Kennedy airport, two burly black porters (red-caps) took our luggage to the exit and waited expectantly to get their tip. We assumed that this was part of the airport service, and on telling them, I had no dollars, they just dumped our battered cases on the ground and went away calling us rude names. Still this did not bother us too much, and all was made well again when Sarah bustled in and hustled us off to a large black sedan.

We had never seen, much less sat in, such a luxurious car, and had never experienced automatic gears before. On the way, we experienced more traffic than we thought imaginable: big cars, mighty trucks and fast parkways. What a contrast to the little winding roads of Ireland where the only dual carriage way was the bumpy Naas road out of Dublin and where the first motorway was still decades in the future.

I suppose that everyone has a different experience when entering the United States for the first time. For us, it was quite thrilling. We had never seen before such traffic, never seen a skyscraper and never met so many fat people! The bustle and noise of Manhattan, the cosmopolitan nature of the popu-lace, the ubiquitous yellow cabs all honking horns, the all-nite diners…so much colour and movement.

In the succeeding days, we would go to the top of the Empire State Building – then the world's tallest free-stand-ing building – and we would visit Time Square, Chinatown, Little Italy, Washington Square, Harlem, the Lincoln Memo-rial, Central Park, Fifth Avenue, the Statue of Liberty and Ellis Island.

But first, we had to get to Sarah's orphanage, feed our three children and come to terms with the fact that we were now really in the world of burgers and hot dogs, of Maceys and Sachs, of cops with guns and of all things big, bright, brash and boisterous.

We eventually arrived at the orphanage. It was a campus made up of several separate blocks, like Nissan huts. The boys occupied the blocks on the left, the girls on the right and the convent was in between towards the back. The blocks were also allocated according to the children's ages and each was self-sufficient in itself with a kitchen, dining hall, recreation room and dormitory. One nun was assigned to each unit and our Sarah was in charge of a group of boys aged between eight and ten years.

I thought of the grim orphanages and boarding schools at home in Ireland. The contrast was stark.

Apparently, the chaplain was on 'vacation' – look how American I am becoming – and so we were given accommodation in his quarters. These were self-contained, with a living area, kitchenette and two bedrooms. It was the first time we ever enjoyed the facility of an *en-suite* bathroom. It was also the first time we had the comfort of air conditioning and the first time we had seen coloured sheets and pillowslips. Everything, down to the smallest item, seemed so much better than at home. Even the telephones were white or green or red, not the drab black that we were used to.

Our little group consisted of Doreen and myself and our three girls, Mary (9), Sallyann (4) and Sibylline (2). Sallyanns birthday, on June 4, was celebrated in the orphanage with a gala party and a special cake. We seemed to live off the fat of the land with fine food and lots of things to do. Sarah brought us to see the sights in New York and brought me to visit Holy Name Hospital in Newark which was run by the same order of nuns. This was a joyful week for us and we were sad leaving for St Lucia, unsure of what lay ahead.

Sarah brought us to the airport in the same black sedan and we felt as if we had been in the United States all our lives! But life is change, and as soon as we entered the departure lounge, we turned our faces south towards the Caribbean determined to make the best of whatever was in store.

Our first stop was Miami where we changed planes but did not leave the airport. I remember we flew with American Airlines and that the air hostesses – that's what the all female air stewards were know as 'back in the day' – were very good to our little ones. I also remember that one of our little ones – I will not mention names – was short taken and that a dark patch of wet stained the seat when we finally prepared to leave the plane after it bumped down on the unkempt runway of Beane Army Airfield in St Lucia, now transformed into a modern international airport.

A sun-tanned American man met us on the tarmac and led us through to the terminal building like Pied Piper. The children were well behaved and probably overawed by all the friendly faces that smiled at them. It was probably the nicest welcome we ever got at any airport. The American had a Chevrolet parked outside and we dumped our luggage into the biggest car trunk I had ever seen.

He talked non-stop for the next fifteen minutes before we pulled up at the gates of the hospital. 'This is it' he said and then got out and asked us to wait while he went to fetch one of the Sisters. Incidentally, we never saw the American or the Chevrolet again.

St Lucia

In those days only a handful of tourists visited St Lucia – pronounced St Lú-shah. It was the island paradise of Hollywood, of the TV series *Death in Paradise*: something out of *Swiss Family Robinson* or *Robinson Crusoe* or *The Pirates of the Caribbean*. Miles of golden sandy beaches, isolated coves, still blue lagoons, gentle foamy waves, the sea teeming with multi-coloured fish, palm trees and a happy exuberant people that seemed not to have a care in the world.

The whole island was cloaked in tropical forest and lush vegetation and was singularly free of biting insects, although it had the usual complement of lizards, snakes and spiders. It is best known nowadays in the travel brochures for its sulphur springs and for the two pointed Pitons, the Petit Piton and the Gros Piton. Both soar about 2,500 feet into the sky from the deep blue waters of the Caribbean near the little town of Soufrière.

St Lucia is a small island (617 km²) with Vieux Fort at the southern end and Castries, the capital, on the northern end. It changed hands between the British and French on so many occasions that people have lost count. The 'native' population is a mixture of many races and includes Creoles, Caribs, Asians, Europeans and Mulattos – and everything in between.

The common language is a kind of debased French, a patois peculiar to the Windward Islands. However, most educated St Lucians speak English.

Bananas grow in abundance and were the main export in 1968. One of the loveliest memories I have is of an evening by the dockside where we watched women with large loads of bananas on their heads marching in single file to deliver them to a waiting banana boat.

All the while, the men sat around chatting and smoking or occasionally joining in with the women in singing a rhythmic calypso chorus uninhibited by any musical constraints. Over the hold of the banana boat, there stood two tall Negro tallymen who counted the bundles of bananas and noted how many each woman delivered. This was for payment later. God knows how many mistakes they made or how much trickery went on. Whatever, there was surely poor pay for a lot of work.

We were too young and naïve to understand these things at that time and merely savoured the scene as if it were something from a Disney movie.

St Judes Hospital

It took but fifteen minutes to arrive at our destination, St Judes Hospital, which lay a short distance from the town of Vieux Fort. After the Chevrolet had deposited us at the hospital gate we stood there wondering what to do, when a fat nun came puffing towards us. She told us she was Sr Zita. Breathlessly, she explained why she could not meet us at the airport but told us that there was a meal ready in the Convent after we had settled in to our quarters.

These were immediately inside the compound on the right-hand side of the main gate. The gate itself was manned by a watchman who seemed to spend most of his time asleep or talking to friends. However, he woke up when he heard the commotion and carried everything to our new home.

This was on the ground floor of a two-storied wing that stretched forward from the main building. It was an integral part of the hospital, designed I think as an on-call suite for a junior doctor. It consisted of a general purpose living room, a kitchenette and two bedrooms separated by a small bathroom with toilet, washbasin and shower.

It suited us fine except for its location. It was situated immediately under the paediatric ward and labour room.

So noise was constant and, when there was a lull, you could be sure it would be the prelude to a screaming chorus of children waiting to be fed. For all that, we were happy in our island paradise and slept soundly at night. Such is youth.

I worked hard enough but nights were generally quiet since only very serious cases made their way there after dark.

Work was easy. I saw the usual fractures, sewed up the usual cuts, did some minor surgery and treated lots of people with heart failure and pneumonia.

Only one case sticks in my memory. It was a girl of thirteen years of age who died from tetanus. We kept her sedated in a darkened room and warned all that anyone making noise in the vicinity would be severely punished (noise brings on the tetanic spasms). She lived for a week.

We were all pleased when she died for her spasms were indescribably painful. I had not seen anything so awful since my time in Nigeria.

Our children thrived. Mary and Sallyann went to the local school and – as the only whites – came in for a lot of notice, none of it nasty. Mary got friendly with a family who taught her to ride a horse called *Suki*. *Suki* was the most forlorn, thinnest and boniest nag you could ever imagine. Yet Mary loved him and she greatly admired Nicholas, *Suki's* owner. Nicholas would let her ride *Suki* whenever she wished.

No doubt that this led to Mary's long-lived love of horses, which later resulted in us buying her a pony when back in Galway. She called that one *Apollo*. Yet there would be only one *Suki!* She cried inconsolably for about five minutes two years later when she heard that Nicholas had died. I have no doubt that at least some of her tears were for the now ownerless *Suki*.

For Sallyann, everything was excitement and fun. She was taken around the wards by Anne, a nurse from Quebec, who took a great shine to the little four-year-old. Anne dressed her up in a nurse's uniform and of course the patients loved to see the two of them marching down the wards.

It seemed that she also made an impression at school as we often heard groups of local children calling 'Sallyann, Sallyann...' after us, when we visited the town to shop or went to the beach.

Nonetheless, Sallyann's outgoing nature was not to everyone's taste. Père Joussemet, an elderly French priest, was chaplain to the hospital. On several occasions, she raided his fridge and took bits of chocolate that he had kept there, presumably as a treat for himself. We could not afford such treats and in truth barely subsisted on the poor rations we bought. The old priest left us in no doubt that stealing was wrong, even in the case of a hungry four-year-old!

Sibylline, the baby, was adored by everyone and even at such a young age had a head of flowing golden blond hair. She was starting to speak and, because she said *Hippie* instead of Sibylline when pronouncing her name, she became known as *Hippie* for some years afterwards. She came everywhere with us and loved splashing in the clear warm waters that lapped Marie Beach, our local swimming place.

We had access to an old Hillman car about twice a week, and made the most of it to go swimming, lie on the sand, visit Soufriere and twice ventured the length of the island to Castries.

Towards the end of our tour, an urgent message came from the US navy in Nassau looking for a doctor immediately. I refused on the grounds that were I to leave, the hospital would be without a doctor for several days. I often wondered afterwards where my life would have led me had I gone with the US navy. It is on such chance opportunities that one's life sometimes hinges.

'If only' must be the most foolish words in the English language. I stayed.

When the incumbent doctor returned, he took us out as a family to a restaurant called to the *Crow's Nest* for a 'Thank-you' meal. It was our first taste of lobster and we have never since tasted any lobster so magnificent as the one we had on that occasion. I cannot remember our host's name but do remember that he was English, and although he was an excellent surgeon, could not practise surgery at home because he never passed his first surgical exam which we called 'the Primary' in those days. I often wonder what became of him in later life.

An Embarrassing Moment

I told you that we lived just below the labour ward so it only took me two minutes to get out of bed and attend to whatever emergency might arise. One night, well after midnight, when I was in a deep sleep, the phone rang and an excited voice told me that a woman had been admitted who was in advanced labour with the baby's buttocks showing. I jumped out of bed and raced upstairs fully awake and fearful that the baby's head would get stuck in the pelvic brim and possibly die. Worse still the mother might rupture her uterus and I would lose both mother and child.

I was upstairs within a minute, gowned and gloved within another minute, and then at the mother's side.

She was in great pain, contractions coming rapidly and regularly. The nurses just stood there looking at me and relying on the 'doc' to do everything. I wonder sometimes if delivering a baby is more an inborn gift rather than an acquired skill. Many midwives have an uncanny expertise in this area of medicine which training alone cannot provide. Although I felt inadequate that night, I knew that there was no time to spare, and that I was better than nothing.

At this stage, there was tension in the air; the two nurses on duty were scared and on edge. I asked one to go to the head of the table and calm the mother as best she could. I asked the other to stay near me and do whatever I asked.

I followed no textbook. I slid my hand under the child's torso and released the little legs. Once I felt the mouth, I gently inserted two fingers and eased the baby's head down towards the floor and then up towards the ceiling while continuing to rotate it until I had the full baby out. I did all this spontaneously and by feel. And yes, the baby came out alive, but alarmingly limp and blue.

'Clamps for the cord... scissors... okay... out of my way please.'

The resuscitation cot was on the other side of the room and so, rather than wasting time giving the baby to the nurse, I raced across to the cot with the baby in my arms.

In my haste getting out of the bed, I had not fully secured my pyjama bottoms which now fell ignominiously to the floor. My gown had come loose at the back and so as I ran with the baby I was virtually stark naked.

Luckily, I reached the resuscitation cot without tripping over my pyjama bottoms which were now around my ankles. No one laughed – just then. That came afterwards.

The baby must have sensed the confusion for he started breathing as soon as I sucked the mucus and meconium out of his mouth. Within a few minutes, all was restored to normal including my modesty.

I would not have been so lucky were the mother to have been a 'primip' – a first child. It was her fourth pregnancy, but she had lost two children already so at least she went home happy with a beautiful bouncing boy and memories of a half-naked white doctor running with her baby in the middle of the night.

The FMI

The local missionaries belonged to a French order of priests called the FMI (*Fils de Marie Immaculée*). These were men solely dedicated to missionary work and most came from families unable to afford to send their sons to the Seminaries that produced priests for the home dioceses.

Pére Jousssemet, the hospital chaplain, was in his seventies when we were there. He was a small man with thinning steel grey hair and a determined manner. He had an iron loyalty to the church and an unquestioning obedience to its laws.

He told of how he would ride his horse around the island in 'the old days' visiting outstations, hearing confessions and praying with the sick. He bemoaned anything new including the motorcar!

His strict adherence to the church rule that no food or drink should pass one's lips after midnight until an hour after receiving Holy Communion the following day is exemplified in the following story. Even swallowing one drop of water was prohibited. People took great care not to swallow any when washing their teeth.

He had spent a Saturday visiting his flock and in saying three Masses. But in the business of the day, he had no time to eat or drink. He expected to be home before 7 p.m. which would give him plenty of time to have a good supper before bedtime. However, just as he was about to sit down for dinner, he got an urgent call to visit a dying man seven miles away.

Undeterred by the late hour – darkness was already gathering fast – he rode off to perform the last rites (*extreme unction*) on the man. He arrived safely and after administering the sacrament he set off for home. In the dark, he mistook the path and went astray. It was almost 10 p.m. before he found the correct path, but he still had plenty of time to get home to his dinner.

He had hardly gone two miles before the heavens opened. The torrential rain was followed by thunder and lightning which frightened both him and the horse and forced them to take shelter for some time in a banana plantation. This further slowed their progress. Despite everything, the faithful horse plodded on sensing the need of its master to get home as quickly as possible. Père Joussemet was due to celebrate the Mass next morning with the last Mass at noon. As he approached his chapel, the bell tolled out midnight.

He had not made it.

He would obey the church rule no matter how unreasonable it was. He smiled in his quaint French way 'The rule has changed since… now I can drink up to an hour before Mass… Indeed at my age I am allowed drink right up to Mass-time.'

Joussemet is in Paradise now where he can drink all he likes whenever he likes.

Henrí Brenon was another French priest who worked in the local parish church. He came from near Nantes where his sister was married to M. Ariau, a wealthy farmer. I mention Henrí because we became very friendly and we did an exchange of our children with his sister's children for several summers afterwards.

I met Henrí by chance, years later, when I was doctor to a pilgrimage that brought sick people to Lourdes. He is now in Bordeaux. We had dinner together and a bottle of *vin ordinaire* and a long chat about old times. I reminded him of Père Joussemet and we both agreed that he was the last of the old missionaries.

I still use an old black-and-white photograph of him as a bookmarker so he is never completely forgotten.

The third FMI we met was a Père Nicola. I remember him chiefly because of the novel way he solved the problem of getting stained glass windows for a church he had built. Of course, he had no money to buy stained glass but instead he got the parishioners to bring him their empty beer bottles. Some of these were colourless, some a pinkish hue and some were deep green. He also gathered a few dozen empty brown wine bottles from the various presbyteries and from the *Crows Nest* – the only decent restaurant in Vieux Fort.

Local workmen cleverly embedded the necks of the bottles in the cement frames of the long narrow window openings of the church. They did this in such a way that all you saw was the body of the bottles which transmitted the sunlight in a medley of colours to rival that of the grandest cathedral in France.

Père Nicola was very proud of his architectural triumph. He had got his stained glass windows, and for nothing.

We returned home in September very pleased with our summer and hoping that some day we would return to our island in the sun. We never did return. I think that we would be disappointed to see how touristic the island has become today. I suspect – indeed I would take a bet – that the locals are no happier.

CHAPTER 11

ANOTHER WORLD

Over the years, I have been lucky enough to examine and teach both physiology and surgery in several Muslim countries, notably Kuwait, Libya, Sudan and Saudi Arabia. These visits brought me into another world, one where people dressed differently and held different beliefs and had different attitudes to life to me, yet one in which it was clear that in our innermost hearts all men and women share the same needs and aspirations.

On some occasions, Doreen or one of the children accompanied me and we have happy memories of those days. It is my opinion that the control Islam holds over people in these places is somewhat similar to the hold Christianity held over Europe in medieval times. And like Christianity, this grip will loosen and finally break in the years ahead and be replaced by a more tolerant and freer society.

Westerners who have visited Saudi will understand more fully the rigidity and severity of strict sharia law. The complete covering of women is mandatory and one of my colleagues, a distinguished woman Physiologist from Dublin, Cliona Buckley, recounts how the religious police hit her legs with some kind of a stick because her ankles were exposed. Western women are shouted at and frequently insulted verbally by young men, even if they wear full Arabic dress, and I have seen this happen frequently when accompanying my wife or daughter on a trip to the souk. On one occasion, while lecturing young doctors doing higher surgical training in Buraydah – a town in the Gassim province of central Saudia – I took a walk outside the hospital compound. It was a hot and dusty afternoon, and my short walk was merely to get a little air and escape from the confines of my apartment. I was passed by a pick-up truck with three or four labourers in the back who shouted what were clearly obscenities at me as they passed by. I ignored them and continued my walk only for the truck to reappear about five minutes later when it pulled up beside me and amid further yelling and fist shaking the occupants doused me in bucketfuls of foul smelling water. Luckily, I was near the hospital gates and beat a hasty retreat to safety. My Saudi students were incensed when I told them what had happened and they blamed ignorant imported labourers for disrespecting a stranger.

Every Friday in Gassim, there were executions and hand chopping for murderers, thieves and other lawbreakers. We all knew about this and I even spoke to eyewitnesses who confirmed these events, but I never attended any of these punishments myself.

Undoubtedly, the punishment fitted the crime as G and S would say, but it seemed that privileged Saudis were somehow above the law. At least that was the impression I got from the stories of Filipino nurses and domestics who alleged that they had been subjected to sexual harassment in exchange for being allowed to stay on in the Kingdom where they could earn twenty times the money they would get at home. I make no judgment here. It seems that people are the same everywhere when given the same opportunities.

Jeddah 1977

In 1977, I was given a sabbatical year in which to write or do research at my leisure. So I started by embarking on a textbook of clinical Physiology and then spent several months in McMaster University and in the Mayo Clinic in Rochester. But undoubtedly, the most interesting part of my sabbatical was the month I spent in the Department of Physiology in Jeddah, my first trip to Saudi Arabia.

I went there as a visiting professor and did so to oblige Kieran Burns the Professor of Physiology in University College Galway. He had contracted himself to work there for a year, but wanted a break. He asked me to go in his place and pretend I was he! He said 'When you go to collect your salary in administration just sign my name, they will think you are me… they cannot distinguish one westerner from another…just as we find it so difficult to identify one of them from another.'

He gave me the keys to his apartment, which he said was on the thirteenth floor of a building which was beside another building that had a large blue neon Sanyo sign at its top, visible for miles. 'You cannot miss it. The sign is lighted and can be seen from all over the city. Oh, just in case you get lost, *mabnaa sakania* is the name of the building where the apartment is ….' Kieran often did unusual things and always surprising ones. He had whetted my interest and he knew it. I agreed there and then to go.

I arrived in Jeddah airport – the old one – after dark. My plane had been delayed, but I felt no anxiety, as it was still only 9 p.m. I got through the airport in about two hours, which was not too bad considering the hassle lone Westerners are normally subjected to by immigration officials in Saudi. But then my troubles started. It was now 11 p.m. and I had missed the last bus into town. Even the aircrew bus had left. Neither were there any taxis in sight nor had I any Saudia reals to pay a taxi man should I have got one. Anyway the airport bank and forex was closed so there I was, stuck outside the airport, virtually in the middle of the night, not a word of Arabic, no useful currency and unsure of my ultimate destination beyond the words '*mabnaa sakani*'.

I started walking towards the city.

It was probably only a few miles, but the journey seemed interminable to me. By the time I started to approach the centre of town, it was two o'clock in the morning. Luckily, it was a fine night, warm but not oppressive, and I was fascinated by the velvet star-studded canopy in which the imperious moon shone out indifferent to my troubles.

Finally, I reached the town centre and was surrounded by fine tall modern buildings and expensive shop fronts. But nowhere could I detect the Sanyo sign that was to be my guide. I think that I did get a little upset at this stage, as I was tired, hungry and hot. There was nobody about and the very stillness of the place started to become intimidating. I looked high and low, walked a bit down every side street and all the time kept gazing skywards in the hope of seeing the Sanyo sign. Eventually, after about 40 long minutes, I got lucky. There, almost above me, loomed the outlines of the word Sanyo, quite dark and unlit. Obviously, the electricity had failed or the bulbs had burnt out. I was really happy to see it and happier still to find my *mabnea sakani* beside it. The entrance was open and no one was around as I took the lift to the thirteenth floor. My key fitted perfectly. At last, I was home. I certainly could not expect Kieran to be responsible for the electric supply of Jeddah. I fell into bed and slept for twelve hours.

While in Jeddah, I immersed myself in teaching medical students. Without exception, I found them all to be lively, intelligent and respectful. I shopped in the Souks and bought brass vases, gold chains for Doreen and the children and old brass coffee pots which I still have.

Jeddah itself was a noisy bustling city obviously suffering from growing pains. Electricity was erratic, water supply hit and miss and the traffic uncontrolled. One afternoon I took a trip to a nearby beech on the Red Sea and despite a covering of clouds got a nasty sunburn. The sea itself was clear as crystal and the coral just below the surface was stunning in colour and variety, although I believe that the deadly stone fish lurks there waiting for his chance to catch the unwary swimmer. Rich sheiks had compounds overlooking the beach surrounded by high walls. One wonders at the goings on in them.

It is said that Eve's tomb is located in Jeddah. It consists of a small non-descript building in the middle of a very old cemetery in the Al Balad neighbourhood of the city. Perhaps it is no coincidence that the word Jeddah means grandmother in Arabic.

I left Jeddah with some sadness. I got to love my students, respect Islam and even learned to tolerate the chaos of Jeddah traffic.

CHAPTER 12

Khartoum

Miracle on the Nile

My first visit to the Sudan had been to lecture in the University of Khartoum in the early 1970s. I returned on several occasions to examine and so was able to see the changes that occurred down the years – some bad, some good. As is often the case, a first trip to a place is the one best remembered.

I don't think that I was regarded very highly by the Sudanese in 1971 for I was young and neither an important figure nor a renowned researcher, but I suppose that I was the handiest outsider they could get at the time, and that suited me very well. I was not put up in a hotel but in a private house, which the university kept for lesser dignitaries. The house had probably belonged to some minor official in colonial times but was sufficiently comfortable and certainly secure enough to satisfy my needs. I was the only person staying there apart from a silent Arab who served my meals and cleaned my room. When I arrived, he pointed to himself and said 'Hussein', and I did likewise and said 'Dom', but that was the end of any meaningful conversation. His silence was understandable for he spoke no English, but we communicated admirably with signs and grunts, and much bowing to each other. Food was frugal but edible. There was lots of coffee (sweet, sticky and strong) and lots of goats cheese and lots of eggs (boiled, scrambled or in omelette form) and of course lots of fish from the Nile.

Once or twice, he made a lamb casserole, but I was not keen on this as the lamb pieces seemed to float about in a sea of grease. Bread (unleavened and dry) accompanied every meal and there were always plates of sticky dates and small pots of jam on the dresser. Happily, I was young enough and healthy enough to enjoy and even thrive on everything Hussein gave me and he smiled in approval when I sat back and rubbed my stomach after I had cleaned my plate.

I walked each day to work and got my first taste of lecturing to classes of many hundreds of medical students. Everyone was polite and helpful, and I soon realised that the Sudanese are extremely intelligent and extremely loyal to their way of life and to their families. All my prejudices about 'Arabs' dissolved as I mingled with them and got familiar with their ways.

However, I did make several excursions to the Sudan Club in the evenings. This club, the centre of the British elite in colonial times, was still mainly used by expatriates and boasted a swimming pool, library, smoking room and bar. It also had air conditioning and the latter was a great relief after the heat of the day, which seldom fell below 40° C. For me, my main delight in the Club was to discover 'The Hobbit'. This brought me to a world of fantasy, which was so far removed from the real world that it seemed even more real than the one I lived in.

Although Khartoum has changed almost beyond recognition, it is still essentially three cities in one: Khartoum city, Omdurman and North Khartoum. These are delineated by the merging of the White and Blue Niles into one great river that continues northward to Cairo.

If you stand on the old bridge that links Omdurman with Khartoum city, you will see the marriage of the two Niles very clearly. The confluence is known by locals as aL-Mogran (المقرن) or simply Mogran. The bridge itself was built in 1926 and has a span of over 600 metres and stands on seven sets of pillars. It must have been absolutely magnificent in 1926 for it is still an impressive structure.

I wonder if the original builders, Dorman Long – the same who built Sydney Harbour Bridge in 1932 – realised the significance of seven sets of pillars for Jews, Christians and Muslims alike.

To stand on the bridge means more than just seeing the Mogran or taking in a panoramic view of the modern city or inhaling fumes from ten-ton trucks. If you look to one side, you can make out the tomb of Muhammad Ahmad (the 'Mahdi) and then swing to the other side and you can see, downstream a bit, Gordon's 'palace', where he was speared to death by the Mahdists in 1885. While this incident is recalled in the history books with horror, it should be said that many at the time, including Gladstone, the British Prime Minister, believed that the Sudanese had a just cause in wanting to be free of Egyptian rule. And the spear was their normal weapon of the Mahdists.

When I first visited, Khartoum life was leisurely and one could saunter across the bridge merely avoiding flocks of goats and herds of camels and a few cars and buses. Today only the foolhardy dare cross because of the constant flow traffic in which the lowly pedestrian is regarded as completely expendable.

Subsequent Visits to Khartoum

Over the years, I had become friendly with both Professor Nasr-El-Din and Professor Youssef Suka who had been co-examiners with me in Kuwait and Benghazi. Both were outstanding academics and administrators and both were living examples of all that is best in the Islamic faith. I liked them greatly and felt at ease in their company. They had that rare quality of listening to the others point of view with respect and understanding.

Now they were back in Khartoum and were instrumental in getting me appointed as a regular examiner in their medical school. The country was poor and I was only given travel and accommodation and a small stipend; nonetheless, it was a rare chance for me to spend time in such a historic place and to experience first-hand true Arab hospitality. Most Western examiners stayed in the Grand Hotel (now known as the Grand Holiday Villa) on the banks of the Nile near the Mogran. That in itself was a special treat.

This was Khartoum's first and oldest hotel and had been the centre of political and business life in Colonial times. The waiters used to wear turbans, jellabiyas and red belts and serve enormous amounts of alcohol to a cosmopolitan clientele. Which all changed in the early 1980s when President Nimeiry introduced a policy of Islamisation. From that time on, the hotel began to fall into decline. It was no longer the centre of intrigue and gossip and certainly not of the hedonism of the past. Yet on my visits, there were signs of a faded victorian Britain everywhere, from the peeling whitewashed columns and arcades to the sedate swimming pool and the adjoining Churchill lounge.

The food was poor, the sanitation doubtful, the bedroom doors were ill-fitting and generally the place was only a relic of its former splendour.

I understand that the new owners have improved it considerably and have tried to banish the shadow of colonial days even to changing the name of the hotel.

There were only 80,000 people in Khartoum on 1st January 1956, the day Sudan became independent of British and Egyptian control. Today greater Khartoum has over five million inhabitants. It is on the way to becoming a megapolis.

This is a far cry from the little settlement founded by Ibrahim Pasha in 1821 who made it the capital of Egyptian Sudan. Ibrahim's father was Mohamed Ali. Sounds familiar?

Nubia and the Pyramids of Meroe

Nubia is that tract of land on either side of the Nile extending northwards from Sudan and well into Southern Egypt. It encompasses the confluences of the White and Blue Niles as well as the area of the Atbara river, the last tributary of the Nile before it reaches the Mediterranean. I mention the Atbara because it was the scene of a historic victory in 1898 by Kitchener and his Anglo-Egyptian army against the Mahdi's tribesmen in fierce hand-to-hand fighting.

The first certain facts about Nubia date from 800 BC. By then it was already the site of the Kush Kingdom which would last in one form or another for over a millennium. Kush was ruled by many famous Pharohs, but the most famous of all was the Pharoh Taharq. Those who read the Old Testament of the Bible will be quite familiar with Taharq for his role in aiding Hezekiah in his battles with Sennacherib and the Assyrians.

Ultimately, Mëroe, about 100 km north of Khartoum, became the Kush capital and many well preserved cemeteries, pyramids and temples bear testament to the splendor of Taharq's reign and to that of his predecessors.

The Pyramid Tombs of Mëroe

The university authorities in Khartoum sometimes brought visitors to see local antiquities and local places of interest so I was pretty sure that they would accede to my request to visit the pyramids of Mëroe when I had a day off from examining. On one occasion when Mary, my eldest daughter, was with me, I asked that both of us be brought to the famous tombs. The authorities were delighted to do so and promised that they would send a driver to pick us up at 6.30 a.m. outside the Grand Hotel the following morning. Mary was by now a dentist and spoke basic 'street' Arabic since her time in the Middle East. This endeared her to the locals.

We waited on the banks of the Nile expectantly at the appointed hour and sure enough the university Pajero appeared right on time. The driver ushered us politely into the back and then introduced us to a slim good-looking young man who was sitting in the front passenger seat. 'This is Mohamed, my friend. He will help with the driving and he will tell you the history of the places we will visit.' The young man grinned back at us and, without further ado, we set off on our journey full of anticipation and delighted to be getting out of the city. Mary had been cooped up in the hotel much of time that I was working and being a foreigner and a woman, she found it impossible to walk anywhere on her own because of the shouts and stares from the locals.

Sequestered with me in the back of the Pajero, she was insulated from all that, and was as bright and breezy as any young woman should be.

Despite the early hour, the traffic out of the city through North Khartoum was heavy and we made but slow progress. Trucks loaded with produce, oil tankers heavy with petrol and busses crammed with workers were both coming into the city and leaving it, so that we could not pass out anything other than hand carts and bicycles until the city sprawl thinned and decent gaps appeared between clusters of oncoming traffic. Always the Nile was in view, but now it frequently disappeared as the road curved away to enter a small town or village.

Mohamed would turn back to us and point vaguely saying 'The temples of Naqa are over there...' or 'The temples of

Mussawwarat are beyond those dunes...' which was all very disconcerting since we had no idea of what we should see, where exactly we should look and how we should respond.

We muttered things like 'Oh yes...' or 'Brilliant... Fab...' and other inanities which exposed our total ignorance of the history of Nubia.

Mohamed soon got tired of educating us and fell into conversation with the driver and to listening to the crackly radio blare out local Arabic music. He kept adjusting the volume and changing stations, while we sat there too polite to ask him to switch the damn thing off.

The road had deteriorated dramatically by the time we were half an hour out of the city. This added to our growing discomfiture and slowed progress considerably. But we were gradually sinking into a world of daydreams, interrupted only when we opened our eyes to watch a train of camels cross in front of us or catch a glimpse of a herder with a flock of goats shooing them to the side so that we could pass. For we were in open desert now and another two hours would bring us to Mëroe.

It was nearly noon when we finally reached our destination. We drove off the road and crossed bare desert for twenty minutes until we almost drove into the first of half a dozen pyramids.

You would be disappointed if you were expecting anything on the scale of the pyramids at Giza. But these were exquisite miniatures many of which were restored to their ancient glory and all of which entranced anyone with a feel for the past. Our driver and Mohamed sat in the Pajero with music on full blast, but we stepped out and asked one of the local Bedouins – who now crowded around us – to act as our guide. One smart looking fellow, who spoke English well, offered his services, so off the three of us traipsed towards the tombs.

I have never felt the desert floor so hot in all my life. Our sandals gave little protection. Burning granules of sand kept getting into our sandals and between our toes. We vainly kept trying to get rid of them by kicking our feet against every rock that crossed our path.

So it was a relief to enter the nearest tomb where the air was cool and our burning feet could calm down. But you guessed it. The tomb inside was pitch dark and we could see nothing.

Our guide explained that there were three cemeteries in the vicinity, two of which were reserved for royalty and one – with over a hundred tombs – for commoners. I wish I could remember anything else he said, but apart from a heat-blurred memory, I recall little else. Not even which cemetery we were in.

On the way back to the Pajero, I bought a few little models of the pyramids, made of brittle red sandstone, by local Bedouins. They are all that I have to remind me of that strange day.

Before leaving Khartoum, our driver had handed us two lunch boxes given to him by the concierge in the hotel. Each box contained a small orange drink, a hard-boiled egg and two slices of dark bread. We now divided them among the four of us and felt well satisfied. There is nothing nicer than a hard-boiled egg, plenty of salt and a long drink of orange juice when you are hot and thirsty and in the middle of a desert.

Shendi

On the way home, we stopped in the town of Shendi. Mohamed had a relation there whom he wanted to visit and he assured us that he would only be a few minutes. We stopped in a spacious square, and while he went to visit his relative, the driver suggested that Mary and I come and visit *his* relation who lived quite near. We duly obliged glad to stretch our legs.

He led us to a small but sturdy looking house. It was white-washed and clean and obviously well cared for by its owner. Having removed our sandals, we had to bend our heads as we passed through the low entrance into the dark interior.

It takes a minute to adapt to the darkness when one passes out of bright sunshine. But after that minute, we were pleased to find ourselves in a neat, comfortably furnished room where there was an old man sitting in an armchair reading an impressive tome, probably the Koran. This was our driver's relation. His granduncle. He spoke English perfectly and bade us welcome. The usual tiny cups of sweet Arabic coffee were produced accompanied by some kind of confection that looked like crystallised gelatin.

We learned that he had been a schoolteacher all his life and that he was a devout Muslim. He told us that he prayed most of his spare time and had saved up enough money to the go Mecca for the Haj the following year. His looked up at us with steady eyes and smiled in the way only old men who have led long blameless lives can. He then told us that he would look forward to dying in peace once he had completed his pilgrimage. We both felt the better for meeting him.

We spent almost an hour in Shendi before resuming our journey back to Khartoum. It seemed far shorter coming back than going out; yet it was 7 p.m. before we finally arrived at our hotel. It was time for supper and bed and dreams of the faded glories of a bygone era. Mohamed and our driver – who never told us his name – waved us goodbye; glad, I am sure to have had a day away from the great city.

During the past year, I met a Sudanese doctor in Galway who had studied in Shendi. I wondered if the old schoolteacher, with whom we drank coffee so many years ago, had taught him when he was a little boy.

CHAPTER 13

TANZANIA, 1984

Land of the Serengeti

Doreen rarely came to Africa with me after our first stint in Nigeria in 1960. She disliked the climate intensely and was fearful of contracting a tropical disease. Regular bites from mosquitoes, our previous experience with an invasion of soldier ants, constant awareness of the dangers of being robbed in our home, fear of bandits on the roads, the annoyance of having to give a *dash* (money) to all sorts of officials, including the police and airport workers, and the difficulty in getting even the smallest job done, were among the solid reasons for her dislike of living there.

And, of course, there were the usual inconveniences of an erratic electricity supply, the need to boil and filter water, the need to take anti-malarials and the regular bouts of dysentery to which we were all subject, despite our best efforts to maintain proper hygiene standards. So I was delighted when she joined me for my last week in Tanzania where I had been lecturing and examining in Physiology in the University of Dar es Salaam.

East Africa is altogether a different place to West Africa. Indeed, they seem to hardly share the same continent in many ways. The people are much quieter and less flamboyant than those in the West, but just as friendly. But importantly, the climate is much more pleasant and the flora and fauna are much more exotic in the East. So this time I was sure that Doreen would be happier than before, for I had planned that we visit Kenya on our way home and arrive in Galway just in time to celebrate Christmas with our children.

Dar es Salaam (Harbor of Peace)

Dar es Salaam (Dar) was clearly a poor city. Shops were badly stocked and prices for imported goods were out of the reach of most people. The whole atmosphere was dispiriting. People seemed to lack any initiative and quite obviously longed for the 'old days'. The city itself showed a strong Arab influence, with many low brick houses surrounded by high walls and protected by elaborately wrought metal gates. Minarets dotted the skyline for Dar had a substantial Muslim population. However, the majority of people were either Christian or followed traditional religions.

A short ferry ride from the city brings you to Zanzibar, which was a major staging post for Arab slave traders in the eighteenth and nineteenth centuries. You embark on the ferry almost directly across from a large catholic church that I frequented daily some years later but you can still easily imagine the horrors enacted where the church now stands in bygone days.

The whole island of Zanzibar, but especially the old slave market in Stone Town, reeks with the smell of those shameful times and the authorities have preserved many of the places just as they were, a reminder to all of what man can do to man.

Julius Nyerere

When we arrived in 1984, Julius Nyerere was the President. Although a devout Catholic, he treated all religions impartially yet at the same time espoused a radical Communism. So committed was he to Communism that he tried to force it on his people and in so doing destroyed his own dream of creating a modern Utopia.

In his Utopia, everyone would share equally in the country's wealth, all land would be held in common and everyone would have an equal opportunity for advancement.

In practice, this had disastrous consequences. Ultimately, Tanzania became the poorest country in Africa.

The people lost everything they owned and starvation was rife. Not because of government corruption or of presidential extravagance, but simply because the people of Tanzania – like all of us – wanted to own their own bit of land and wanted to keep a fair share of their hard-earned profits.

Nyerere's failed experiment was motivated by the highest ideals, but his policies were ruthlessly implemented. Not only were people forced out of their villages and sent to collective farms, but their homes were also burned down. No motive – however good – justifies evil methods.

I feel sad that such an intrinsically good person – who showed no favouritism to his own daughter when she failed her 'Second Med' – should have stooped so low, for he must have known what was happening in the towns and villages throughout the land.

Tanzanians have told me that they forgive him, not for what he did but, because eventually, he courageously admitted that he had been wrong.

More a Holiday than Work

We spent a very pleasant time in Dar es Salaam. It was December and the weather was warm and humid, but not too oppressive. We were quartered in an old-fashioned hotel overlooking the Indian Ocean but, since all the rooms in the main building were occupied, we had to sleep in the overflow accommodation which was one of several picturesque wattle huts close to the seashore. These were well appointed with mosquito nets and electric lights, running water and a functional toilet.

At night, the only sound you heard was the gentle lapping of water as the tide ebbed and flowed. In the morning you were awakened by a dawn chorus of tropical birds, all bidding you welcome into another glorious sun-filled day.

But the downside was that the moment you left the security of your mosquito net a swarms of voracious mosquitoes were waiting to pounce and sample the delights of your virgin blood.

I had some immunity to malaria, but Doreen had little if any. We were lucky that neither of us got ill there.

Since the university was several miles away, they gave me a small Honda car to use. This enabled us to get around a bit and gave us a chance to explore the city and its environs. I had wanted to see the University Hospital at Muhimbili and luckily met up with Sr Margaret Hogan MMM – from County Clare – who was working as a psychologist there. She gave us a tour of the hospital, proudly explaining all that had been achieved in the last few years.

The MMMs in Tanzania were centred in Arusha but a small number of them lived in Dar, so Margaret was seldom completely alone. I had the pleasure of meeting her in Dar over 40 years later when lecturing for the College of Surgeons of East, Central and Southern Africa. She was still working in the same hospital and still as proud of it as ever.

Another MMM, Dr Margaret Garnet, had worked in Tanzania long before our visit. I mention her, because her name is legendary among many Tanzanians as someone who had toiled fearlessly and unselfishly for their betterment for many years. Margaret was a lady to her fingertips. That's a cliché, but it describes her perfectly. Tall and regal in appearance, she seemed at first glance distant and austere. But... Oh so wrong! Margaret was a gentle, kind, talented person whom everyone loved. And no, she was not Irish. She was English, and had actually been reared an Anglican. I think of her often and know she was one of a kind.

During our brief visit, we also became friendly with staff from the Irish Consulate, later to become a full embassy. We spent several easy-going afternoons with them and one Sunday we all picnicked on an island, a short row from the coast.

Those were halcyon days. We were cocooned in a world of sunshine, palm trees, and fragrant flowers. We strolled on golden beaches, picked up exotic seashells, let the grains of sand crinkle between our toes and took the occasional dip in the warm waters of the Indian Ocean. It sounds idyllic now and it was idyllic then.

People were poor but not living in poverty. Houses were small and uniform but not hovels, and the city was quiet and not threatening. Nobody called us names, nobody hassled us for money and nobody made us feel unwelcome. Yes, Dar was a contented lazy sun-drenched oasis at the time, but then we did not see behind the veneer of politeness and graciousness that was so evident everywhere, and I am sure that we might have come to a more realistic appraisal had we stayed on longer.

In any event, we had to move on and although we were sad to leave Dar, we were also excited at the prospect of our next assignment, Kenya.

CHAPTER 14
JAMBO TO KENYA

We were seen off from Dar es Salaam's Julius Nyerere International Airport by our new Tanzanian friends amid lots of 'don't lose touch' and 'see you in Ireland' exclamations, intermingled with hugs and handshakes.

I have never been good at 'good-byes' and prefer to slip away as quietly as possible, but they are a necessary part of life, and I think women do them much better than men. Be that as it may, we were both glad to get seated on the plane, for much as we had enjoyed Tanzania, we were glad to be 'on the road' again.

I had been to Kenya several times before and so was not apprehensive, but I could sense that Doreen would have much preferred to go home directly. However, I wanted to see – with my own eyes – some development projects in Kenya for which I had raised money at home. I also had some money to give, 'as I thought fit', and I wanted to be certain that it went to really deserving families.

In any case, I had bought our air tickets from *Solar Travel* in Merrion Row in Dublin and had got hem very cheaply. We were booked home via Nairobi and Moscow, due to arrive on an Aeroflot flight to Shannon on the 22nd of December, and that was that. Our tickets were fixed and unchangeable.

When you fly from Europe to Kenya you are rewarded by looking down on the endless sand dunes of the great Sahara desert. But we flew north from Tanzania and so missed this spectacle. It had been dark when we left Dar but now, as we descended into Nairobi, we could see the sun rising like a majestic golden ball above the eastern horizon. It had climbed well up in the sky by the time we entered the crowded arrivals hall.

Jomo Kenyatta airport is one of my least favorite airports in the world. At that time, nothing was safe there. Checked baggage was regularly rifled, and rifled expertly. Locks were of little use and zips could be un-zipped and re-zipped without leaving a trace. The service of completely wrapping your cases in broad plastic sheets had not yet come in, and so you carried all valuables by hand. These included your alarm clock, electric razor, camera, jewellery, transistor radio and any item that might be sold on the black market even down to good shoes.

The prices in the airport shops were – and still are – higher than in most places. And while the staff were courteous, they were obviously overworked and this showed in the peremptory way they sometimes treated people. The final insult of the airport was the first-class lounge that I used twice in my life. It was little more than a grotty room.

A few years ago, the airport was burned down allegedly by traders who had shops in the duty free, and were being subjected to protection rackets and exorbitant rents. I hope the new airport will be a safer and more welcoming place.

But when Doreen and I landed, we were just happy that the flight was over and were pleasantly surprised when we got nothing but smiles from the immigration officers and passed through a meticulous customs inspection without a hitch. It was a true *Jambo* – welcome – to the smiling face of Kenya.

It is always a bonus to be met at an airport and a special bonus to be met when you are hot and tired and not absolutely sure where you are going.

A Carmelite priest/doctor , a friend of mine, Fr Robbie McCabe, was there to meet us, and so we walked calmly past the many touts, tour guides and taxi men who offered to carry our cases and bring us to town at 'a very very cheap price, just for us'.

It is one thing for someone to say that they will meet you; it is another for them to turn up on time, especially in a country where being held up by getting a puncture or running into a traffic accident is almost the norm. However, Robbie was there, in the waiting crowd and any apprehension we had evaporated immediately.

Robbie had worked for many years in Rhodesia (now divided into Zambia and Zimbabwe) before taking up a doctor/priest role in Lokitaung, a small town in the Turkana desert in northern Kenya. He had promised to take us there and I was looking forward to seeing this remote place about which I had heard so much from him.

Normally, when visiting Nairobi, I would stay in the Flora Hostel run by the Consolata Sisters, on the Fifth Ngong Avenue, but this time I wanted to go a bit upmarket with Doreen, and had asked Robbie to book us in the nearby Fairview Hotel, on Bishops Road.

Once initial greetings had been made and the usual questions about 'how was the trip?' answered, we went outside and got into Robbie's vehicle. It was a pick-up truck, roofed and closed at the back, and we all fitted into the front cab comfortably.

Driving into Nairobi

You get a preview of Kenya on the way in from the airport to the centre of Nairobi. The road may be very modern, but it is crowded with all kinds of conveyances. These include mule carts, battered Toyotas, sleek Jaguars with shaded windows, black and yellow taxis and grossly overcrowded trucks, buses and *matatus* (mini buses).

In the midst of all this, there are people J-walking, quite nonchalantly, with enormous loads balanced on their heads. You see cyclists on old black bicycles carrying seemingly impossible loads and there are always those – including children – darting in and out between the traffic, impervious to the horn blowing and curses of the drivers.

Even here street vendors ply their trade and pester you with offers of all kinds of useless items from cigarettes and watches to bananas, chewing gum and wooden carvings. They pounce on you every time the crawling traffic slows to a stop. It is a mistake to buy or haggle with them for this draws swarms of other hopefuls, none of which have change.

Sometimes you find someone, either selling or begging, who truly tugs at your heartstrings. It might be a young boy who drags himself on his buttocks because he has no power in his legs, it might be an old man who is naked and has a wild look in his eyes, it might be a mother with children clutching to her skirts and a pleading look in her eyes; in those cases, it is best not to deny your better self.

After all, you are just a tourist.

Close to the city, on the left-hand side, you pass the Nairobi National Park, a small game reserve, which is home to a large variety of animals, including elephants, lions, zebras and giraffes. It was looking out through the rather dirty window of Robbie's pick-up that Doreen got her first glimpse of a giraffe 'in the wild'. We had never seen a giraffe in Nigeria. Even in 1960, the numbers of West African giraffes had decreased dramatically. Here in Kenya, giraffe abounded everywhere.

Nairobi

Nairobi is a new city founded on the banks of the Athi River by the British East Africa Company in 1899. The film *Out of Africa* depicted its importance as a rail depot and starting place for a *safari*. It also brought the Norfolk hotel, the first hotel in Nairobi, into sharp focus. Many famous people have stayed there since it was built in 1904. They include Theodore Roosevelt, Winston Churchill, Richard Leakey, Kofi Annan and a host of popular 'celebrities'. I have a nostalgic memory of the famous thorn tree in the lobby where one pinned up messages for ones friends. The mobile phone killed off this practice many years ago.

Today Nairobi is a very large city of over 3.5 million inhabitants and its roads are as congested with traffic as any other great city. But when we were there, the population was not more than half a million. Yet, even then, it was an impressive place and the centre of town, the business area, was already sprouting a few skyscrapers.

Our hotel, the Fairview, was small, quiet, compact and clean. It was situated in the lovely greenbelt area of the city off Valley road, not far from Uhuru (Freedom) Avenue. Nowadays, it would be called a boutique hotel, although when we stayed there, it was far from the sophistication that the term boutique implies. When we arrived Robbie thoughtfully left us alone so that we might rest and promised that he would return next morning to show us the sights.

The hotel staff were quiet and gentle in a way that is almost unique to Kenya. They led us to a room looking out on a garden full of flowers and sporting a small non-functioning fountain in the centre of a patch of rust coloured grass. It was an oasis of peace, which we both relished. However, we wanted to explore the city and, after a wash and a short lie down, we decided to take a walk outside. I suppose that we were restless and just wanted to be up and doing.

It was now afternoon and the sun was beating down relentlessly on streets which were almost deserted. We had not gone far before I decided to take a few photos to mark our first day in Nairobi. But unfortunately, some policemen saw me and demanded my camera. They informed me that photography was forbidden in the centre of the city and it was clear they were not open to any arguments. We were both upset by the incident, but the history of colonial repression and the arrogance of many white people in the past was still fresh in local memories and, I suppose, made the rudeness of the local police to us more understandable.

In the event, we were let go with a caution after they examined our passports and checked our visas. Needless to say, we were polite and compliant throughout.

We told Robbie about this next day, but he merely shrugged his shoulders and said that life was getting more difficult day by day, and that we should never dare cross authority even in the slightest way. He also explained that downtown Nairobi is not a safe place after dark, and told us that seasoned travellers never walk there at night even if in a group.

Robbie had joined us for breakfast in the hotel and the three of us piled into his pick-up shortly afterwards. Instead of showing us fine streets and fine buildings, he brought us to see Kibera, then, as now, the largest slum in Africa. We were happy to do this. Our first stop was on the Langata road. Here we pulled up under the shade of a tree and waited for Robbie to make the next move. He got out, scanned the area and spotted a boy who was sitting on the wall watching us.

'Will you mind our car for a half an hour?'

The boy grinned broadly and said he would be sure to do so.

The boy was delighted for he knew the strangers would pay well. And then, with that important business concluded, the three of us took a side road, which led directly to the shanty-town.

Kibera was the first real shantytown that I had walked through. It seemed to be a mass of cardboard and corrugated sheet metal shacks, scattered randomly on a vast muddy field. And although it was teeming with people no one stopped us, no one hassled us for money, and we saw no beggars anywhere. Nor did we feel threatened in any way.

Perhaps they knew Robbie, perhaps they thought that we were all missionaries or perhaps the rarity of seeing three walking *mzungus* took them unexpectedly. *Mzungus* are expected to be driven or at least drive themselves. Never should they be seen walking.

After twenty minutes or so, we returned to the pick-up, where our young watchman was busy cleaning the windscreen. I gave him a few dollars and his eyes lit up as if he had won the lotto. I am not sure that Robbie approved of giving so much and that is understandable. If you live in a place, you cannot give out money continually to everyone.

In any case, our pick-up was intact and our windscreen was clear as crystal, and we had the long day ahead to see the rest of the city. Robbie drove us back to the centre of the city where we visited the Basilica of the Holy Family in City Square, bought a few books and post cards in its excellent bookshop and then went to see the up-market residential suburb of Westlands. Here we had a leisurely lunch in the Jacaranda Hotel where we all enjoyed a lovely kenyan steak with mushrooms and pepper sauce. The day went by easily, and eventually we retraced our journey to the Langata road and made our way to the foothills of the Ngong hills.

Robbie's Cousins: Kevin and Carla

We stopped just beyond the pretty village of Karen which is believed to have been named after Karen Blixen, the well-known Danish lady of *Out of Africa* fame. It was here that Robbie's cousin and his wife, Kevin and Carla Craig-McFeely, lived, and he was anxious that we meet them.

Kevin was an architect who had come to Kenya after the Second World War and, loving the climate and the lifestyle, had decided to settle down there with his new found Dutch wife. They were obviously well-off but, like many of their expatriate friends, they were now living in fear of the numerous bands of armed thieves who ravaged the land, plundering homes and murdering white settlers.

The settlers defended themselves stoutly and used every form of security they could think of. Many had no hesitation in shooting dead anyone who entered their property unannounced such was the fear they had of intruders.

This was the first time we had seen security at such a high level. It was the first time, we saw armed guards with vicious looking dogs and our first encounter with remote-controlled electric gates. It was the first time we had to communicate and identify ourselves to the owners of a house by radiophone. It was the first time we saw electrified fencing set at a voltage high enough to render anyone who tried to climb over unconscious.

Robbie told us that the most dangerous trespassers were roving maverick elements of the Mau Mau who were now 'out of work' since Kenya achieved its independence in 1964. Perhaps we should not be too hard on those settlers who shot first and asked questions afterwards.

Kevin and Carla had lived in Kenya for many years. Their house was beautifully situated on a rolling pasture with the

Ngong hills forming an unforgettable backdrop. We spent an hour or so on the back verandah taking in the lovely view – and making trivial conversation – until dusk fell and the buzz of mosquitoes drove us inside. It was now time for sundowners, which we had in true colonial style, before night descended and darkness enveloped everything.

A uniformed houseboy padded towards us and announced that dinner was ready. So, with a scraping of chairs, we all got up and retired into the dining room where a highly polished mahogany table was laid out for five. The centrepiece was a sparkling Waterford cut glass vase in which there was an elegant arrangement of freshly cut flowers. Unfortunately, the flowers blocked a clear view across the table. This made conversation difficult as our heads kept bobbing from one side to another in an effort to speak to each other rather than to the flowers.

Dinner was served silently and gracefully. I cannot remember what we ate but I do remember the portions dished out were small. There was certainly nothing generous or *flathuileach* in the hospitality, but we have long since learned that posh accents and expensive tableware often presage parsimonious hospitality. One couldn't but notice that while Doreen and I were offered small drinks, the architect filled half a tumbler with Glenfiddich for himself and was equally generous with his wife. I do not say this in a carping or backstabbing way. That was the norm in most colonial households where so many uninvited guests would drop by, often to merely drink as much free liquor as they could cadge.

Unfortunately, there is a sad sequel to this story. The January following our visit – a mere month – both Robbie's cousin and his wife were brutally murdered by robbers who were attempting to break into their home. So much for security.

Robbie later told us that the robbers actually shot Kevin and Carla as they halted their car prior to opening the gates. I am not sure that the true story will ever come to light. Some men were tried and hanged for the double murder but there seems to be doubt as to whether the real culprits were ever found.

I understand that Kevin, who was the town planner for Nairobi, was seriously thinking of leaving Kenya early the following year after being offered a position as an architect in Dublin.

Kevin was described by his neighbour, Desmond Fitzgerald, in his book *Many Parts* (2007), as an 'aesthete' and a lover of classical music. His wife, Carla, was devoted to him and vice versa.

Poor Kevin and his plans to come back to Ireland! How true for Gay Byrne, Ireland's most popular broadcaster at the time, who said on his morning show: 'Man proposes and God laughs'.

On an earlier visit to Kenya, I stayed in the village of Karen. In truth, I had bunked down on the floor of the front room of the local presbytery because there was no spare bed. But I was rewarded every morning by the vision of a pride of lions, outlined by the rising sun, on the Ngong hills. They stood motionless in a line, headed by a big male, whose mane glowed and shimmered in the early light. He had a haughty powerful air about him which reminded me of Aslan in *The Lion the Witch and the Wardrobe*. But there was no imagination about the reality of the Ngong hills, the lions and the village of Karen when I stood there awestruck, those far off mornings.

Karen is now a well-to-do suburb of Nairobi, but I saw it as it was in Karen Blixen's time. Now a thing of the past, just a poignant memory, it still evokes misty memories in me whenever I hear the score to *Out of Africa*. More poignantly, I am reminded of Robbie's cousins; those two sad souls murdered

without reason and now long forgotten. And with the crass-
ness of human nature, I also think of them when I see a bottle
of Glenfiddich.

We Visit a Cemetery

Before leaving Nairobi, we made a visit to the missionary
cemetery. This is where great numbers of missionaries are
buried, both Catholic and Protestant. It is beside St Austin's
church, in the suburb of Muthangari, and is easily accessed
from the road between Nairobi and Nakuru.

I especially wanted to visit the grave of Edel Quinn. Edel
was born in Kanturk, Co Cork in September 1907 and died of
tuberculosis in Nairobi 37 years later. She had toiled during
the last 8 years of her life all over Central and Southeast Africa,
tirelessly spreading the message of the Legion of Mary and
founding Praesidia of the Legion wherever she went. Back
in Nairobi, a sick and dying woman, she still summoned the
strength to attend the funeral of the legendary, Bishop Shanahan, who died on Christmas morning 1943. She would join
him forever the following May. Her body now rests in a grave
close by Bishop Shanahan's 'first burial' plot.

Fr Aegidius Doolin, a Dominican priest, a Waterford man
like me, lies further along the same path. Aegidius Doolin,
mostly known as Giles Doolin, was a noted scholar and author.
His book, A *Philosophy for the Layman* (1954), is probably the
most popular of his works. Aegidius spent the last thirteen
months of his life in Nairobi as chaplain to the Dominican
nuns there. I understand that he died in the Mater Hospital
Nairobi that the Irish Mercy Sisters from Dublin had established in the late 1950s.

I have visited St Austin's cemetery many times and each
time I experienced something special as I kneel beside Edel

Quinn's grave. I think of her young age, of her fearless deter-
mination to help others and of her struggle with sickness and
pain all borne with courage and serenity to the end. And I
know her spirit lives on.

On the Road

Doreen and I only stayed a few days in Nairobi. Robbie was
eager to leave and besides he had already filled his pick-up
with all kinds of supplies including bed linen, a new mattress,
medicines, canned food, several bags of rice and a three
months supply of coffee and tea. We did not know, of course,
that he was going to take an American nun on the trip, and
since we would also have a driver, it was obvious that we would
be consigned to sitting with all the luggage in back of the pick-
up with only one little rear window to give us a view of Kenya!

Our journey to Lokitaung would take several days and the
prospect of being squeezed between suitcases, bags of rice and
cartons of food and the back window was not one to be relished.
You will appreciate this all the more when you consider the
stifling heat and the continuous shaking and bumping that we
were to endure. The bumps would get worse and the potholes
deeper after the tar road ran out when we entered Turkana.
However, we were young and strong and happy to be together,
just the two of us.

This was to be Doreen's first real safari in Africa and would
prove an unforgettable experience for both of us.

Nairobi to Nakuru

The road from Nairobi to Nakuru is nowadays one long traffic jam. A ninety-minute journey can take anything up to five
hours. Happily, there were far fewer cars about when Doreen and

I took the trip. So despite the narrowness of the road, the many potholes, and the sudden unexpected bends, we made good time. The scenery is quite spectacular as you drive along the rim of the Rift Valley but, like any journey, you soon get used to the passing view and very quickly concentrate on your personal comfort.

It is amazing how the body adjusts to the being squeezed between packing boxes and how you can get yourself into a reasonably comfortable position. That is what we did, and although we could see nothing when we were crouched down, we did see the odd giraffe and zebra through the back window whenever we craned our necks upwards or moved about to stretch cramped limbs.

As we travelled northwest to Nakuru, we came across the town of Naivasha, which lies deep in the Great Rift Valley. Naivasha today is a sizeable town, but it was more of a bypassed backwater when we passed through.

Its claim to fame comes from a local lake which is the breeding and feeding place for hundreds of thousands of flamingos. Here we marvelled at the masses of these beautiful birds, standing in the shallow water, heads bowed beneath its surface like monks in prayer. At rest, their delicate pink plumage merges into an undulating sheet of colour that covers the lake surface like an exquisite living tapestry. And then suddenly, without warning, first one then two and then hundreds of birds stretch their long necks and fly skywards wheeling around and swirling like aerial ballet dancers.

It is truly a never to be forgotten sight.

Yet, close up, flamingos are raucous and quarrelsome and anything but the graceful birds that you see pirouetting in the sky above. I suppose that no one can look elegant when fighting over food.

Many volcanic lakes dot the basin of the Rift at this point and extend well beyond Nakuru. These lakes are home to many creatures including hippos. However, we only saw a few hippos during our whole trip and nothing like the numbers I was to see in the Zambezi on a later trip to Africa.

Time was passing, but our next stop – at my request – was the Irish Franciscan brothers Agriculture College, just outside Nakuru. These religious brothers are based in Mountbellew, Co. Galway, my home territory so to speak, so it was natural that I would want to see them in their African setting. My connection with the brothers was not just geographical. I was the one who prepared them for overseas assignments by giving them vaccinations against yellow fever and typhoid and other tropical diseases. And when they returned I was the one who treated them for malaria and dysentery.

No medicine and no advice can prepare the traveller for all eventualities. So it was with deep regret that I learned later of the murder of one of the brothers, Larry Timmons, a favourite patient of mine. I understand the murderer got away with paying twenty Kenyan shillings, but was later imprisoned for 10 years.

As we did everywhere we went, we gave money to the brothers for their work. This was not just my money. It was mostly money given to me by generous people at home who wanted to be certain that every penny went directly to the most needy without any middleman. We had several thousand dollars to disperse and I think we made every cent count.

Nakuru

Nakuru itself seemed to be just one wide street lined by rather dilapidated wooden shops and houses. I have been there since and the difference is incredible. Today it is a thriving little city with lovely hotels, a booming tourist trade and many institutions of learning including a university.

Like many cities in contemporary Africa it has a drug problem, an alcohol problem and an AIDS problem. Poverty – the firstborn of all overcrowded urban communities – is rife in Nakuru, and I wonder if affluence and technology have brought more evil than good.

My most recent stay in Nakuru was in 2013 when I was part of a team from the College of Surgeons in Ireland that was providing post-graduate training for young surgeons. I normally travelled with Mary Leader (Pathology) and Clive Lee (Anatomy) and the three of us used to teach in different African countries three times a year.

It was my habit to remain behind after the others had gone home so that I could spend some time in various mission hospitals, do a little work and help in any small way that I could. This was about all I could offer in my old age.

Eldama Ravine and Eldoret

Eldoret was the next big town on our journey. However, a few miles out from Nakuru we detoured to the right to Eldama Ravine where I had connections with the local hospital which was run by the Mercy Sisters. At that time the Kerry Doctors Group, of which I was a part, raised considerable amounts of money for this hospital. In addition, the group provided doctors to work there on a voluntary basis. As a bonus some of my voluntary service abroad (VSA) medical students from Galway had done 'electives' there. So I was only too happy to visit in person and see how things were going and give a little money.

Maura O'Connor, a red-headed Irish lady doctor, greeted us with delight. She invited us to her quarters (one room) and offered tea and biscuits and a drop of the *cráytúr* (Irish whiskey), which she had brought from home. We accepted her hospitality with alacrity and spent a lovely evening with our newfound friend. Doreen and I slept in a room that was obviously vacated by someone for our benefit. Robbie and the American nun returned to Nakuru promising to pick us up at ten o'clock next day.

This gave us time to do rounds in the morning and see the work of the hospital first hand. Everywhere was crowded; wards, outpatients and emergency room. Everyone was busy, yet everyone had time to greet us and make us feel welcome. Maura explained that the outreach clinics were being supplemented by the establishment of primary health care centres (PHCs) scattered strategically throughout the hospital's catchment area. She claimed that this had brought enormous benefits to isolated rural communities and she was right. All now agree that PHC centres play a significant role in promoting health in rural Africa. I am also convinced that when the HIV epidemic hit sub-Saharan Africa, the devastation would have been on a far greater scale only for the presence of local health centres.

Robbie, the nun, and our driver, called for us close to eleven o'clock next morning. Unexpectedly, most of the hospital staff – including a few patients – waved us goodbye. It is very touching when you get thanked for just visiting a place. You leave feeling warm and good inside. That's the way Doreen and I felt that morning. Indeed, we were happy, almost a merry party, heading for Eldoret, the chief town of western Kenya.

Politically and tribally, Eldama Ravine and the Baringo (lit. *lake*) district are home to the Kalenjins, a small tribe who live peacefully alongside the Kikuyu (the largest tribe in Kenya) and their cousins, the local nomadic Maasai. Daniel Arap Moi, the second president of Kenya, was a Kalenjin. But his power was based on his backing the Kikuyu, yet, although always conscious of this, he gave unabashed preference to Eldama

Ravine, Eldoret and Kabarnet (his own part of the Rift Valley) – much as our politicians favour their own electoral areas.

He also pushed kenyanisation aggressively. Ultimately, those of English and Afrikaan descent left one by one so that today few are left. To Moi's credit their departure was marred by little violence compared to what happened in Rhodesia. However, the almost indecent diversion of funds into developing the Baringo district led to much resentment on the part of other Kenyans and sewed the seeds of tribal unrest that culminated in the murderous riots of the late 1990s.

Entering Karamoja

After Eldama Ravine, we rejoined the main road to Eldoret. We had left the Aberdares range on our right-hand side and had briefly caught sight of 'Treetops Lodge' where Queen Elizabeth, then Princess Elizabeth, had stayed in February 1952. His father died on 6 February, so it was at Treetops that the young 25-year-old princess became Queen of England. Soon we passed through the thriving town of Eldoret which the brash favouritism of President Moi had transformed from a sleepy rural centre to a bustling little metropolis with a University – Moi University – and an airport.

We did not stop but instead continued on until we reached Kitale. This proved to be a rather dilapidated place which was much smaller than Eldoret. Any development is due to it being a starting point for tourists and explorers who plan to hike in the nearby Cherangani hills.

The countryside was changing. To the west lay soaring Mount Elgon with its five volcanic peaks. These sit astride the border between Kenya and Uganda. The highest peak, Wagagai, is solely in Uganda and at 14,000 feet is second only to Mt Kenya (17,000 feet) in height. Like Kilimanjaro it is accessible nowadays to all reasonably fit climbers. The crater of Wagagai is an astonishing five miles wide.

Karamoja

We did not stop in Kitale but pressed north to West Pokot. All this part of Kenya – including the adjacent parts of Uganda – is loosely known as the 'Karamoja' and its people are called the Karimojong. They are constantly on the move to find water for their cattle, their most treasured possession. But they are no passive nomadic herdsmen. They will raid, cheat and fight for their cattle, and political boundaries mean nothing to them.

The Karamoja is one of the poorest and most deprived areas of Africa to this day. Its existence illustrates well the artificial division of Africa by Colonial powers who frequently divided up much of that great continent without reference to existing tribal lands. This artificial division of Africa sowed the seeds for many a future conflict.

The Maasai and Massailand

Although many Maasai people live in Karamoja, many also live in adjacent lands with no regard to political borders. Consequently, Maasailand is not a place you can see on a map, but more an indefinite term that embraces all Maasai wherever they live in Central and East Africa.

However, we can be definite about the Maasai themselves. They have been the subject of books and movies down the years and I can add little to what is already known about them except to say they are among the most colourful, fascinating and intriguing of all the people that I have met in Africa.

At one point, I was invited into a Maasai house, a *manyata*. The simplest manyata is a temporary affair which the women build of sticks and leaves in a single day. Other *manyatas* are more permanent and are reinforced with mud and cow dung. When grouped together and encircled in a fence of thorn bushes – to keep wild animals out – the settlement is called a *boma*. However, many use the terms *manyata* and *boma* interchangeably. Individual *manyata* are mostly used for sleeping and, if there is a storm, for cooking. Traditionally, the passerby can seek shelter in the nearest *manyata* where food and drink is offered gratuitously.

Visiting a Maasai *manyata* or *boma* today has become something of a tourist attraction but when I first went to Maasailand, outsiders never visited them unless specifically invited. Indeed, it was quite an honour and a gesture of acceptance to be allowed into a Maasai home.

I was happy to have such a privilege, and went along accompanied by two *moranis* (young Maasai warriors) one on either side. The inside of the *manyata* was dark and it took a few minutes for my eyes to adapt. Gradually, I began to see the smiling faces of my hosts and to make out their scarlet and purple robes and the beautiful ostrich feathers in their headdress. We all sat hunched on the floor, which looked as if it were made of hardened earth mixed with straw, but was actually made of dried cow dung. On closer inspection, and as my eyes adapted to the darkness, I could see that the floor was alive. Yes, alive with little insects of all sorts. It crawled with cockroaches, lice, bugs, fleas and mites and with things I could not name.

Indeed, the whole floor was a living entity the inhabitants of which must have gazed with awe and dread on us humans who must have seemed like giant Gods. I was one of those giant Gods, sitting in shorts on this teeming world of tiny creatures, and this barelegged God was anything but comfortable doing so.

But more was to follow. I had treated several Maasai recently for serious fever (presumably malaria) and had cured a few children of meningitis so, as an honoured guest, albeit a foreigner, I was asked if I would like to drink something.

I knew it would be – not just impolite – but downright insulting to refuse. So I agreed, despite protesting that I was not thirsty. Someone went outside to fetch my drink and during the interval that elapsed before he returned the conversation lulled and we all just smiled at one another blandly, without saying a word. The drink came in. It was in a chipped enamel mug, with no handle. I assumed it would be their special home-brewed beer. I asked what it was and they told me it was milk.

Milk is a special commodity for the Maasai because – as for all Karimojong – the cow is prized above all animals. I already knew a few things about the Masaai and cows. I knew that the number of cows a Maasai owns is an index of his wealth and of his ability to feed his family. I knew that chunks of meat are sometimes cut from the living animal so that the family gets good protein, yet does not lose a cow. I knew that cows are an important feature in the Maasai dowry, and that you need to give four or five cows at least to the future bride's family before her father will allow your son marry his daughter.

But it was something else about cows that bothered me now. Maasai keep milk fresh by adding cow's blood to it. This they do by nicking a vein in the cow's neck and adding the cow's blood to milk which is already in a gourd. The gourd, containing blood and milk, is then placed in a cool place in the *boma* or buried under sand until needed. I knew all this at the time and I knew too that I was now expected to drink some of this milk.

To my shame, I put the cup to my lips and pretended to drink.

I may indeed have sipped a little but I am not sure. However, I am sure that I stood up saying I had cramp in my leg and rubbed it vigorously while making my way to the door. I quickly emptied the cup into a tuft of wild grass and came back into the hut with the cup to my mouth, as if drinking the last drops.

To this day I do not know if they guessed what I had done. I think they did. I was politely offered a refill but this time declined, saying firmly that I had more than enough and that it had been delicious. Afterwards I got to thinking. Don't most of us in the West eat black pudding? Many eat tripe, many eat octopus, lobster, cows tongue, snails. The list goes on and on.

I squirm now when I think of that afternoon. Because the whole village must have found out afterwards what I did to their precious milk. There are always eyes watching you in Africa, and I have no doubt that someone spotted what I did when I went outside the *manayta* with my cup in my hand.

I never expected to enter a *boma* much less a *manyata* again, but of course I was wrong. The next time was to spend a night in one. I did so at the behest of Mike Meegan about whom I shall speak of shortly. Mike had asked me to do a few clinics for the Maasai in the Kajiado, which is near Nairobi, claiming rightly, that although these Maasai were living near the big city they were even more neglected that those who lived far away. And so, after doing clinics all day, I was shown to a *manyata* where I could sleep for the night.

I had been given a *manyata* to myself, a signal honour, and my bed, which was little more than a few planks covered by a thin quilt, was thankfully raised a few inches from ground level. My mattress was some kind of animal skin stretched over a low wooden base. I found it difficult to sleep. There were all kinds of night noises from the wind in the acacia trees to the eerie howls of hyenas outside the *boma*.

It was a long night. I was fully clothed, bathed in sweat and eaten alive by mosquitoes. I also felt itchy, perhaps from my animal skin mattress, perhaps from my overactive imagination.

You can imagine how happy I was to see the sun break the darkness and feel the stirrings of life as the camp awoke next morning. I was happier still when I got home and had a through scrub in cold water.

Masaai Marriage

We often think that 'uncivilized' (forgive the word) tribes have little respect for the institution of marriage. This is not so. Indeed it is far from the truth. In any remote place that I have been, and in places scarcely touched by 'civilization', marriage is looked on as a serious business and strict sexual behaviour is not just expected but is demanded. The Maasai are no exception. When a young Maasai man is circumcised he is expected to marry. At this stage he is a junior warrior and, until banned by the Kenyan Government, he was expected to kill a lion single handedly – with a spear – before he becomes a senior warrior. At no stage does he choose his wife to be, and he almost never sees her until their wedding day. So there is no question of pre-marital sex. Promiscuous liaisons are unknown.

Families will only unite if they are of the same standing in the community. Standing means history, social position, health and wealth. If compatible in these four areas the respective fathers meet and arrange things. They choose which boy will marry which girl, they extol the virtues of their own child to each other and, most importantly, they settle on a suitable dowry which the prospective groom must pay the bride's father.

These negotiations are conducted in a serious manner and usually end in an agreement that satisfies both families. The bride's family will not attend the actual marriage ceremony. The dowry of cattle, and perhaps cash, will always serve as a reminder of their daughter.

Once married, the wife becomes completely subservient to her husband – who may take more wives as he gets older. She is also subservient to any sons she bears and to the local elders. Widows are not allowed re-marry. The concept of gender equality does not exist in the Maasai tradition.

In truth, girls and women are treated as slaves from the time they are circumcised (11–12 years old) to the time they die.

But it is not all completely negative. Maasai marriages last much longer and are far more faithful than our Western ones.

Following the Great Rift Valley

After leaving Nairobi we had journeyed northwest along the Kenyan part of the Great Rift Valley, with the Aberdares on our right or east side and the Mau escarpment on our left or west side. The floor of the valley is dotted with lakes such as Lake Naivasha and Lake Baringo and ultimately ends at its northern extremity in Lake Turkana. The Ngong hills – which I already mentioned – lie southwest of Nairobi, on the eastern ridge of the valley. This brief recap may make it easier for you to remember how we got to Eldoret after leaving Nairobi.

We had now driven steadily northeast from Eldoret, passed through the town of Kitale, and left Mount Elgon well to the left as we headed towards Ortum, our next port of call. Before we came to Ortum we passed through a town called Kapenguria. It wasn't much of a place in those days although it was – as now – the administrative capital of the West Pokot region. The town is probably of greatest interest to those who espouse freedom, for it was here that the Mau Mau fighter Jomo Kenyatta and his companions were jailed in 1953.

No one should condone violence, nor do I, but the Mau Mau had ultimately a noble aim, that of freeing Kenya from colonial rule. I don't know why freedom almost invariably comes at the cost bloodshed, violence, torture and evil. Why can't we talk our way to a solution? Why can't we see the other person's point of view? We never learn.

By leaving West Pokot we were moving further and further from civilization – as we knew it. Now the countryside became bleaker and drier and sandier, and the *bomas* became fewer and fewer. Thorny acacia bushes were scattered in clumps here and there and, apart from a few goats and camels, we saw little of livestock much less of wild animals.

But probably the most striking thing was the number of people we passed who were on the move. Many of these were bringing loads to market or going to another town to visit friends or merely passing through.

Among the walkers were women with large gourds on their heads fetching water from the local well, going to the market or the health clinic or else going to work a plot of land. Children were walking too, often in small groups, making the long daily trudge to school. The walking starts before dawn and continues all day long. I often think it seems as if the whole continent is walking. The numbers walking increases as one approaches a town. So it was easy for us to know that we were coming close to Ortum, the last real town before Turkana.

Ortum, the Gateway to Turkana

Ortum was an unremarkable place, indistinguishable from thousands of similar towns scattered throughout sub-Saharan Africa. The main street was unpaved and lined by the usual stalls where you could buy anything you needed or didn't need. Bags of flour and rice were stacked outside little shops and fruit stalls were heaped with pineapples, passion fruit, mangoes, oranges and bananas. Children played on the sandy 'sidewalks' and the odd mangy dog was either asleep in the shade of a broken down car or had his nose stuck in one of the many piles of garbage that were left to rot by the roadside.

Nothing seemed to have been painted since it was built so that the painting was now cracked and peeling to reveal dun coloured mud and brick walls beneath. There were the expected garish signs proclaiming The De Luxe Hotel, God's Barber, Serious Dentist, Lucky Taxi Company and Happy Eating Place. We did not stop to try their wares.

No description of Ortum can adequately convey the stifling heat, the mixture of smells from smoldering charcoal fires, the roasting chickens and the decaying garbage. Nor can the written word depict the groups of men standing or sitting around discussing the day's events or the groups of elegant graceful women carrying enormous loads on their heads.

Bicycles were obviously a prized possession, probably a status symbol too. They were uniformly coloured black, typical 'high nellies', with a basket in front and a carrier behind. Nearly all were laden with goods of one sort or another. Sacks would be slung over the cross bar and the rider would have a calabash on his head and maybe a basket full of live chickens in front.

As always, children milled about, happy, long legged and friendly, yet shy. Some of the older ones would run to the windows of our car proffering trays laden with cheap watches, charms and trinkets or cigarettes, minerals and fruit. To buy from a particular one was a matter of sheer chance and while the lucky vendor was all grins, the rest would turn away downcast and glum.

Anyone who has travelled in rural Africa, especially 40 years ago, will immediately recognise this description. And there is little change since.

The Catholic mission hospital in Ortum was a busy place. At that time, the resident doctor was Tim O'Dempsey who later joined the staff of the Liverpool School of Tropical Medicine and who has appeared many times on Channel 4 television as a presenter in the series *Bugs, Bites and Parasites*.

I understand that when Tim went first to Ortum he was so much against killing any living thing that he would even shush away mosquitoes that landed on his bare arm. I also understand that after he got an attack of malaria he drastically modified his views. I did not meet Tim at the time but got to know him in after years because of our mutual interest in Tropical Medicine.

My only other remembrance of Ortum hospital was of the matron, a nun, Sr Gabriel Mary, who was a super-efficient American. Everyone knew her as Sr General Motors or GM.

She allowed me visit some wards that evening and there were many cases I would dearly have loved to photograph and use back home when teaching my students.

However, I have taken few photos of 'cases' during all my years of travel. I always found it distasteful and downright insulting to photograph sick or deformed or starving people. How dare we photograph our less fortunate brothers and sisters just because they are defenseless and maybe dependent on our dollars. I suppose one can justify this if the pictures are used to raise funds to help alleviate poverty. But there is certainly no justification in taking pictures just to show our friends at home how 'the other half lives'.

I have often been appalled in the past by patronizing 'Westerners' (including Japanese and Chinese), with expensive cameras hanging around their necks, taking pictures of the 'natives'.

However, I have no problem with taking a photo of places, things, birds, animals or flowers.

Samburuland

We were shortly to leave Ortum and head north out of West Pokot towards Lodwar, the capital of Turkana. But first I must say something about Samburuland, which lay to the east, which is to our right-hand side, across the 'Rift'.

Samburuland is a vast chunk of northeast Kenya that stretches right up to Lake Turkana. Its people, the Samburu, are colourful nomads closely related to the Maasai with whom they share the same language, Maa.

The Samburu are an ancient and colourful people who have had little contact with the outside world until recent times. Hollywood was one of the first major external influences to bring them to the attention of the rest of us. But it did so in a way that was crass and exploitative. Everything they highlighted was flamboyant, exotic, fantastic and primitive.

Western audiences were regaled with wild dancing, drinking orgies, naked women, spear-throwing warriors and made-up invocations to all manner of idols. It was a form of tasteless cultural debasement, done solely for the entertainment of the masses, which lacked the one thing we owe everyone; respect.

And yet I do not think there was any evil intent. I truly believe the filmmakers only wanted to boost box-office receipts. Ethics, culture and good taste played little or no part in their thinking.

However, the Samburu know the meaning of the word respect, albeit a sort of selective respect. They show this in the extraordinary respect and deference for their elders (all men of course) so much so that experts have labelled their culture a true gerontocracy. Like the Maasai and the Turkans, Samburu men are absolute despots in their own homes and like them it will take many years before women take their rightful place in Samburu society.

The Samburu respect wealth. A man's wealth is judged, not just by the number of cattle he owns but by the number of wives he possesses. Since each wife is allotted a different hut or *manyata* you can tell at a glance how wealthy a man is by counting the number of *manaytas* he owns in a particular *boma*. I suppose this practice helped maintain an orderly and peaceful hierarchy of wives within each family.

Settlements of *manyatas* were, and still are, similar in structure to those of the Maasai, and, like them, are constructed of mud, manure, bamboo and wattle.

Things are changing, but Samburus still retain much of their traditional lifestyle and guard their cultural inheritance jealously.

In respecting wealth the Samburu differ little from any other society.

The Samburu and Maasai are Nilotic people and speak a very similar language. Both are proud and fearless peoples with a long tradition into pre-history and it is an amazing fact that both have survived down the millennia in such a harsh and hateful environment.

Isolation of Samburuland and Turkana

One of the most striking things about Samburuland, and even more so about Turkana, is their remoteness and isolation from the rest of Kenya and hence from the outside world.

Their isolation became enshrined in colonial policy after the end of World War Two. The Government in Nairobi had many more pressing things to think about than the constantly warring tribes in a distant and impoverished places where the inhabitants gave them no allegiance in the first place.

This positive neglect by officialdom resulted in a failure of development and a lack of basic infrastructure throughout Turkana and to a lesser extent in neighbouring Samburuland.

In some ways isolation from the rest of us was good, since it allowed the Turkans and the Samburu to maintain their ancient cultures unadulterated by outside influences. In other ways it was bad, since it deprived them of basic education, basic health and basic housing. Many will tell you that the so-called development of recent times has resulted in more crime, more infighting, more corruption and more unhappiness than in the past. Perhaps it is the speed of change that is responsible for this rather than the change itself.

Not long after leaving Ortum the hardtop road gave way to laterite and compacted sand. Our journey to Lodwar would take less than half a day, so there was no rush. Initially, we went through the Marich Pass which has since become famous, not just for its beauty but also as a location for field trips and nature study. Doreen and I saw little of it through the back window of Robbie's pick-up. In fact, we were unaware of its presence until told about it afterwards.

The Lost World

Having left the Pass, and a few miles beyond Ortum, there is a large rock. It is more than a rock; it is more like a massive lump of stone with almost sheer sides and flat top – like a mini plateau.

A solitary tree, with outstretched branches, grew on top. The tree looked like a prophet of old, perhaps Moses, lifting his arms up to the Lord. I managed to get Robbie's attention and got him to stop while I took a photograph. The image of Conan Doyle's *Lost World* haunted me. I wondered what strange things inhabited this plateau, which seemed so inaccessible to those who dwelt in the flat desert below.

My lost world was indeed the gateway to the real Turkana, a true dividing point between the busy man-made world I was leaving and another less complicated one where Nature had the final say in everything.

Thoughts Approaching Turkana

The Turkans are almost, but not quite, as flamboyant as the Samburus. Though not as beloved by Hollywood, nonetheless, the Turkans are striking, not only in their physical appearance but also in their distinctive dress. They often carry a spear and, like the Samburu, almost always have a sheathed razor-sharp wrist knife (*ararait*) that is sometimes used to gouge out an opponent's eye.

The *enkitchalon*, or headrest, is an invariable accouterment for Turkans. It consists of a short smooth piece of curved wood on which you lay your head. This 'wooden pillow' is nailed down to a three-inch upright, which is mortised into a rectangular base making a little portable pedestal. When tired, you simply place the *enkitchalon* on the ground, lie down and rest your head on the concave upper surface of your wooden pillow. They grease this surface with oil, and rub it in well, so that it becomes weather proof and will last for a long time. An *enkitchalon* is surprisingly comfortable.

For clothing, the men use lion cloths and often little else. In company, if travelling, or if the weather is cold, they add a wrap-around tunic, slung over the right shoulder. This is of great protection if one is caught in a sandstorm when it can be used as a makeshift tent. Both sexes wear neckbands although not as many as the Samburu. Women usually have an animal skin (*yorfas*), around their bodies often dyed red and tied at the neck with a leather tong. Children go naked.

Turkan Beliefs

The Turkans have a deep spirituality and a striking sense of their own dignity. Indeed they are first and foremost a deeply religious people. Primary to this is their belief in One supreme God, the great Creator and Giver of all good things. They call him – it must be a 'him'– *Akuj*. And *Akuj* is not just up in the sky. No, he is a personal God. He takes a strong interest in the lives and welfare of each individual Turkan; each man, woman and child.

It is a curiously advanced religion with many features in common, or at least in parallel, with Judeo-Christianity and Islam. The devil or evil spirit (*Akipe*) is also an important part of their tradition and he continually interferes in the way people behave to one another in everyday life – pushing them always towards evil. Like the Maasai, they too pray that the 'Creator will give them children and cattle' to which they often add 'and give us rain'. They do not overdo it. They usually ask *Akipe* to let it rain just 'every few years'!

Although humble before *Akipe*, the Turkans will not bow to any man. This is a fiercesome and courageous people and going to war is almost a natural pastime for them

Turkan Wars

The Turkan people do not consider themselves to be Kenyans. They live in a virtually independent Turkan nation which has little truck with Nairobi. However, while they live in peaceful co-existence with the official Kenyan authorities, they are constantly bickering and skirmishing with their neighbours. Much of this is due to frequent forays – made by all parties – in which cattle and sometimes women and children are stolen. They engage in these mini wars mostly with tribes from Ethiopia and the Sudan.

In these squabbles limbs are lost and great gashes are inflicted with knives and chests are impaled with spears. Uncivilised in the twenty-first century? Of course! The civilised world has far smarter ways of killing and mutilating people than these uneducated barbarians.

A Simple Life in an Unpolluted Environment

Simple life? Nothing could be further from the truth. Life is harsh: drought, famine and pestilence are perennial. The climate is unforgiving, facilities are few, leisure is rare, and luxuries are non-existent. That is the truth of things for the Turkans even today.

Life expectancy is not much over 40 years, less than half that for people in Switzerland. You say there is no pollution? Wrong. Go inside a cooking hut and the steam and smoke is choking. You say there is no external pollution? Wrong again. Since oil has been discovered in the region, chemical waste and gases from the so-called perforations of the surface waters of Lake Turkana have resulted in serious contamination of the atmosphere. Some link this to the discovery of cancer (not seen before) and the apparent ease of disease spread (more marked than before).

Our romantic ideas about the idyllic lives of those living off nature are sadly amiss.

Lodwar

A Desert Trading Post

Lodwar is the capital of Turkana. But when we arrived it certainly did not look like much of a town much less the capital of anywhere. The main street was unpaved as were all the roads in Turkana, and what passed for sidewalks, were merely slightly raised strips of laterite that were bordered by dilapidated one roomed wooden stores. These boasted exotic names such as The Excelsior Supermarket, Heavens Rest Hotel, Fifth Avenue Emporium, and Hotel for Happiness. Barbers shops, general grocers, dentists and doctors – with alleged cures for everything and real cures for nothing – were all represented. All had colourful signs displaying their wares or services.

You did not have to be able to read in order to know the business of each shop. A tailor or barber might have a sign hanging outside with a drawing of a large scissors, a dentist would have a drawing of a large tooth while a doctors sign might show an enormous syringe or a distorted stethoscope.

Items for sale were usually displayed on cardboard boxes or packing cases outside shop entrances, while traders without premises would set up stalls anywhere they liked loaded with fruit, yesterday's fish, dubious meat, live chickens and bags of rice. No extra charge for accompanying flies.

A few lean dogs stalked around, seeking whatever morsels they might find from rummaging in the mounds of garbage and offal that lay everywhere. They obviously wanted a change from their normal diet of rats and mice. They also gorged on the abundant droppings and discarded bits of sheep, goats, camels and pigs that came to town for slaughter.

The people stared at us curiously but, unlike experiences elsewhere, they did not pester us to buy counterfeit videos, imitation leather belts, single cigarettes or second-rate radios.

Women walked elegantly despite – or perhaps because of – the large loads on their heads; men cycled sedately on old black bikes, and children chased one another – all the time shouting and laughing as children do everywhere.

Lodwar seemed like another Ortum only larger and more run down. It had not changed a lot since 1933, the year that Shah Mohammed founded a small trading post on the site. It had merely enlarged in concentric circles as more and more people drifted into town and added to the squalor.

The town was of special interest to the Irish because it was to Lodwar that Fr James Good went to manage a famine camp in 1975 and it was here that Bishop Lucey of Cork, then 78 years old, came to join him in 1980. That was a clear message of reconciliation between the two. Fr Good had left Ireland because Bishop Lucey had reprimanded him and curtailed his priestly activities in Cork after Fr Good's open objections to *Humanae Vitae*. The media, including the *Irish Times*, had always referred to Fr Good's departure to Turkana as *an imposed exile*. Noel Browne, the controversial ex-Minister for Health, but at that time a Senator, added fuel to this controversy by castigating the Irish Catholic Church without mincing words. Lay people in Ireland were divided on the issue.

Whatever the truth behind the 'exile', it is a fact that James Good worked tirelessly for the Turkana people and won the hearts of many by his dedication and good humour. I like to think we would be more sympathetic to him today than in the early 1970s.

We stayed with Jim Mahon, another Irishman, and the first Bishop of Lodwar. Jim had spent 32 years in Turkana building a network of schools, feeding centres and health clinics throughout the vast area. At the time Fr Pat O'Sullivan was his vicar General, and we remember Pat as a tall lean Kerry man who gave us a warm Kerry welcome. They received us kindly, gave us a decent meal and took the American nun off our hands!

The reduction of our travelling party to three – our driver and the nun would stay in Lodwar – was a great relief to Doreen and I. We could now sit in relative comfort on the long front seat of Robbie's pick-up and view the countryside with ease.

This freed up space in the back of the pick-up so before making our good byes we took on more supplies in the line of a bag of flour, two cans of cooking oil, sugar and a few loaves of freshly baked bread. Most importantly, we loaded up a barrel of diesel which Robbie would keep outside his house. Finally, four large cylinders of gas were squeezed in which would keep Robbie's cooker, gas fire and gas light going for some months.

Everything was loaded by willing hands who were reluctant to take the dollars we gave them. I was told that Turkans believed that everyone should help everyone else without looking for any reward. We were learning fast that the unlearned have a lot to teach us about how to treat one another.

On the Road to Lokitaung

'Do not throw away the water you have because the sky is cloudy, it may not rain; use what you have wisely' Turkana Proverb.

Robbie was now our driver and we duly set off for Lokitaung in high spirits.

The road from Lodwar to Lokitaung was marked as a 'track' on my map of Kenya, and so it was. Yet at this time of the year the sand was firm and although there were many bumps, there were fewer potholes than in the tarmac roads further south. We were now making a steady 50 mph and it felt as if we were flying along. Our journey was all the more pleasant because there was room in front for the three of us: Robbie, Doreen and I. A haze limited our vision, but in any case, the view was monotonous. Gone were the mountains, forests and lakes. Now there was only sand, dry scrubland, isolated thorn bushes and an occasional herder with his sheep. It was hot in the cab and we dare not open the windows fully because of the dust that kept blowing in.

Indeed, the dust is a real problem here, and as we went along, I began to understand why trachoma was so prevalent among the Turkans.

Despite the bumps and the dust, we were happy to be sitting on a seat instead of being thrown around in the back with boxes, crates and bags of rice. Unfortunately, it was difficult to distinguish the hard ridges of impacted sand that crossed the track at irregular intervals, and so, in order to avoid being propelled forward towards the windscreen, we had to keep a constant grip on the rim of our seats. I offered to do the driving but Robbie, although obviously tired, insisted on staying at the wheel. That was fine by me. At least, Robbie knew where he was going.

CHAPTER 15

LOARENGAK/LOKITAUNG

It was close to 5 p.m. when we approached the end of our journey. The mad heat of the day was beginning to abate and a barely perceptible dimming of the sun was signalling the night animals to stir in their lairs and the day creatures to seek a safe sanctuary in which to rest. As we slowed down and moved towards Robbie's house, we could smell the freshness from Lake Turkana and almost taste salt in the air. For Robbie this was home, home at last. It was only now we learned that we would be staying in Loarengak where Robbie had a house almost on the shore of Lake Turkana. The town of Lokitaung is about seventeen miles further inland and was marked on the map. Loarengak was not. No wonder it was often confused with Lokitaung by outsiders.

Robbie's house was only a few hundred metres from the lake and at first sight looked a decent enough place. It was made of cream coloured concrete blocks and had a red tiled roof. We were to find out later that the space under the roof was a favourite habitat for hundreds of bats and that the house itself was a favourite resort for all kinds of rodents and God knows how many different kinds of insects and creepy crawlies.

It was dark inside. The main door (difficult to categorise as a 'front door') opened directly into a rectangular space (hard to call it a 'room') which was obviously a living-dining-office-cum-kitchen room, indeed an anything-you-like room. Two small bedrooms – with open doors – faced across from the entrance, and a third smaller door between them led to a cubicle in which there was a privy.

One bedroom was Robbie's; the other was spare, presumably for occasional guests. It was also used as a convenient dump for books, journals, spare bed linen, spare cutlery, a coil of rope, old biscuit boxes filled with receipts and letters, assorted screw drivers and pliers and general *bric a brac*. There was little space left for furniture. In the centre of the main room there was a low heavy colonial type wooden table and four chairs, at least one of which was the victim of someone trying vainly to stop a wobble by cutting pieces off each leg in turn. An age-darkened 'dresser' stood against the right gable wall. Two thin jet-coal cats were curled up on top of the dresser and only their eyes moved as we entered. They reminded me of the Cheshire cats in *Alice in Wonderland*. We were obviously too large to eat so they soon lost interest in us and returned to whatever bored cats do.

As we entered, a large Turkana woman, who had a runny-nosed child clinging to her leg, greeted Robbie effusively. When she turned around to let us enter we could see she was carrying another smaller child on her back.

Robbie assured us that she was a treasure and that she took care of everything to his complete satisfaction. That meant she cooked, washed, cleaned and generally ran the place seven days a week. This is not as hard as it sounds. Most of the time she would be minding her own children, minding her own man, doing her own cooking and feeding her own chickens. Most likely, she would discreetly appropriate food for her family from Robbie's store room, a shed-like appendage stuck on to the back of the house. Clearly she was in control. Clearly she had the key to the storeroom. Clearly Robbie depended on her and trusted her totally.

I knew Robbie was punctilious, even excessively so. He had shown a meticulous attention to detail and planning ever since we met him. We wondered how on earth he could accept the kind of sloppy standards so evident in his housekeeper. But we were in for another eye opener.

After getting boys to empty the back of the pick-up he brought in the loaves of fresh bread that we had bought in Lodwar and put them on the top of the dresser beside the cats. 'Rats cannot climb so high' he assured us, and then he left us to rest while he went to his room to practice yoga. Since there was no proper door to any of the rooms we saw him doing yoga and I have no doubt that he derived great soothing of spirit from his exercises.

However my attention was diverted elsewhere when Doreen pointed to the dresser. 'Look, look at the cats'. I followed her pointing finger. Sure enough both cats were now wide awake and actively engaged in sniffing, pawing and then snapping bits out of the bread Robbie had just put beside them. At least the rats didn't get there first.

I fear we ate little of the stew the housekeeper left for us that night 'Your appetite goes in the heat' Doreen explained when Robbie expressed genuine surprise at our reluctance to take second helpings. However, Robbie delightedly dipped chunks of bread into the stew 'to give it substance'.

After supper we retired early. There was not enough light to read in comfort, nor frankly were we in a mood to talk much. We all needed rest.

The guest room was small, dark, airless and not particularly clean. But, after the bumps and jolts of the long journey, we were tired, and happy to lie down anywhere.

We fell asleep to the gentle lapping of the lake only interrupted now and then by the distant cry of a hyena or the thud of some larger animal going to the lake for a midnight drink.

And we slept well, wondering what new delights were in store for us on the morrow.

There is nothing nicer than getting up just as the sun rises. And there is no sunrise more majestic than that which lights up the calm waters of Lake Turkana which slowly changes colour from dark grey to pale green, to light blue, to aquamarine and then finally to a deep rich blue topped with frothy white waves. But even the blue is not static. As the waves begin to ripple they act as prisms splitting up the sunshine into a thousand different hues. And as the clouds sail overhead they cast fleeting shadows so that the many different shades mix together in a shimmering mantle that stretches to the horizon.

Lake Turkana has several different names. Older people still call it Lake Rudolph as it was known in Victorian times. The more romantic call it the Jade Lake because during the day its colour varies so much. I do not think all the colours it displays have actual names.

The next few days were a pleasure for us. I did clinics every morning, assisted by Doreen, which we both thoroughly enjoyed. Although the work was tiring, the heat oppressive and the crowds endless we kept going from early morning until after two in the afternoon.

The medicine was the usual. We dispensed large amounts of vitamin tablets, worm medicine, aspirin, antimalarials and cough syrup. Iron tablets and folic acid were given to the pregnant. Sores and ulcers were cleaned and dressed. Amoxyl tablets were given to those with pneumonia and chloramphenicol to those suspected of having typhoid. Injections of penicillin were reserved for the very sick or those with gonorrhea.

Fortified food was given to those with malnutrition. We had a small supply of antiseptic eye drops and of tetracycline eye ointment. These were dispensed sparingly. The people were courteous, patient and grateful.

From time to time we would dish out sweets to the children. The adults wanted some too, so we had to make our supplies of goodies stretch further than we expected. Eventually, arms and hands were poked through the window of the hut hoping they would get something – anything – from us. And, judging by the noise, there was lots of arguing, jostling and vying for position among those outside.

One mother, to whose child I had given a handful of little sweets called *Love Hearts,* particularly moved Doreen.

The mother was anxiously asking something of our interpreter so Doreen turned to her and said. 'What is she asking?' The interpreter started to giggle but became serious once she knew Doreen meant to get an answer. 'Oh..Madam... she wants to know how to take these tablets; is it once or twice a day?' Now it was Doreen's time to giggle. Neither mother nor child had ever seen candy or sweets before.

'Give her two four times a day' Doreen smiled indulgently and winked broadly at the interpreter who was now not sure whether or not *Love Hearts* were some kind of new medicine.

We only spent a week here and although we worked hard we always had late afternoon and evening time to ourselves. One of the highlights was walking to the edge of the lake when the sudden tropical night was about to fall. By six o'clock the surface began to assume a deeper hue, something like purple, and then, as night fell, it became laced with the silver rays of the rising moon. The light seemed to dance as it spun from one ripplet to the next before eventually fading as the water reached the shore.

Soon the dome of heaven would glitter with a myriad of stars and the harsh outlines of the thorn trees and the native shanties become blurred and softened.

When night finally fell the whole scene became suffused with a fairytale, almost an ethereal atmosphere, in which mortal man seemed very small indeed.

Fishermen launched their boats at a night. Their silhouettes only added to the impression that what we were seeing was not actually real. There was little sound except the murmur of the water and the gentle swish of paddles as the boats moved away from the shore. I wish you were there to experience the peace, tranquility and naturalness of those nights. My description falls very far short of the real thing.

Lake Turkana

It is worth spending a few moments talking about Lake Turkana, the largest desert salt lake in the world. Although known to Europeans since 1888, it is still too remote for the average tourist, and thus retains an aura of mystery for most of us. However naturalists, ecologists, biologists, geologists and other scientific folk are constant visitors and between them have built up an impressive corpus of knowledge about this extraordinary mass of water.

One puzzle they think they solved is the question of why there are so few species of fish in lake. Only eleven indigenous species have been found apart from those imported from the Nile. This they claim is due to the low amount of salt in the water thus making it unsuitable for both strictly salt or fresh-water fish.

On the other hand, humans can drink from the lake without becoming pickled, and I have no doubt that animals with better salt handling capacities than us can drink it without any ill effect at all. Turkans do not eat much fish yet the lake is overfished nowadays – for commercial reasons.

However, there is one reptile that thrives in the waters of Lake Turkana and that is the Nile crocodile. You will find more here than anywhere else in Africa and their numbers are estimated at between ten and twenty thousand. We did not see any during our brief visit but were assured they were congregated near the two large islands of the lake, the North Island and Crocodile Island. When the rains arrived they would disperse.

Bird life is plentiful but not as colourful as further south where the climate is less harsh. Sometimes one sees big animals such as lions, cheetahs, zebra and giraffes coming to drink in the evening, but they avoid humans as much as possible, so that you would have to travel some distance away from human habitations in order to observe them in large numbers.

In the past ages, the lake was much larger and the hinterland far greener than today. No wonder then that the surrounds have been the source of significant anthropological finds. Richard Leakey spent many years searching for evidence of early human life around Lake Turkana and his efforts were suddenly crowned with glory when he discovered a hominid skull there in 1972.

He named it *homo rudolphensis* after the earlier name of the lake, Lake Rudolph. Leakey had a very colourful, you could say extraordinary career, and his biography is more fascinating than any novel. It should be read by anyone who has a dream and means to follow it no matter what the cost.

Lake Turkana was first discovered by Europeans when Count Teleki and his secretary Lt. von Höhnel led an expedition into Turkanaland in search of a rumoured desert sea somewhere to the north of Baringo.

Von Hohnel recoded their astonishment in the following words: *'....we gazed in speechless delight ....we were spellbound by the beauty of the scene....the glittering expanse of the great lake seemed to melt on the horizon into the deep blue of the sky.'*

They named it after their sponsor, Prince Rudolph, heir to the Hapsburg Empire. It is far more appropriate that it is now known by the name of the people who live around it. However locals actually call it *'anam'* lit. The great pool.

Anam means soul in Gaelic, a coincidence?

CHAPTER 16

ON THE ROAD TO KAKUMA

Blood and Sand

Robbie, Doreen and I set off on the road to Kakuma in good spirits. We had little cargo as we were merely carrying some medicines that Robbie had bought in Nairobi and was delivering to the MMM hospital in Kakuma. The road was almost due west, into the heart of the desert, and was more puckered, bumpy and potholed than anything we had driven on before. Robbie asked me to drive; he looked tired, and was tired, and obviously wanted to sleep. So there I was, driving for the first time in Kenya, no license and probably no insurance. But I was glad of having something active to do and off we went in a cloud of dust.

Everything went well for the first hour but then the road got even worse and the jolts became more frequent. I tried to avoid the larger potholes by zig zagging as I had done when driving in West Africa. But it was impossible to achieve anything resembling a smooth drive. Robbie was now deeply asleep with his sun hat tipped down over his forehead covering his eyes. Doreen was holding on to the edge of the seat and warning me to 'take it easy for heavens sake'. However I was happy and, despite the dust, I had my elbow sticking out the open window.

The thrill of speeding through pristine shimmering desert was intoxicating.

Unfortunately, I had just managed to avoid a particularly nasty looking pothole when I drove straight into a deeper one that sent the three of us rocketing up and forward. I held on to the steering wheel, Doreen had her eyes wide open and grabbed the dashboard but Robbie went skyward and cracked his head off the metal roof of the cab.

Blood trickled down his face and by the time I pulled up the trickle had become a stream. Luckily there was a large first-aid box under the seat and better still it had never been used before. It was a Red Cross emergency kit and contained local anaesthetic, sutures, swabs and sterile forceps. I laid Robbie down on the seat and stitched up a deep gash in his scalp.

Scalp wounds bleed profusely but heal quickly if managed properly. I had no need for the novocain as Robbie was in shock and could feel no pain. I used it anyhow. I think we were all in shock, but once the bleeding was controlled we all calmed down. Doreen kept reassuring Robbie that it was just a slight scratch but he must have known it was more than that. Doreen was so convincing that I even began to believe her and joined with her in assuring him it was just a minor scratch and that I was being over cautious by stitching it. However, he was either too polite or too upset to contradict us and after a short while he settled down again. This time he slept with his eyes open.

We continued our journey at a more leisurely pace amidst intermittent apologies on my part for not seeing the pothole. I dared not say I was driving at 60 miles per hour when our mishap occurred!

Kakuma

We came across Kakuma quite suddenly, as if it had sprung out of the desert. In Swahili the name 'kakuma' means 'nowhere' and this is very appropriate. It lies in the dusty northwest corner of Turkana almost 200 km from the Ethiopian border and 100 km from both Sudan and the Karamoja region of Uganda.

The town itself was poor, even by Turkana standards. Rain falls a few times a year and, when it does fall, it comes in torrents that wash away the meager soil and destroys local homes. This is not surprising since houses are mostly made of dried mud, held in place by a flimsy mesh of bamboo laths. Temperatures can soar into the forties and the nights are not much cooler. For example, the night temperature when we were there in December – the coldest month – averages 21° C.

Drought, crop failure, starvation and hunger affect crops, man and beast, but little attention is paid to the sufferings of the people by the central government in Nairobi, much less by the rest of the world. Curiously enough the climate has recently changed for the better because of global warming. Warm air, laden with moisture, now blows in from Ethiopia and this greatly increases the chance of rainfall. As a result, crops have a chance of growing in land that could never sustain them in the past, and the dry riverbeds or *lagers* hold more water – and for longer – so that animals and man have extended access to better water.

Unfortunately, all this is counterbalanced by the need to feed a growing population. Refugees from the Sudan, Ethiopia, Eritrea, Uganda and the Democratic Republic of the Congo (the DCR) have been seeking safety here since the late eighties. So many came that Kakuma Camp, with 200,000 inhabitants, was the world's largest refugee camp until the Syrian conflict started in 2011.

At the time of our visit, the Turkana camp was a disorganized shambles and the UNHCR (United Nations High Commission for Refugees) was just becoming involved in putting a structure on it. However, we had limited time and so we drove on and headed for the hospital where the MMM Sisters were expecting us.

We were pleasantly surprised to find that the hospital itself was a fine structure. It seemed to rise out of the desert like a challenge to all the poverty we had passed in the Camp. It had been built with Germanic thoroughness and built to last. Funding had been by the German Agency *Misereor*, and, at the time of our visit, it was administered by the MMM Sisters.

We were greeted with enthusiasm and, on the first night, entertained on a rooftop – where there was at least some breeze. Some Tuskar beer was produced for the great occasion and it tasted like nectar.

As we sat and chatted about home, we felt as if we were on another planet, isolated and insulated from the hustle and bustle and cares of this world. Two of the Sisters, Rina Hanrahan and Rita Kelly, were quite young, and although far removed from the outside world, they both exuded the kind of fun and laughter that only young people possess. We definitely enjoyed those few hours more than any other part of our Kenyan holiday.

Next day, I viewed the hospital and did medical rounds.

The 'Lost boys of Sudan'

The Kakuma refugee crisis came to international prominence in 1992 when the outside world learned of the 'Lost boys of Sudan'. This refers to the thousands of people, mainly young boys, who had fled from the Sudan to escape death – and worse.

The harrowing stories these lost boys told of torture rape and pillage beggars description. It was a time when the civil war in the Sudan was at its most barbaric, and when the Sudanese army went on the rampage in the south of the country; burning villages, raping and enslaving women and children and hacking old people to death. Many thousands of children, perhaps as many as twenty thousand, escaped and ran for their lives into the bush. Here they hid from the marauding militia and eventually trekked across the border into Kenya finding the first port of safety at Kakuma.

The UNHCR acted quickly to provide a haven for these children but the camp was now so big that it had to be divided into four self-contained sections. The sections were pragmatically called Camps 1, 2, 3 and 4. Currently each camp is a little town in itself, with all the amenities of a town, such as local governance, local police, churches, mosques, cinemas, supermarkets, and, of course, local dens of vice. The Irish Jesuits sent a small mission there, which was meant to be temporary but which still functions, decades later.

You might get the impression that people in settled camps are reasonably content. This is not so. They are far from content. Above all they dream of escaping to 'freedom' in the West, choosing to ignore its exaggerated attractions and possibilities.

CHAPTER 17
THE GIRL WITH NO HANDS

When you work in an isolated hospital it is always a joy to have a visiting doctor who can affirm you in what you are doing and offer advice about problems that seem impossible and diseases that have stumped you. I had nothing but admiration for the skill and dedication of the staff from the top down, but I confess that I added little in the way of medical expertise. However there was one patient, who was not a patient so to speak, who caught my eye.

I could not help remarking on a girl who had no hands. She was a slim good-looking girl probably nineteen or twenty years old. She wore the simple blue dress that all the nursing aides wore. It was tightly buckled at the waist and showed her figure off to perfection. Sadly both her arms ended in stumps, which, to me, seemed curiously like amputation stumps. I enquired about her and an old Scottish nun, Sr Evangelist, who was reputed to be as active at ninety as others were at twenty, told me this story.

Apparently the girl, let's call her Mary – because I have forgotten her name – was a refugee from Ethiopia who stumbled into Kakuma a year previously. She almost collapsed into the arms of some locals; exhausted, dehydrated, penniless and alone. They carried her to the hospital where Sr Evangelist – there was no doctor there at the time – rehydrated her. She cleaned and dressed the festering gangrenous stumps, all that remained of her hands.

Many thought that Mary would die. She had septicaemia on top of everything else and penicillin was the only antibiotic available. But the little Scottish nun never despaired. She virtually adopted her charge and watched over her day and night until her fever abated and she started to sit up in bed and take food. Bit by bit she improved and after a month she was well enough to manage herself and get around unaided. At this stage a surgeon from AMREF (the flying doctor service of Kenya) arrived and performed a bilateral above-wrist amputation. The amputation stumps healed nicely, by first intention, as we doctors say.

During all this time she gradually revealed her story.

It seems she belonged to a tribe who lived in the remote southeastern Ethiopian highlands. It was a very traditional tribe with a multitude of laws governing all aspects of life. In no aspect of life were these laws enforced more strictly than in the ritual of marriage.

Mary, being of a good family, and being very presentable, was betrothed to an elderly Chief for whom she was destined to become a junior wife. Mary's family was happy about this because it meant honour for their daughter and prestige for themselves among the community. So when Mary came of age the marriage bargain was made and she became officially the property of the Chief.

It is important to remember that when I say property I do not wish to demean or rubbish this contract. Men were bound to cherish, protect and care for their wives as their most valuable property. This placed women on the highest pedestal that was possible as far as men were concerned, but of course it condemned them to a life of subservience, which is anathema to any right way of thinking.

I am sure Mary would have accepted her lot without demur had she not fallen madly in love with one of the Chief's sons.

It seems that her feelings were reciprocated, and they began a furtive relationship, which led to terrible and unforeseen consequences. How they expected to keep their liaison secret in such a small tight-knit community is a mystery. The truth is they were so blinded by each other that they took unnecessary and often outrageous risks. Being found out became inevitable.

They were caught by a pair of village elders *in flagrante delicto* one night, and immediately dragged before the aging Chief. The Chief was angry beyond words. As Mary was describing his face, suffused with anger, eyes glaring with hate and neck veins bulging, her confidante, Sr Evangelist, confessed that she herself trembled. In biblical terms, it reminded me of the two old lechers who accused Susanna of adultery after she had repelled their lustful advances. No doubt the Chief was looking forward to ravishing Mary himself. So what a shock to think she was with one of his sons.

Unfortunately in Mary's case there was no Daniel to adjudicate. The Chief, surrounded by a few sycophants, hastily summoned a meeting of the village elders to discuss the matter. About half the Council attended. One wonders where the other half was.

However, the depleted Council proceeded with its business and the evidence of the two accusers, who alleged they had caught the young pair red handed, was accepted unanimously. What need of further proof?

The grim-faced Chief stifled and dismissed out of hand all protestations of innocence by the terrified pair. It was now late, and nothing definitive could be achieved until all the elders were present. So he ordered that both young people should be immediately incarcerated in irons and kept in separate huts without food or water, until final judgement could be passed.

News travelled fast. It was a long time since such excitement had gripped the people in a place where one day is as drab as the next. The fact that it was the Chief's son and the Chief's betrothed that were involved made things all the more thrilling. And, of course, the case was titillating by any yardstick.

People came early and jostled for position next morning. They knew that the Council would meet under the shade of a large tree in the centre of the village and, in the scramble for places, the more agile climbed its branches to get a bird's eye view.

The full Council gathered by nine o'clock and waited impatiently for the Chief to emerge from his hut. He kept them waiting – as usual – for about half an hour, and then appeared in full regalia. It was an impressive sight. Silence descended on the babbling crowd and all eyes were fixed on the Chief and then on the two huts where the prisoners were held. At a sign from one of the Elders, Mary and the Chief's son were led out and made kneel with heads bowed in front of the Council.

The accusers were then asked to speak. Both explained that they happened to be passing a derelict hut at the end of the village when they heard voices. Surely it was a man and a woman speaking? This surprised them. Who could be in the hut at this hour? They felt duty bound to investigate and on entering the hut they...well they could hardly say this...but they saw the accused 'in each others arms...in a most unbecoming way' (I am paraphrasing to avoid shocking you.)

Everyone – and that includes the onlookers – gasped and self-righteously protested loudly that such a happening was unprecedented and was a matter of the gravest shame for the village. Some spoke at length proclaiming their shock at such a gross betrayal of trust and at the appalling insult this was to the Chief and the whole village.

I have no doubt that many were secretly enjoying listening to the details of the affair with all its sexual implications.

The talking went on and on. The accused were given no chance to speak. Their guilt was obvious to everyone and the whole gathering seemed to be taken over by a single desire to inflict as much pain on the offending pair as possible.

There were many who taunted and spat at the two miscreants who answered not a word for fear of worse treatment.

By late afternoon, the Chief was getting tired and anyway he had made his decision the night before. He called a halt to the proceedings and after a few minutes pretending to consult with his Council members, he pronounced judgement.

His son was partly guilty but had been led on by the woman slut. So he indicated that his son be taken away and be dealt with by his family at a later date. For now he would deal only with Mary.

He gave his judgement with dignity and deliberation. Gone was the fiery anger of the night before. Instead there was a cold hardness in his voice that both excited and frightened the onlookers.

Brushwood was gathered and set alight. Little tongues of flame licked the dry branches, which crackled and spluttered as the fire took hold. Now the tongues of flame coalesced and shot up sending hot fiery sparks into the air. But as quickly as the conflagration had started it began to die down, and all that remained were the smoldering red-glowing embers of the thicker parts of the branches.

Mary watched in horrified fascination, mesmerized by the dancing flames and unable to think, pray or say anything. She made no resistance when her shackles were opened and the two accusing elders caught her arms and led her towards the fire. One of them spoke loud enough to be heard over the spluttering embers. He spoke of the Chief's justice and mercy in giving a punishment short of whipping and beheading. He was interrupted only by the sound of sobbing and gasps from some of the on-looking women. 'Your hands will never lead your body astray again', he said.

Mary cannot remember the exact words. But she does recall the other elder grabbing her two arms and plunging them into the red-hot embers. She remembers screaming and screaming and she remembers pain so intense that her whole body writhed and convulsed in a manic effort to tear herself away from her captor's grip.

Then she passed out and remembers nothing until she awoke in her father's hut sometime later that night. Her mother had dipped her burned useless hands into palm oil and bound them with leaves, yet the pain was intense.

But not so intense as the shame and misery that she now felt as her father spat on her and reviled her as a devil's woman and a lasting disgrace to her family.

After a few days lying inside the hut and too ashamed to venture forth, her father explained what he must do now. It would not clear the family name, but would at least show that he was as shocked as everyone else by his daughter's behaviour. She was to be expelled from the village late at night so that no one would ever see her again.

Her mother remained quiet while she received her sentence. She obviously had no say in the matter. We do not know what happened to the Chief's son but it is likely that his sentence was far less severe.

And so, a few nights later, when darkness had fallen, Mary left home. She was given a gourd of water and some maize, and brought to the outskirts of the village where she looked at her parents for the last time. They turned their backs to her but she was all the time conscious of her mother's sobs. Then she moved into the darkness. No word was said. Being alone, facing the terrors of the night, facing the unknown and not knowing where she would go caused Mary to turn around and call back. But there was no answer. She walked on.

She walked for many days crossing the Kenyan border and then trekking across the relentless hot sands of the Turkana desert until arriving at Kakuma and finally falling into Sr Evangelist's arms.

We listened spellbound to Evangelist's story and discussed it far into the night. We had given money to Robbie and now gave the remainder to the Sisters, but money in itself would not help Mary.

However, I believed I could get Mary artificial hands. Even if they were only cosmetic appliances they would make her feel more like a normal person. Besides she could always use them as claws and so do lots of things she was unable to do with two blind stumps. With this in mind, I took plaster casts of both stumps and carefully measured her forearms, knowing that these measurements were essential in making prostheses that would fit snugly when we went back to Ireland.

Alas, on our returning home, I was told that 'since the patient does not have a medical card she is not entitled to these appliances'.

I got quotes for the cost of two modern prostheses and they were well beyond my means at the time. I then went in person to the National Rehabilitation Hospital in Dun Laoire, but got no help there either. I even wrote a letter to Barry Desmond, the Minister for Health, but to no avail. Finally, I explained my dilemma to the MMMs in Drogheda who sent my casts and measurements to London where they managed to get the new hands free of charge.

It shames me that the Irish, vaunted for their generosity, were so tied in bureaucracy that they did not consider my Mary as a real person. It took the British to show us up.

We said goodbye to Kakuma and started on the long trek back to Nairobi. This time there was only one stop and that was south of Ortum, where a severe drought had destroyed the maize crop and the local population was in dire need of food. Fr Paddy Hyland, of the Kiltegan Fathers, was the missioner here and after the usual greetings and offer of a bed for the night he brought Doreen and I off to a feeding station where he was distributing food to families who were worst affected by the lack of rain.

As we drove with him we could see that the maize was brown and the land was dusty and bone dry. Paddy explained that a decent harvest was vital, so that the menfolk could feed their families over the next twelve months. 'In a good year any surplus maize can be sold to buy a little meat and fish', he explained. 'Now they have lost everything…they borrow from neighbours who have little to spare…and they even steal at night….' Money was also needed to buy clothes and other essentials such as firewood, and cooking utensils. 'You know they have to pay for schooling for the children, for hospital attendance and for any medicines they need. And now look at this…this disaster.'

Doreen and I helped Paddy dole out rice and grain from the large sacs that were in Paddy's pick-up. It was the first time Doreen had done this and she was greatly moved by the whole experience. But, of course, we all know that this sort of paternal benevolence is not the answer to poverty; it merely prolongs dependence under the guise of charity. Yet there are occasions in which it is the right thing to do and where abstract theories are as drops of water in the face of a forest fire.

Paddy died in Ireland in 2016. He achieved the oft-repeated prayer of all Irish Missionaries, *Bás in Eirinn*, Death in Ireland.

We left Paddy in chastened mood yet conscious of the rising excitement we both felt at the prospect of going home and seeing our five children again. We had left them under the care of the eldest daughter Mary, and although we were sure she could cope under normal circumstances, who knows what sort of emergency she might have to face.

We had seen many new places, met many new people and had many experiences of which only misty memories now remain. Our Kenyan adventures were at an end and we were returning home and counting every minute until we would see the little patchy green fields of Ireland under the wings of our plane once more.

I have visited Kenya many times since, but no trip was as memorable as the one I made with Doreen, my dear wife and companion.

We finally parted from Robbie at the airport with more than a tinge of sadness in our hearts. The last time I met him was in the RCSI in Dublin when he launched his book *Desert Nomads,* shortly before he died in May 2011.

Sheremetyevo Airport

I should be writing that our journey back to Ireland was smooth and uneventful and that it culminated in the great joy of being reunited with our children in Galway and in a very happy Christmas.

And most of that is true with one exception. Solar Travel in Dublin had issued our tickets and assured us that we would fly direct from Moscow to Dublin on 22 December. But when we arrived in Sheremetyevo airport, we were told that our tickets would only get us to London and that we would have to make our way home from there. We were polite at first but less so when they came back with the news that all flights from London to Ireland were fully booked over the Christmas period. 'We are sorry' they insisted, but we cannot do anything.

I persisted. 'But Aeroflot flights from Moscow stop in Shannon. Can't we pay the difference and go on one of them?'

'Sorry, passengers are not allowed disembark…it is a fuel stop only…and you have now lost your place on the original flight to London which is where your tickets were issued to bring you' the lady snarled. That was final. Solar Travel had not done us any favours after all.

The finality was emphasised when two burly security men ushered us into the airport transit hotel. I suppose we should have been grateful that we did not have to spend the night on hard-backed airport chairs.

Our escorts led us along a bare corridor which ended in an old-fashioned rickety elevator with a sliding metal lattice door. It creaked and squealed when one of the men pulled it open. Clearly oiling hinges were not a priority for the USSR. However, it lumbered us safely to the fifth floor where it groaned to a halt. Here we got off and were shown into a small bedroom, sparsely furnished in true communist style.

We sat on the bed and looked at each other wondering what was going to happen but the two minders left without a word and locked the door after them. We should have protested but did not. Instead we meekly lay down and fell asleep.

We were awakened an hour later by the sound of the door opening and the entrance of a large lady in a well-stretched Aeroflot uniform who was brandishing our passports and tickets.

She spoke with a heavily accented but good English and her manner was sympathetic not aggressive. She returned our passports and said she would do her best to get us to Shannon. In the meantime, we were free to take a closed bus into town and see the sights but not free to leave the bus. Food would be provided downstairs for a nominal few dollars and she hoped we would enjoy our stay. She told us to report to her desk in the main airport at nine each morning and then left us sitting there, on the bed, and somewhat bewildered, but also somewhat cheered up.

We cheered up more when we took the trip into the city that the lady had promised. We were impressed by Red Square, marveled at St Basils, were overawed by the Kremlin and disconcerted by Gorky Park the scene of so many alleged KGB killings.

All the time we were watched by a security guard and all the time we were subjected to a commentary in English by a small swarthy Russian lady, extoling the achievements of the USSR. She poured out statistics about the number of tractors, the number of wheat bushels and the volume of milk produced by Russian farmers. There were six other people in the bus with us, probably in similar situations to ourselves. None of them spoke English, yet the guide kept on reciting in English a litany of Communist achievements since the Great Patriotic War. All this was incomprehensible to our fellow travellers and boring for us.

Next morning we were at the Aeroflot desk in the departure lounge at 8.30 a.m. Our lady did not appear until after ten o'clock and was obviously in no mood to help us. She firmly told us what we did not want to hear, but relented somewhat at the end and said we should try again tomorrow, Christmas Eve.

We spent a long dreary day in the Transit Hotel filling the hours with desultory conversation and picking up and leaving down our novels. We still believed everything would turn out fine. How wrong we were.

The following morning we were at the desk, well before nine o'clock, and were delighted to see the same lady sitting there checking in people. There was little of the Christmas spirit in her voice when we asked her once more if we could board the flight to Shannon. She used all the restraint she could muster when telling us what she had told us several times already that 'no passengers can disembark at Shannon'.

It was then that Doreen started to cry and threw her tickets across the floor tearfully wailing that there were five children waiting eagerly for their mother to be with them at Christmas and that there was no one to mind them….This was not an act. Doreen was genuinely in tears and genuinely distraught.

A small crowd of tourists gathered around the desk and looked on in sympathy. I explained what was happening and you could sense the waves of support we were receiving. The lady at the desk got up and went somewhere, presumably to confer with a superior, because she returned all smiles a few moments later with two boarding passes for Shannon. But the plane was leaving in less than an hour. We should hurry up!

A murmur of approbation rippled through the onlookers as Doreen and I picked up our things and hurried towards the gates. Russians are no different to anyone else. They have hearts too.

Christmas 1984 was one of the best I can remember. Little did we know at the time that 1985 would plunge Ethiopia into a famine that was to dwarf anything we had seen in Kenya with Paddy Hyland.

CHAPTER 18

TALES FROM CANADA

The call of travel and exploration had intrigued me since childhood and the long summer university holidays allowed me indulge myself. But there was a more practical side to this as well. If I could earn enough money working for the summer in Canada then I would be able to fund volunteer work in a developing country the next year.

I worked in many different places in Canada and saw more of the country than the majority of Canadians. Most of the places I worked in were small rural towns and all of them provided medical challenges that were beyond anything family doctors faced in Ireland or the United Kingdom at that time. I purposely sampled life in as many different places as my medical registration allowed. These different places included Parry Sound and Hagersville in Ontario, Foam Lake, Wynyard and Melville in Saskatchewan, Lytton, Lillooet and Ashcroft in BC, Norway House and Churchill in Manitoba and Jeffreys and Stephenville in Newfoundland.

Sometimes I went alone and sometimes one or more of the children came with me, leaving Doreen to manage things in Galway. Mostly it was financial constraints that decided on how many would go and how many would stay. But when we could, we travelled as a complete family, and if this was a trial to fellow travellers, imagine what a trial it was for us and for the airlines.

We had one trial that may be amusing in retrospect but certainly was not at the time. We had flown from St Lucia to Miami and then to JFK to connect with our flight to Shannon. So you can imagine how weary we were. Doreen and I and three children, from nine years down to a two years old. We had to immigrate and change terminals in JFK and then check in again for our flight to Shannon. I was alone with Sallyann (4) at the desk 'foustering' with our check-in luggage which was overweight. Doreen and Mary (9) and Sibylline (2) were some distance away keeping extra luggage out of sight, which we would later carry aboard as hand luggage and so avoid paying exorbitant overweight charges. And of course there was a long queue of passengers behind me obviously impatient with the delay I was causing at the desk.

Eventually, I was allowed heave my bags on to the carousel and watched nervously as the lady stuck on the appropriate labels. When suddenly I heard loud shouts behind me. 'Hey... hey ...look at the kid....' I looked up. Then I saw her. Our four-year-old daughter was sailing away happily on the moving belt heading for the depths of the airport. By the time I spotted her she was already disappearing from view under a black rubber flap. I was horrified and spellbound for a moment and then, ignoring everything and everybody, I sprang over the counter knocking bags out of my way only to find I was just too late to snatch her. Instinct rather than mind took over. I caught sight of a door a little further on and without thinking I raced over to it pushed it open and half stumbled down a grey metal stairs. Presumably an alternative route for staff to transport the luggage should the carousel fail. As I clattered down I was conscious of luggage moving down on a wide black belt to my right.

I was almost at the last step when I saw a big black baggage handler staring in amazement at the little girl who had just landed in between large travel cases. He lifted her up and handed her to me. I don't know what he said. I think he was speechless with surprise and shock. So was I.

We all have very happy memories of those days and laugh about the chaotic journeys we made. Everyday in Canada now seems to have been sunny and every trip we made seems to have been exciting. Memory is selective and in truth we behaved like any other family, loving and hating and laughing and crying, yet now all I can recall is the fun and happiness of those bygone days. Doreen used to joke that she 'would be collecting the old age pension and the children's allowance at the same time'. In retrospect it was all worth it.

We spent two summers in Parry Sound. This is a pretty little town that lies on the Georgian Bay, an inlet of Lake Huron. It attracted an influx of tourists in the summer time giving it a festive atmosphere. Our children were young and as there is no better way of integrating with a community than having small children we quickly got involved in all kinds of activities from swimming galas to concerts to picnics and excursions on the bay.

On free weekends we would drive to the Niagara Falls or go on a shopping trip to Sudbury or Toronto. We also made several excursions to Fantasy Island (an embryonic Disney-land) near Buffalo NY and I will never forget those locals who helped us when our car broke down in a seedy part of Detroit.

One Sunday, we made the trip to the shrine of the Canadian martyrs, Sainte-Marie among the Hurons, where six Jesuits and two lay people were tortured and murdered in the 1600s. This was the first time that our eyes had been opened to Canadian history. I think Europeans are generally ignorant of the rich history of North America, which they still consider to have only started when Columbus landed in Hispaniola – that is if they know where he landed.

Probably the most memorable excursion we made from Parry Sound was when we went to Quebec. I had five days off work and so Doreen and I and the children packed into our rented VW and hit the road. The weather was glorious and the Algonquin Nature Reserve, our first port of call, never looked better. Our next stop was Ottawa. Here we saw the lovely Government Buildings but actually remember Ottawa better for having had our very first Chinese meal there. The children loved it.

Then we drove all the way to the shrine of St Anne de Beaupré and explored a bit of the Gaspé peninsula.

Here we circled back via Montreal, the mighty St Laurence and Quebec city ending up in Valleyfield, where we stayed with the LaFontaines, friends of mine since my time in Liberia. We arrived back in Parry Sound tired but delighted that we had used our time off so well.

Later in the summer, we made several excursions on friends boats to one of the many islands in Georgian Bay and Lake Huron. My colleagues vied with one another as to who had the biggest, sleekest and most powerful boat but it was all the same to us and frankly most of these trips ended in everyone being drenched in spray and eating gritty tuna sandwiches and drinking from paper cups. We tried to avoid invitations to go on the lake after the first few outings.

We marvelled at huge size of Canada, its mountains, its prairies, its forests, its rivers and its lakes. Nowadays people pay to see the aurora borealis (northern lights); this was a free nightly display in Northern Canada which rarely raised a comment from the locals no more than did watching brown bears catching fish in the wild torrents that course through the Rockies.

The Prairies

The Prairie Provinces of Canada appear to be extraordinarily peaceful and calm. In summer, the view is the same whatever way you look. There are limitless acres of fine golden corn reaching beyond the horizon on every side. In the distance, you may see the tall grain elevators standing like accusing fingers pointed upwards to the clear blue sky. Size is vast. The quietness is tangible and heavy in the summer heat. It is broken only when a Ford pick-up speeds past you and then disappears in a cloud of dust. In winter everything is covered in a blanket of snow. Rivers, streams, lakes and ponds are frozen. The ice is thick enough to bear the weight of a heavy truck but occasionally there is a mishap and you hear of vehicles plunging into the icy waters beneath. Remarkable tales of survival for days in ice-cold water are told but most victims die from hypothermia before they can be resuscitated.

The Holy Frog

I think you will enjoy reading about the Holy Frog and I tell it here almost exactly as it was published in the Canadian medical journal *DIAGNOSIS* in November 1984.

It was titled by the Editor *A Frog In My Ear* and sub-titled *Can a Saskatoon Frog Sound Like Niagara Falls?*

Here goes.

'It was almost five on the office clock when the big burly preacher came in. He had no appointment. I was not pleased to see him. The hot day at both office and hospital had left me just a little short tempered. Besides, it was Friday, and the thought of a sun-drenched week end in the heart of Saskatchewan, where I was doing this locum, was making me feel less and less like facing any unsuspected medical problems.

I heard him before I saw him. He had thumped heavily up the wooden stairs to my office.

'I have a frog in my head' announced the big man without any preamble. His voice was shrill. I suppose I had expected a deep sonorous voice to go with his bulk as much as his calling. 'I just can't stand it any more.'

'Help me' I thought, 'not a nut case at five o'clock!'

I looked through his notes; he had been here – and gone to other doctors – several times previously. And yes, he had complained of the same thing many times during the past year. But aside from being rather obese, nobody had found any abnormality on physical examination.

His blood tests were absolutely normal and, significantly, he had no history of mental illness nor was there any history of mental illness in his family.

His work as an evangelist, travelling around the small towns of Saskatchewan, resulted in a rather unorthodox life-style and this was reflected in his character by restlessness, which verged – it seemed to me – on impatience with himself and with everyone else. He had marched up the stairs almost aggressively, been brusque with the receptionist and demanded to see me without any delay.

He fidgeted as I went through his notes. He had been given tablets to lighten, depress, elevate and alter whatever mood he might have been in when seen by my predecessors. Two different Psychiatrists in Saskatoon had seen him. They both thanked the GP 'for sending along this pleasant and interesting man', but they had no clear answers. It could be any number of things. Anxiety? Tension? Pressure of work? Obsession? Why not?

It occurred to me that he might have wax in his ear. Anyway I had to be seen to do something, so I pulled back his fleshy pendulous ear lobes and examined first one side and then the other with my auroscope. All clear. Maybe he had high blood pressure. No, his pressure was normal.

'When does the frog start acting up?' I asked this more to use up time than for any other reason. At least he would feel I was taking him seriously.

'Especially at night when I lie down' he replied 'I suppose that is the time for frogs and toads to start making their noises', he trailed off. This was clearly a misfired joke but it showed me a side to his character that I liked. Up to now I had actually disliked him and felt he was either a mental case or a fraud.

But you know he didn't look crazy. His eyes were normal, his gaze steady and his whole demeanour was now somewhat subdued, perhaps resigned to hearing the same old doctor's spiel.

I don't know why, but I got up rather resignedly from my chair and did a full examination of his cranial nerves.

There are twelve of these on each side. We were now gone over fifteen minutes. I was ready to give up.

'Is it there now?' I asked more from not knowing what to say next, than from sympathy or from medical ingenuity. 'Could I hear it?' (another joke, this time from me).

'Sure, it's there now, maybe not so loud as when I came into your office but it's there all the same… '

I rose again and felt foolish as I placed the bell of my stethoscope on his head. I listened.

It was like Niagara Falls. Rush..rush..rush…cascading torrents of blood coursing from a large brain artery to a nearby vein. What we call an arteriovenous fistula.

I was perplexed, then excited, and then happy and ready to laugh and cry all at the same time.

We moved him to the neurosurgeons in Saskatoon where they operated on him within a week. He made a full and complete recovery and, as far as I know, continues – minus one frog – to evangelize the good people of Saskatchewan to this day.

For me this was, I suppose, a petty triumph. For my patient it was the luckiest meeting of his life. For at least two psychiatrists, a case of two red faces.

Doreen was always cheerful despite the constant travel and the constant settling into new places. She loved everything about Canada especially driving on the long straight prairie roads. I think it was in Foam Lake, Saskatchewan, that she drove over 100 mph on a prairie road with seven-year-old Sallyann fast asleep beside her.

No harm done, but it took some nerve.

In Saskatchewan, there was little to see that lay within driving distance. Here we confined our leisure to visiting local farming families, having barbecues and listening to the price of corn and wheat and to constant complaints about the government ignoring the prairie provinces.

One incident shows the kind of people who lived there. It was our second visit to the little town deep in rural Saskatchewan. We lived in the basement of the doctor's house and, while he and his wife were away on holiday, I was given the use of his second car. An old banger. His brand new Cadillac – the only one in town – was parked sedately in the small driveway and I was explicitly forbidden from using it.

Imagine my distress when I rushed out of the house one evening in answer to an urgent medical call and backed the old banger into the Cadillac. The doctor was due back in three days and news of the damaged Cadillac spread rapidly. It was like a death. All my patients expressed sorrow about 'the accident' and everyone wondered what Mrs Doctor would say when she returned.

I approached the local mechanic with my problem and he merely said 'Leave it to me doc'.

He phoned the Cadillac dealers in Saskatoon got them to send a complete new front grille by courier and replaced the damaged one all within 24 hours. My total bill came to 200 dollars. When the doctor and his wife returned a day later they neither saw nor heard anything about what I had done to their treasured new car.

Churchill, Manitoba

Churchill, called after John Churchill – an ancestor of Winston Churchill – lies on the west side of Hudson Bay in Northern Manitoba. People first lived there all year round in the early 1700s when the Hudson Bay Company set up a small trading post on the mouth of the Churchill River. Today it contains a mixture of races. Those of European origin live peacefully side by side with descendants of the original Cree and Chipewyans.

These native races were there long before the Danes, English or French. The Europeans came to exploit the riches of the Arctic seas and export grain in summertime from the Prairie Provinces to the rest of the world. They certainly had no love for the frozen Arctic wastes and had no care for its unique wildlife and even less for the locals.

The locals are today called Inuit, an amalgam of native tribes, and are, I suppose, the 'Eskimos' of Northern Canada.

I was on a sabbatical year and applied to work for the University of Manitoba in their outreach sector during the winter months. And so I was sent to Churchill.

Locals spoke of 'down south' when referring to Manitoba as if it was in a different country. Certainly, the Inuit population had little in common with the average Canadian and had little or no allegiance to Winnipeg let alone to Ottawa.

They lived lonely lives in remote and often nomadic settlements, and we only saw them in town when they were sick or buying provisions – well subsidised by the Ottawa government.

On the whole, I liked and admired them. But I also liked the townspeople. It took a special sort of person to live in the harsh climate of this place. Life was not easy. Most were 'government men': administrators, teachers, medical and paramedical staff, mounties, geophysicists, survey takers, ecologists, weathermen and engineers. The rest were traders, hunters or casual hands who kept the airstrip clear and who cleaned the streets.

For many, Churchill was self-contained and would be their home for life. Families were raised and marriages made. People lived and died, got drunk (the liquor store was always busy) and went wild, just a little more so than in other parts of the world. The extreme was the normal and the normal was the extreme.

The beautiful white polar bear was a regular visitor to the town. But nobody liked these visits because of the savage unpredictability of these creatures.

Children in particular were taught to 'play dead' if they were cornered outdoors and spotted a polar bear. It was believed that the bear would be fooled and just pass by harmlessly. I am sure that this ploy might work but I would not have the courage to try it.

However, it was the nuisance they caused that annoyed people the most. They would often come at night, knock down fences, trample anything that was not well protected and scatter garbage all over the place. Wisely, no one interfered with these near nightly rampages.

The Mounties or Royal Canadian Mounted Police (RCMP), in their distinctive hats and red jackets, had an outpost here and protected us from our fellow Canadians as well as from renegade Inuits and Indians. We were all very happy to have the Mounties around. I dread to think what sort of place Churchill would have been without them.

The medical facility in Churchill was very up-to-date and was staffed mainly by Canadian graduates. They were young, enthusiastic and conscientious and were only sent up North if they chose to go there – the hardship posting.

The medical staff of the health centre, which now included me, flew regularly on the Artic run to Rankin and Frobisher where we held clinics for those who could not travel to Churchill.

There were no roads, so one had to travel either by sled or snowmobile or by air. The 'Artic pilots' were absolutely brilliant and flew us safely in little Cessna planes in all sorts of weather. Storms, blizzards and 'white outs' were not uncommon, but when the sky was clear and the sun shone, the view from the air was stunning and the majesty of the landscape was awe-inspiring.

We would land on temporary airstrips which in winter were marked out by bright flares. In summer, in daylight, one might more easily land on water in a nearby creek.

Of course, every night the sky was lit up by the Northern Lights. The different colours and the way they dance and mingle with one another are simply beautiful. I had always wanted to see the Northern Lights and the Southern Cross. This was one half of my dream come true. I had to wait until 1989 to fulfil the other half.

The Sad Mountie

In winter, Hudson Bay is completely frozen over. You breath out and your breath freezes before your eyes.

Low temperatures and the isolation of the place make you feel completely cut off from the rest of the civilised world and it was a Mountie's unexpected response to these of that I speak of now

The Mountie had been in Churchill for six months and was from the 'city' (meaning Winnipeg). He was brought in to our medical centre one evening by his colleagues who said that they had found him slumped in a chair in the RCMP station with a discharged revolver in his hand. It was a clear case of attempted suicide and they put it down to 'cabin fever'. Unexpected, but in retrospect not unpredictable.

Cabin fever is a type of psychoneurosis brought on by being isolated in a specific location for a prolonged period. It appears to be common in Arctic regions where the boredom of long periods of inactivity and lack of social intercourse can make you irritable, restless, depressed or even suicidal. Our man was almost certainly such a case.

Luckily, the bullet had skidded across the outer plate of his skull under the *galea aponeurosis* and I could extract it easily under local anaesthetic. The man was stunned but became fully conscious within a short time. After filling out reams of reports, I eventually got a chance to talk to him.

I found him to be a really nice fellow. He was single, in his mid-thirties, and from a very respectable family in Winnipeg. Yes, he missed home badly and was rather isolated up here in the wilderness where there was no social life – except drinking. There were, he said, few people of his own age to talk to.

However, he liked his job and was both happy and proud to be a Mountie. After a while, he admitted that he had tried to kill himself, well not really kill himself for he was now glad to be alive. What he wanted most was to move back home into his natural surroundings and meet up with his pals and family again. Then things would settle down. However, he knew and accepted that he would have to attend a psychiatrist and probably a counsellor and at least get an assessment of his mental status. Would I recommend he be sent back to Winnipeg?

I visited him a few times and we spoke for about fifteen minutes each time. His head wound healed (I had made it larger when probing for the bullet) and in less than ten days he was as fit as ever. I recommended, in writing, that he be sent back to the city and receive appropriate psychiatric assessment there. I hoped that he could stay on as a Mountie. Informally, I got solemn assurances from him that he would never attempt self-harm again and would do all I recommended once back in Winnipeg and away from the dark and dismal frozen north.

Three weeks after his return to Winnipeg, he shot himself again and this time made a final job of it.

I was devastated. How could I have been taken in so easily? Why did I believe him? Why did I not commit him to a mental hospital in Winnipeg once he left Churchill? It is no excuse to say that I was young and inexperienced. I was simply taken in.

Like many things in life, you have to experience them for yourself in order to appreciate them. It is difficult to explain the long dreary days, the incessant persistent cold, the same conversational topics over and over again, and the numerous petty squabbles that occur daily in an isolated far North outpost.

Of course, I am really trying to excuse myself of all guilt by saying these things. Then again, without self-deception, most of us would find life intolerable.

Although our biggest excitement was the arrival of the *Transair* plane from Winnipeg three times a week, weather permitting, going to church on a Sunday was the major social event, and most of the community attended one of the three little wooden churches that attested to the supernatural.

Fr Peter was the local catholic priest. He tended his small flock with great compassion and kindness. He was an ascetic looking man who probably loved living alone, for his life was surely one of extreme isolation from humankind. Thin and gaunt, with a short pointed beard, he looked just as one would imagine the desert fathers of old must have looked.

I hardly knew him, but the townsfolk spoke well of him, which is more than can be said of the way they spoke about each other.

The Bird Call Contest

Churchill is a renowned centre for nesting and migrating birds. Many such as the Loon and the Grey Goose have a really distinctive call. During my stay there, everyone gathered in the recreation hall, which was part of a complex that housed the medical centre and shopping mall, in order to hear contestants mimic animal and birdcalls.

The performers were mainly Inuit and were skilled in this art. The snowy owl and sandpiper figured prominently among the bird calls that year, and the whole population of Churchill and its surrounds, almost 1,000 people, crammed expectantly into the hall and cheered vociferously almost non-stop. As is the custom in most of North America, everyone took off their shoes when entering and left them on the floor near the wide entrance doors.

I remember arriving late and for some inexplicable reason decided to mix up all the shoes knowing well the havoc this would cause when the show was over and everyone wanted to leave.

I bubbled with suppressed laughter when this happened after the final birdcall. But got a little uneasy as people started getting angry when they could not match their shoes or squeezed their feet into someone else's. I was just as indignant as the rest of them muttering imprecations against 'Whoever did this stupid thing…no joke…needs a kick in the backside….'

Strangely, they never found out who played this dirty trick on them. Now they know.

British Columbia (BC)

BC is such a contrast to the Prairie Provinces that they could belong to different planets. One is washed by the ocean, is mountainous, forested, full of swirling rivers and has a bustling colourful cosmopolitan capital city.

The others are land-locked and flat and Saskatoon, Winnipeg and even Edmonton are provincial compared to Vancouver.

Asian immigrants have greatly influenced the life of Vancouver, while in the prairies most people are the descendants of Europeans who came to Canada at an earlier date and retain strong emotional links with their ethnic origin be it the Ukraine or Germany or Poland or Britain.

My first locum in BC was in 1977 in the little town of Lillooet. This was probably because they could get no one else to go to such an out of the way place. But the offer was good and the accommodation was free. This time I was alone except for Danielle – our six-year-old – and she was the nicest company one could have.

Lillooet is situated on the Frasier River about 250 km from Vancouver with which it was linked by a rickety railway. The small gauge track clung perilously to the towering sides of the Canadian Rockies. It was one of the most frightening journeys I ever took, although Danielle looked out the window quite unperturbed by the possibility of plunging to perdition far below. The train traversed fairy-tale bridges that joined seemingly impossible ridges of rock on cliff faces that soared thousands of metres above.

Most of the time our engine was sounding its horn to scare away any living creature that would be foolish enough to live on the side of the mountain. And then the train stopped – as if finally out of breath – in one of the most beautifully situated places I have ever seen.

The township was nestled between a towering green mountain and a tranquil blue lake and sat there as if on a man-made shelf. The mountain was part of the coastal offshoot of the Canadian Rockies and the lake one of the many that graced the might Frasier River system. Clouds gathered half way up the mountain like a fluffy white scarf. But the peak pushed itself so high that you could see it clearly against the deep blue sky. Everyone in Lillooet forecast the weather by looking at the mountain. If you could make out the tree line then showers were expected, if the clouds obscured them, then a storm was brewing and, if the colour of the mountain suddenly changed, then 'we were sure in for a surprise!'

It was in Lillooet that Danielle started to cook for her dad and mind our house – a three-room apartment joined to the medical centre. Most of the time she played with her toys or went apricot picking with me. There was a marvellous tree laden with sweet juicy yellow apricots just behind the clinic at the foothills of the great mountain. However, the legacy of Lillooet will always remain with Danielle for another reason.

It was here that she slipped at the swimming pool and broke a front tooth, unfortunately a permanent one, which was not long erupted. In today's world, we would make an insurance claim, but in 1977, the thought of claiming insurance never entered my head.

Happily modern dentistry has replaced Danielle's tooth so that she can smile normally again.

I have a special affection for Lillooet not just for its beauty but chiefly for the welcome the people gave Danielle and I and for the way they helped us settle down during our stay there. Small communities do that in a way no big city can ever manage.

A few years later, I brought Sallyann, Danielle and Serryth with me to a small town called Ashcroft. It was summer and the grass was green and the evenings mild despite us being quite far north in BC.

Doreen was at home and Sibylline (no. 3 daughter) was in France. I was working hard and could only manage to give the children the same boring food each day, but they never complained. Fathers were not expected to be able to cook in those days.

None of us starved and things got easier when Sallyann got a job as a waitress in Hungry Herbie's, a fast-food joint somewhere out of town. At least she could eat there and that meant I only had the two smaller ones and myself to manage. But the days were long and boring for them and that worried me.

A Camping Trip

So when I got a weekend free, I decided to give everyone a treat and take them camping. I borrowed a tent and cooking things and, on the Friday afternoon, we all set off happily in a packed car. Our first stop was to be the city of Kamloops. We took the lower road via Logan Lake because it was more scenic than the normal route via Savona. It was also longer, narrower and less used.

The day was fine, the children laughing and singing, and the car was chugging steadily along when suddenly I noticed a distinct loss of power as if the engine was failing. Several lights showed on the dashboard, but then they were always blinking at me. However, it was now late afternoon, and I felt that the car needed a rest before bringing it to a garage. So I pulled off the road into a grassy clearing which I decided was an ideal spot to pitch our tent for the night.

It was near a lake and surrounded by lovely Canadian forest. I erected the tent as best I could, although it looked a little lopsided when it was finished. The children helped me do this and thoroughly enjoyed the whole business. We then ate ready-made sandwiches and tried to warm water on a primus stove with no success. However, we had enough coke to satisfy all our thirsts and went to bed very happily at about nine o'clock, as there was really nothing else to do. It was of course quite bright outside and would be bright for many hours to come.

Sometime during the night, the wind picked up. This woke me. At first, I felt very secure and comfortable listening to the sounds of a brewing storm outside. There are few things more comforting that being tightly snuggled up in bed while a storm lashes the outside world, the window panes rattle, the wind whistles through nearby trees and branches groan under the weight of wet leaves. But there is nothing more alarming than when your little world crashes down about you and your haven of bliss becomes a whirling twirling maelstrom of ferocious gusts of wind, while cascades of rain soak you instantly and blur your vision. Add to this nearby claps of thunder and flashes of fork lightning, and you can understand the mayhem that ensued. The tent collapsed on top of us, the children started screaming and I started frantically trying to extricate us from ropes, canvas and drenched blankets.

Happily, the storm passed as quickly as it had started, and after much re-arranging, we bundled ourselves into the car, switched on the heater and huddled together for the remainder of the night.

We returned to Ashcroft next day tired, hungry and vowing never to go camping again. The mechanic said that the car had seen better days and that there was really nothing much he could do with it and charged me 50 dollars. He wondered if I would like to buy a new one.

Mr Jackson

Monday was my day on call and I was still tired and irritable when the hospital phoned before midnight to say there was a man from 'the South' (that meant the USA) who was asking to see a doctor because he had got something in his left eye. The guy's name was Jackson. I had only just laid down in bed and nodded off but answered the call promptly. I have always found that taking a minute or two to snooze after being called is a disaster. You have to get up anyway. So you may as well do it immediately. All doctors share the phenomenon of 'on-call' syndrome. That consists of hearing the phone *before it rings* or worse still imagining you are being called when you actually have a night off.

In any case, I arrived at the hospital within ten minutes of the call and in only fairly decent humour.

'Where are you from?' I snapped at the rather frightened, olive-skinned young man who was waiting in the emergency room (ER) for me. 'Indiana', he replied, 'I am here with my brothers... doing a show for the night and some goddamned thing got into my eye. I don't know. Maybe a flying insect...it hurts like mad.'

'I charge $15 US dollars to non-Canadians plus ten for a night call.' I always stated my terms to anyone from the South.

They would reply that I could claim it from their insurance. But I had been caught out too often in the past either to trust their Insurance Company or to trust that they were actually insured, or, if not insured, to trust that they would pay cash into my hand after they had received treatment.

Besides, I was dubious about this guy. He probably hadn't a cent on him and probably had no insurance.

I was wrong, of course. A man who was sitting patiently outside the ER now came forward and paid me in hard US currency saying 'No problem Doc, just give me a receipt.' This was a big strong and pleasant looking black man who was obviously with my patient and probably his manager.

I took the money, gave a receipt and got Jackson to lie down so that I could check out his eye. 'What's your first name?' I enquired as I washed out his left conjunctiva sac with saline. 'Michael' he replied and then added 'Where are you from Doc? You from the East?'

'That's right', I responded. I get tired telling people that I am from Ireland because that leads to all sorts of questions and exclamations such as 'How do you like it here?… I visited Cork once, my great great grandmother came from Cavan, our family doctor is married to an Irish girl….'

It was only some days later that my daughter Sallyann told me that the Jackson I had treated was Michael Jackson of the Jackson Five. Poor Michael Jackson. His life was to be a turbulent one filled with highs that were too high and lows that were too low. A life that ended in dark tragedy a few years later.

Norway House

Norway House was originally built by Norwegian ex-convicts in the early 1800s and lies about 20 miles north of Lake Winnipeg. The location is stunning. It lies in thickly wooded countryside which is sprinkled with hundreds of lakes all interconnected so that the locals travel around mostly by boat until winter comes when the lakes freeze and they resort to dog sleds and snowmobiles. As an important centre for the Cree Nation, all basic services including medical care are provided by the Federal Government in Ottawa.

I first worked there in 1980 and was given a place to live close to the clinic. The clinic was situated on a spit of land that was surrounded on three sides by water with a landing jetty on one side, a small, sandy cove on the other, and a blunt end that the extended into the lake. There were several wooden canoes and boats tied up at the jetty and one was for the exclusive use of the staff.

The only other doctor was an elderly Australian who wanted to explore isolated parts of the world, but like myself wanted to get paid for it! We shared the roster equally and in truth the work was easy and enjoyable. We had a few beds for inpatients and minor emergencies, but anything major was airlifted to Winnipeg. He was accompanied by his wife, while I had brought two daughters, Mary (21) and Danielle (9). I cannot recall a glum face or a nasty word between any of us. We lived in a little Shangri La of our own.

Mary was a dental student at the time and made friends with the local pilots who would smuggle beer into their house about a mile from the clinic. They often gave her a bottle or two to give me since alcohol was strictly forbidden on the island for fear of its effect on the local Indians. I treasured these little treats. But the pilots also caused us trouble.

One evening they let Mary take the wheel of their car which she duly totalled taking a bend too fast. Luckily, I was on duty in the hospital and thank God she was not hurt badly, only bruised and shocked. Everyone was sorry for Mary and the whole incident was hushed up including her visit to the emergency department! All records of the incident disappeared miraculously from the ER logbook.

Just couldn't happen today.

Danielle had an adventure too. When not with me, she spent her time with Donna, a little Cree girl, and they became close friends. They often splashed around in the water of the cove and I would sit and watch them, just looking up from my novel now and again to make sure that they were all right. I must have been quite engrossed one afternoon when I was roused by sounds of shouts and screaming.

There was my Danielle pulling Donna out of the water! I was paralysed with shock, but leapt up and chased down to the water's edge. No need. The two were fine. Standing there, dripping wet, hair like limp spaghetti and both crying. I made light of the whole affair and Danielle still believes that she did nothing extraordinary.

On a less than happy note I remember, on at least two occasions, removing leeches from Danielle's skin, after she had been playing with Donna in the reeds and bushes. I had forbidden them to ever play in the cove so they moved to a kind of small swamp further up which was apparently the favourite haunt of leeches.

The Cree people are tough, stoic and fiercely independent. Nonetheless, many live on welfare but native pride gives them an inner strength and a way of life which outsiders seldom appreciate. Being a doctor, and serving their body needs, gets you close to them, but only if you can genuinely show respect and care. Like most people that I have worked with, they quickly see through the patronising smile and strongly resent it.

Most of the people live in reservations, which are financed by the Federal Government in Ottawa. There is ample fishing and logging and hunting in the area for them to live on, but federal money has eroded much of the native skill for survival and replaced it with the conveniences of modern life including TVs, motorised snowmobiles and alcohol. Alcohol was the curse of the reservations. There was much drunkenness and a high level of unemployment.

The Mounties tried to prevent liquor entering the reservations but met with as much success as prohibition did in the United States.

Twenty years after I left Norway House an ex-student of mine from Galway, Deirdre O'Flaherty, became the MO there. Deirdre moved on to Churchill further north where she became the chief of medical staff and has since served as the President of the Manitoba College of Family Physicians. Deirdre is from a well known Galway family. I knew her late father, a pharmacist, 'back in the day'. Small world

Newfoundland

I landed in Stephenville, on the island of Newfoundland, in June 1986, thus completing a coast-to-coast experience of Canada.

Stephenville is a small town that lies on the southwest coast of the most easterly Province of Canada and relies mainly on fishing for its livelihood. It was singularly devoid of any architectural character, but the inhabitants were warm, welcoming and generous despite so many living on welfare. My first few nights were spent in a dreary hotel in the main street which was furnished like the kind of place Jack Reacher would use. Totally cheap and tawdry. The doctor who met me, an aficionado of the official health service, was tall, thin and colourless, and boringly enthusiastic about 'the system'. I did not care. I was interested in sampling life on the east coast of

Canada. I had already sampled it in the prairies and on the west coast.

Gander, on the northeast tip of the island, still resonates with memories of past glories in the presence of shabby buildings and a scattering of older people associated with its famous airport. The Second World War had brought an influx of military personnel into the region, who spent their dollars liberally. But that time was long since gone and all that remained was a precarious living to be earned from the sea, modest farming or life on welfare. Today Gander is bypassed as modern jets fly longer distances without refuelling.

Many Newfoundlanders have roots in Ireland, Scotland and in the Nordic countries, and in scattered villages people still play typical Celtic music and speak in Celtic and Breton dialects. It is quite a shock to hear locals speak English with a distinct Irish *brogue*. As you can imagine my accent evoked no comment from anyone.

Labrador, to the northwest, is part of the Canadian mainland and is separated from Newfoundland by the Strait of Belle Isle. They were amalgamated into a single province in 2001 under the name 'Newfoundland and Labrador', but many are unhappy about this marriage not least because of the cumbersome name. I did not visit Labrador, but one warm afternoon decided to have a swim in the straits which looked blue, unrippled and inviting. The water was freezing. I am used to the gentle waters of the Atlantic that wash the shore of Galway and swim there all year around. But the waters that wash Labrador are a different matter and I was hardly in before I was out.

I had taken up a contract with the Provincial government and was initially assigned to the hospital in Stephenville. The work was light, but on-call at night was irksome, because of the frequent demands to tend trivial complaints such as someone with a sore throat or a nosebleed. This was a far cry from the sort of emergency one was called at night to see in Africa.

However, after a week, I was sent to the west coast of the island, to a little village called Jeffreys. Here I was installed as a district medical officer for the surrounding area and given a nice house and surgery overlooking the sea.

A car was essential so I bought one in the local garage for 200 dollars with a guarantee that I would get my money back after three months. I am not a businessman, but that looked as if I was given the use of the car for nothing.

However, the garage man was no fool. It cost me far more than 200 dollars on repairs during my time there and eventually I returned a car to him in a much better condition than when I got it.

Sibylline, our third daughter, joined me in July. She was a trainee teacher and was delighted to get to Canada for the summer. She kept house, answered the phone and did general reception work during the day, and in the evening, we would walk on the cliffs and watch the sunset across the Gulf of St Laurence and distant Labrador.

Once a week, we would go to Corner Brook, the local big town, to do shopping and buy presents for home. On a warm day, we would dally in the main drag, sit on public seats and eat large Canadian ice creams covered in chocolate and cream.

Occasionally, we went to local functions where the men barbecued steaks and burgers and the ladies handed around plates of apple pie and homemade cookies. The doctor was expected to attend such functions which were usually held in the British Legion Hall.

All that was missing was a couple of fellows playing fiddles and we would have had a real barn dance like you see in old Western movies.

I had always thought that Dr Finlay, Marcus Welby and their successor Doc Martin were idealised TV characters who worked themselves to the bone and cared for everyone. My job in Jeffreys made the same demands and had the same rewards. I was expected to do everything, listen sympathetically to everyone and be available at all times. In return, the people would stand by me, mind me and invite me to everything. Such is life in 'A country practice'. And I enjoyed the job – for a few months.

Canada: Land of the Brave and Free

Doreen and I loved Canada, not just because it provided me with money to work in Africa, and not just because it gave us so many happy memories, but also because Canada was – and still is – a land where colour, race or creed do not stop you from achieving a full and contented life, a land where there is fairness for all and especial care for the underdog. May it always remain so.

Leabharlanna Poibli Chathair Baile Átha Cliath

Dublin City Public Libraries

APPENDIX 1

ROBBIE AND MIKE

There were many people I met in Kenya who were talented, unusual, eccentric, maverick and even heroic. I mention but two who were in many respects similar but in other ways completely different.

One was Robbie McCabe, the Carmelite priest/doctor with whom Doreen and I shared a memorable safari. The other was Mike Meegan, the energetic, charismatic humanitarian who became more Kenyan than the Kenyans themselves.

Robbie's Roots

Robbie was born in Mallow, Co Cork, in July 1926. His grandfather was a distinguished surgeon who was knighted for his services to medicine. His father, Col. Fred McCabe, was also a doctor and served in the Boer War, the Great War and afterwards in the Irish Free State Army. He was a keen sportsman. Robbie's mother was a distinguished person too. At one time, she worked in the War Office in London and during the Great War made it clear that she was devastated by the scale and wanton loss of life, so much so that she incurred the displeasure of senior officials.

Robbie inherited characteristics from both his parents. He had sport and medicine and traditional army values from his father and a strong sense of compassion for the sick from his mother. He excelled in all these fields.

He studied medicine in University College Dublin but had to interrupt his studies for six months because he contracted TB, for which – in those days – there was no specific treatment. Nonetheless, he graduated with honours and went on to do his internship year in the Mater Hospital Dublin.

But medicine did not satisfy the young doctor. He wanted to fulfil, indeed he needed to fulfil, a call that medicine alone could not satisfy, and so, after much thought and soul searching – as he told me himself – he spoke to the Carmelites in 1954 about his desire to enter their order.

Catholic priests were not allowed practise medicine when Robbie was ordained a priest in 1961. However, religious Sisters had been emancipated from this rule and this paved the way for Bishop Donal Lamont, a fellow Carmelite, to get permission from Rome for Robbie to work as both priest and doctor in his diocese in Rhodesia (now Zimbabwe).

Later Robbie would go to Turkana in northern Kenya, where he spent most of his missionary life working to better the physical and spiritual health of the indigenous people. His visits to Dublin, in particular to lecture in the RCSI, were something he cherished, and which gave him time to rest, think and write his magnum opus 'Desert Nomads'. Sam McConkey, professor in the Department of International Health and Tropical Medicine, facilitated Robbie and delivered a glowing citation on his death.

Perhaps his main contribution to health in Turkana was his unrelenting fight against hydatid disease, the perennial scourge of the local population. Many of us in and outside the RCSI supported Robbie in his work both financially and with medicines. Some Irish doctors, like Dermot MacDonald an ex-Master of Holles St and a classmate of mine in UCD, considered Robbie a 'saint'. But whenever I hear someone say 'so and so is a saint', I think of my Doreen's saying 'The Saints are in Heaven.'

Thomas Michael Elmore-Meegan

Thomas Michael Elmore-Meegan or, more simply, Mike Meegan was an even more extraordinary person than Robbie.

Mike was born in Liverpool and raised a devout English Catholic. He was educated in the United Kingdom and France and later in Terenure College, Dublin, and by the time he left school in 1977, he appears to have been someone on a mission and in a hurry.

His mission was to bring clean water, sanitation and health to deprived areas of the world, starting with East Africa. And he wanted *to do it now*.

It was natural therefore that he was attracted to a missionary life and so he spent some years in and out of different Catholic Missionary Orders, easily achieving a degree in Philosophy from the Jesuits in Miltown Park.

But patience and obedience were not his strong points, and he did not fit in to the rigid routine of seminary life and finally left it behind when he became a full time student in Trinity College Dublin. Here he took an MSc in Community Health basing his thesis on Diarrheal Disease in the Maasai.

In pursuit of his ideals, Mike decided to go to Kenya in 1979 and do something concrete rather than merely theorise from the comfort of Dublin. However, he quickly found out that to win the respect and confidence of the local Maasai, he needed two things: one was to speak their language and the second was to actually cure disease.

Consequently, Mike did not dismiss the contribution of missionaries and other humanitarian expatriates; indeed, he befriended and helped them whenever he could.

Mike had a powerful personal charism. He was a born leader who combined his ability to speak passionately with an obvious willingness to dedicate his life to helping others. It was logical that he needed an organisation to back his work, and so in 1979, he gathered a small group around him and was the prime mover in founding The Community for the Relief of Starvation and Suffering (CROSS). In 1984, he expanded this by founding ICROSS – the 'I' standing for 'International'.

Dr Joe Barnes (Dublin), Wilfred Koinange (MOH, Kenya), Vincent Kenny (a technician in the RCSI) and myself were among those who joined the executive committee. Indeed, one of the first meetings of ICROSS took place in my home in Galway.

Nonetheless, I had reservations about Mike. He seemed too good to be true. Perhaps that is what niggled at me. And, although I had no evidence to the contrary, the accounts he gave of his activities in Africa seemed to me somewhat exaggerated. Then again, perhaps I was a little envious.

He spoke Kiswahili fluently and had made his home among the Maasai and had opened a 'medical' clinic in Kajiado, virtually in opposition to a nearby Catholic Health Centre. The missionaries contended that he could have opened his clinic elsewhere where there was none.

He was also seen by the missionaries as someone who was practising medicine without having any formal training in it. And they were quite right. But in reality, he was probably well able to cope with most of the patients he saw. In a short time, a kind of mythology arose about 'the white healer'.

Mike's Cinic

So, before committing myself fully to ICROSS, I wanted to see him working first-hand. Shortly afterwards, I found myself in Kenya and got that opportunity. Not only that but he asked me to take a clinic one morning in Kajiado and see things for myself. I did so with alacrity.

What I saw impressed me, in particular, the way he spoke to people, the way he listened to them and the way he solved their problems. As for medicine he had the usual antimalarials, antibiotics and antihelminthics as in most rural clinics. He sent obviously sick people to Nairobi and he could certainly manage minor routine cases well.

During the morning, he asked me to see one of his most trusted helpers and naturally I was happy to oblige. The helper was a handsome Maasai warrior of about eighteen years of age, a favourite of Mike, and had the frank, spirited manner which characterises his race.

He complained of recent backache, which he put down to changing a wheel on Mike's jeep. I have an experience of changing wheels on stranded jeeps in Africa and I can tell you it is no easy task. Indeed, a backache is a small price to pay for successfully changing a weighty wheel when you have few tools and no jack. However, this man's pain had persisted and was radiating down his left leg. He also had a slight fever, which Mike had told him was probably due to malaria. Coughing aggravated the pain and his left ankle jerk reflex was reduced. I felt sure that this was a prolapsed disk, probably at the level of L5/S1, at the junction of the lumbar and sacral spine.

However, the presence of fever bothered me. I did not think that he had malaria and I was not entirely sure that this was a simple disk prolapse. Fever is not a feature in such cases, and it is all too easy to regard every case of fever you see in Africa as being due to malaria

Normally, I would have prescribed analgesics for pain, valium to relieve muscle spasm and complete bedrest to allow the prolapse to settle. However, since we were near Nairobi, and since this was Mike's special helper, I decided to get an X-ray. I assumed that this would be a waste of time or at best merely confirm disk narrowing.

Ultimately, when I saw the X-ray, it was clear that he had severe TB of the spine. I am happy to say that he recovered fully after a prolonged course of anti-TB drugs while remaining ambulatory and useful to Mike's work. This was one misdiagnosis that turned out well *by my being lucky*. It made me realise too that medicine is a pyramid and that the bulk of common diseases can be handled by those who do not necessarily possess a full medical degree.

Mike Drives Me to Nairobi

I think Mike's maverick nature first impinged directly on me on the day before I was to leave Kenya. Mike was driving me from Eldoret to Nairobi when our land rover suddenly swerved out of control and almost toppled over before it stopped. Mike seemed very calm, got out and inspected the damage. I climbed out my side glad to be alive and intact and outwardly calm.

'No problem Dom, just a flat tyre'

I was unhappy but relieved. Somehow when Mike said no problem, it meant that it was a problem that he could solve but unlikely that I could solve. However, neither of us could solve it this time. We carried neither tools nor a spare tyre.

Mike was unabashed.

'I guess we will wait until we can hail down help', he grinned. It was now 5 p.m.

We waited and waited. One or two cars sped past us but failed to stop. Bandits and carjacking are very common in these parts, and no doubt, one does not stop unless it is absolutely essential.

It was now 6.0 p.m. Darkness was descending like a blanket and we were in the middle of nowhere. We climbed back into the car and made ourselves as comfortable as possible. It got cold as night wore on and that added to our discomfort. Neither of us slept. All was still except for the occasional call of a night owl and the distant roar of a lion. Rain-heavy clouds covered the sky. They hid the moon and stars so that outside was pitch black until the first streaks of dawn signalled the birth of a new day.

We got out of the car, yawned and stretched and waited. Mike's optimism was justified. Hardly an hour passed until we heard the unmistakable sound of heavy traffic approaching. Soon a line of grey trucks appeared, an army battalion on its way to Nairobi. We hailed them down expectantly and Mike turned on all his charm.

He spoke to the commander in Kiswahili and explained our problem jerking a finger in my direction from time to time. I presume telling the officer that I was a doctor and needed to get to Nairobi in a hurry to catch a flight.

Meantime the men jacked up our vehicle and loaned us a wheel on condition they would get it back later that day. We willingly agreed to this and after profusely thanking everyone drove on to the city without further mishap – wondering if a Western army would have been so obliging.

Our first stop in Nairobi was at the house of Mohammed Amin – 'Mo' as he was commonly known. Mo was an internationally known journalist cum photographer who had received much acclaim for his coverage of African coups, wars and disasters. For some, his best work would be associated with Michael Buerk's reporting of the Ethiopian famine in 1994. But for most, his best work depicted the spectacular scenery and daily life of man and beast in the Sahel.

His house was lovely. It stood secluded in a jacaranda lined suburban avenue and was fenced in by a profusion of glorious multi-coloured bougainvillea. It exuded serenity. We pulled up in the gravelled driveway and were instantly met by a houseboy who informed us that Mo was away but that madam was at home.

She had heard us talking and came around the side of the house with a secutaire in one hand and a bunch of freshly cut flowers in the other. She was tall, blonde and charming.

She greeted Mike like an old friend and bade us both come around the back of the house where there was a spacious patio with a couple of glass-topped tables and several garden chairs.

'Mo is away again on assignment' she told us as we all sat down 'So I am glad of company.' She then had a servant bring cool drinks and bowls of macadamia nuts and turned to me and asked what I was doing in Kenya.

Once she realised that I was a doctor she expounded at length on the wonderful work Mike was doing with the Maasai, and soon I began to have renewed respect for my companion. Mike took all the compliments in his stride merely smiling enigmatically as she continued her eulogy. She was obviously one of Mike's admirers. But she impressed me. Here was someone who must really know about Mike's work.

From where we sat, there was a clear view of Kilimanjaro, the highest mountain in Africa. The mountain itself was snow topped and looked like a very large inverted ice cream cone. So clear was the atmosphere that I could even make out the green-covered lower slopes. It was hard to believe that we were viewing something in Tanzania over 300 km away.

We spent about an hour in this oasis of peace before I suggested to Mike that it was time I got to the airport. Besides, he had to return the wheel and get the old one fixed. I am always far too early for my flights. I count that a virtue not a fault.

'Man invents talking to stop thinking' Agatha Christie.

You may then wonder why I dropped out of ICROSS. I was worried from the start by the volatile personality of its founder, by his unorthodox history, by his Walter Mitty life style and above all by his smooth talking. Mike could carry you away with his words.

So I left ICROSS because I could not continue to support an organisation that had doubtful financial accountability that was essentially a one-man show and in which that man was doling out medicines without any formal training.

Reputation Matters

If you Google 'Michael Meegan' you will find that his reputation has since been sullied by allegations of impropriety against vulnerable native people, by a misrepresentation of his qualifications and by a misuse of donated money (he raised huge monies). Paul Cullen's article in the *Irish Times* in April 2010 is just one of many questioning the activities of Mike and of ICROSS. And yet it must be clearly said that *the Courts have cleared Mike of these charges* and rightly awarded him compensation for unproven allegations.

In summary, I say this. Mike had a deep and generous nature and was prepared to do things to help his fellow man that I would not dare to do. Once you met him, you could never forget him.

ANIMAL ENCOUNTERS

Never Smile at a Crocodile

Many of us have a picture of Africa in which there is a constant danger of being attacked by a wild animal or being bitten by a snake. This is a hangover from the stories brought back by the early explorers and later immortalised and exaggerated by Hollywood in the Tarzan movies and more recently in the Indiana Jones ones.

The truth is that you may visit Africa and never see anything more frightening than a lizard and never have been bitten by anything bigger than a mosquito.

Indeed, I have had more frightening brushes with animals outside Africa than inside Africa. So I have gathered a handful of them together, from Africa, the Middle East and Europe, in the hopes that their telling will show that you do not have to be a big game hunter to tangle with creatures that have as much right to the earth as we.

I will begin with the most innocuous tale, a story about my encounter with dogs in that most civilised of cities, Brussels.

I was going there to a board meeting of Medicus Mundi International (MMI), on which I was the Irish representative. MMI was originally founded as an agency for sending doctors to developing countries and for addressing poverty and inequality between the 'third world' and the 'first world'.

Several European countries had come together originally to form MMI and the President, Dr Edgar Widmer from Zurich, was keen that Ireland should join. But first, we had to have a national branch. I managed to get this going and was soon on the International Board.

Everyone could speak French and so we did our business in that language. It was only then that I regretted learning Greek rather than French in school, but somehow I muddled through.

Part of my job was to attend meetings in participating European capitals and this story is about attending one in Brussels.

On the Aer Lingus plane from Dublin, I sat beside an ex-pupil of mine, now a successful doctor. He told me that he was a confirmed atheist. 'Cannot understand why you, such a clever man, still believe in all that religious bunkum.'

'I know it is difficult, but I suppose that is what Faith means', I replied. I always think of great answers too late.

'But you can be a good, a great Christian even, without going to mass and obeying all those archaic church rules.' Of course, I sensed an inherent truth in what he is saying.

'Ah, but I need the discipline. Otherwise I would drift into believing nothing, or worse still in believing anything – provided I found it convenient. I really need the Church to keep me on the straight and narrow.'

I am sure that I did not convince him. You don't convince anyone by pushing arguments on them.

After that, we drifted into a pleasant conversation and drank lots of coffee spaced with several little bottles of good Irish whiskey. Alcohol was plentiful and free on board European flights in those days.

On reaching Brussels, I got a bus to the centre of the city and then decided to walk to my lodging about a mile from the beautiful Central Square, the Grand Place or Grote Market. It was a lovely May evening, and although it was only 8 p.m., the streets were quiet and almost deserted. Half way to my lodgings, the coffee and whiskey started to work and I got a sudden irrepressible call of nature.

Massive EU buildings and lots of faceless office blocks surrounded me. More importantly, there was no hotel, no café, no pub and no public convenience in sight. This only made the urge of nature stronger and now a sense of panic began to grip me. However, salvation loomed around the corner in the form of a tree-studded park, surrounded by a high wrought-iron railing.

The gates were locked, but I quickly looked around, found that there was no one in sight, and then scampered over the railing. I was almost finished watering a majestic oak tree when I heard them coming. Dogs. Guard dogs.

There must have been four of them and as they came, they snarled viciously. I raced like mad to the gate, launched myself over it and left the dogs seething and frustrated and scraping the rails as they leapt upwards.

My sudden relief was short lived. Unbelievably, but without doubt, one of the dogs had scaled the railing and was now perched on top ready to launch himself at me. He was barking furiously, but I did not wait to see what would happen next.

It was a no-brainer; dignity flew out the window and I took to my heels and ran. What a relief to see my lodgings come in view. I was too scared to look back but I imagined I could hear the dogs baying not far behind.

I slid open the porch door and closed it firmly behind me and from the safety of my sanctuary looked up and down the street. It was empty. Not a dog or a cat or a mouse in sight. I then rang the bell and tried to look calm when my host opened the door.

But he must have sensed my distress for he produced a bottle of Bordeaux 'on the house' before sitting me down to a very welcome evening meal.

In bed that night I promised myself that I would take a taxi if ever I arrived late in Brussels again.

The Kingdom of Saudia Arabia:
لسعوديةا العربية مملكةٌ
The dogs of Jeddah

It was 1977, my first time in Jeddah, and I was a passenger in a pick-up being driven by a North of Ireland fellow who was working there. He was bringing me home from the university and I was very glad of the ride. We were almost there when suddenly a pack of wild dogs appeared from nowhere and scrambled up on the back of the vehicle. They were barking and snarling furiously and, although it was dusk, I could clearly see their snouts pressed against the back of the driving cabin. More worrying was the fact that some of them started pawing and scratching the Perspex window that separated us.

My Irish friend, inured to riots and chases in Belfast, reacted swiftly by speeding up, braking sharply and taking corners at speed. It worked. I could sense the thud thud thud as one by one the dogs lost footing and were flung mercilessly on to the road. The last one stuck on grimly and he only managed to get rid of him by making a series of sudden stops and starts.

When we finally halted, we just sat motionless. 'Happens all the time' he intoned 'Usually it is easy to get rid of them. Tonight, I don't know… they must be extra hungry…maybe doing their version of Ramadan.'

'God that was scary.' I meant it. His joke about Ramadan had fallen flat.

He laughed and without another word drove slowly to my apartment building. I carefully opened the cab door and gave my companion a wave. I never saw him, his pickup or the dogs again.

Fear in India: Satan or Rabies?

Fear and cowardice are not the same. But neither are pleasant things and, although my next story is far less dramatic than the one about the dogs in Jeddah, it was as frightening at the time.

We were in India, Doreen, my sister Sibyl and myself. The three of us were coming down a mountain on the way back to Mangalore having spent the night in a kind of ashram guesthouse. I was in the front with the driver, Doreen and Sibyl were in the back. We had almost reached the ground level when a large lean black dog appeared on the road just ahead. He stood motionless staring at us.

This time there was no immediate threat, we were safe in our vehicle, and there was no way the dog could attack us. Yet there was something sinister about the dog with his drooping mouth, hanging tongue and staring eyes. He exuded a sense of evil, evil incarnate.

I believe that we all felt this, including the Indian driver who stopped as if commanded to do so by some unseen power. Was this fanciful? Were we tired and overwrought after the night in the ashram? I told the driver to drive on, get away. He obeyed automatically but reluctantly.

Later I wondered if this dog had rabies, which is very common in dogs in India. But an uneasy feeling always comes over me when I recall that morning and our encounter with that forlorn creature.

Beware of Sleeping Crocodiles

When you travel from Jomo Kenyatta airport to the city of Nairobi, you pass a small game reserve on the left-hand side. It contains many of the animals you would expect to see in East Africa with giraffes and zebras predominating.

A rather polluted muddy creek used to run on the Nairobi side of the reserve and one sunny afternoon, when I was walking along its bank with some friends I spied a large crocodile, fast asleep on a small rocky island, in the middle of the stream. I should explain that steep grassy slopes bordered the stream and that we were walking on the top of the slope, enjoying the sun, just like the crocodile.

I bent down, picked up a stone and aimed it at the crocodile's head. 'That'll wake him up', I said carelessly.

As I bent down to find another stone, I became aware of a movement from the corner of my eye. It was the crocodile.

I straightened up and suddenly realised that the croc had slipped off his rock, had splashed into the shallow water and was just about to climb the slope in our direction. I need not tell you that we all took to our heels. I did not look back until I was sure that I was safe. My last memory was of seeing him slip back into the water, doubtless disappointed at missing a tasty meal. I have never disturbed a sleeping crocodile since.

I did learn a bit more about crocodiles sometime later from a young missionary nun, who was working at the time in Baluba, which was a TB and leprosy centre on the northern shore of Lake Victoria.

She spoke of how cunning crocodiles are, how they mimic a dead log while in the water, and then pounce on their unsuspecting prey. She told me of one experience when she was chased for twenty metres inland by an exasperated croc and of course told me of the number of natives who had lost arms and legs to their savage jaws while fishing on the lake. Never take a crocodile for granted.

> The Nairobi game reserve has been developed in recent years with guided tours, display centres and a rather expensive entrance fee.

Other Animals

During my trips to Africa, I have come across many of the animals that you see in nature programmes on TV. I have been lucky to have seen the massed flamingos on Lake Naivasha, to gaze in awe at a pride of lions in the early morning mist on the Ngong hills, to have been startled by a fearsome cobra when getting out of my car at night, to have had a viper strike – and miss me – in Zambia, to have been frightened by the headlong rush of a wild boar in Uganda, and to have seen crocodiles in Lake Turkana and hippos in the Zambezi. Giraffes, zebras and water hens are probably too common to mention.

The ostrich is a strange fellow. Generally, he runs away when you approach, but they have been known to turn and attack a small car and, since they can easily out-run a man, I have always been wary of them. I am told reliably that the kick of an ostrich is even worse than the kick of a kangaroo. A large dent in the side of my car proved that.

I have only once seen a leopard in the wild, I mean the real wild, not a game park 'wild'. They lie comfortably and well camouflaged along the bough of a tree and, and if in the mood, they will leap down on you without warning. You cannot outrun them, you cannot outjump them and you certainly cannot outmuscle them. They are solitary, secretive, elusive and ferocious animals.

The fact that they appear to care deeply for their young – and even for the young of other animals – is of little consolation if you are attacked by one.

And then there are the birds of Africa. So many, so colourful, so noisy. Even the African starling is beautiful. Or take for instance the solemn cranes siting like a row of High Court judges on the roof of a rest house beside Lake Edward in central Uganda. The slim still white egrets, so very common in Africa, are especially abundant in West Africa where they sometimes dot the fields like praying Cistercian monks. However, I never could get to like vultures with their bald heads, beady eyes and crimson mouths. There is something definitely blood curdling about the way they hover around dying animals or tear dead carcasses to pieces. Hyenas are even worse. I have seen a boy's arm half hanging off from a hyena attack when I was in Ethiopia during the great famine.

Monkeys of every sort abound and they chatter, swing, jump and generally make a nuisance of themselves. Indeed, on one occasion, they definitely threw coconuts at

Doreen when we entered a part of a forest in Nigeria that they considered their private domain.

Naturally, smaller animals such as geckos and lizards and chameleons abound, but their numbers are insignificant when compared to those of insects such as cockroaches, ants, scorpions, mosquitoes, butterflies, midges, gnats, sand-flies blackflies, tsetse flies, fireflies and a host of others.

Holy Obedience

I recall vividly two stories, both true, that involve fireflies in one and a snake in the other.

I was sitting one night chatting with a few MMM sisters in one of their houses in Nigeria. As is often in such situations, the talk centred on 'the old days' and 'what it was like compared to today'.

'What were your first impressions of Nigeria?', I asked, expecting the usual replies such as a dread of being bitten by a snake, a fear of disease such as yellow fever or malaria or typhoid or fear of being robbed or simply homesickness.

One sister piped up and said 'On my first night in Lagos, I lay scared in bed by clusters of little moving lights that surrounded me.' She went on 'The Sister in the next bed was deeply asleep but I shook her awake and whispered that I was afraid.' 'Sister...I'm afraid... All those moving specks of light... Are we on fire? Is there someone in the room?' She sleepily answered me, 'Sister, you are a silly goose...those little lights are just fireflies. Like flying glow-worms but much brighter.' After which she promptly turned her back to me and fell asleep again. Of course, this became a standard joke at my expense for months afterwards. Afterwards I was ashamed of myself.

There was a pause before another Sister spoke, 'You know' – she started in a delightful Cork accent – 'how strict things were in the old days. Well I sailed from Liverpool with four other Sisters, sometime in November 1957. I remember the ship; it was called the *Apapa* and you all know that the *Apapa* and the *Auriol* were the two vessels of the Elder Dempster Lines that served West Africa in those days.' She paused for effect. We had all travelled on the Elder Dempster Lines and those twelve or fourteen days on board were always a real rest and marvellous holiday. Indeed, I took and framed the dining room menus from my first trip home and they now hang proudly in our living room displaying a colourful series of West African birds. Doreen and baby Mary and I had sailed on the *Aureol*, a nicer and more modern ship than the *Apapa*, but both were equal as far as passenger comfort was concerned.

The sister continued. 'Yes' she mused 'things were tough in those days and being a nun was a demanding vocation that taxed your obedience and often your common sense.'

She paused again gathering her thoughts. 'We arrived in *Apapa*, the port of Lagos – after which our ship had been named – hot and tired and apprehensive. As the *Apapa* entered tropical waters, it became hotter and hotter, but this was really a welcome change from the cold damp of Ireland, and on deck, there was always a light breeze to cool you off. We had all got our shots from Dr Joe Barnes, so we knew that we were protected from the deadly yellow fever and we had all started our chloroquin and paludrine that would protect us from malaria. At least that side of things was covered. Besides we would be under the care of our own sister doctors should we fall sick. But I digress.' She stopped, hesitant to go on, perhaps in my presence. We waited expectantly. We were all familiar with the dangers of disease, tropical disease – especially of yellow fever – and all knew the old rhyme. 'The Bight of Benin the Bight of Benin, few come out though many go in.' Yellow fever, more than malaria or dysentery, gave that part of West Africa the unhappy title of 'The white man's grave'.

'I will never forget that first night', her voice trembled as she closed her eyes to conjure up the memory. 'The five of us slept in an upstairs room which was stifling. Not a breath of air. But of course we had to be modest and be fully covered as we lay inside our mosquito nets. This was my first time seeing, never mind using, a mosquito net. Once I had it well tucked in and was safely inside, I felt secure and at peace, despite the fact that I wanted to throw everything off and go to the window for air. In any event, I settled down calm and serene and insulated and somehow isolated from the real world. I was in for a shock.'

It must have been an hour after we went to bed when I felt it. I had lain awake pondering what the future might hold for me. My mind was full of thoughts about the life I was going to have in this strange country, when quite suddenly I sensed something like a cold hand moving across my left foot. It was not imagination. I was completely awake now and frozen with fear as the something moved slowly along my other leg and started to creep up towards my tummy. I whispered loudly to the Sister in the next bed, 'There is something crawling across me... Sister... Sister... Please Help Me! Can you put on the light Please...?' I had forgotten that we had no electricity, only a bush lamp, and I am not sure any of us could manage one. 'Shssh... Sister, go to sleep.... You are breaking the grand silence ...Wait until morning and let us all get a nights rest... for God sake!'

I lay there petrified. Not moving a muscle.

'The "thing" crawled up my chest and appeared from under my sheet. I kept my eyes closed and stayed stock-still and prayed and prayed. It moved slowly towards the head of the bed brushing my neck in the process. I waited and waited never sleeping a wink all night. Dawn came. The grand silence was over and we all got out of our beds or I should say all extracted ourselves from under our mosquito nets, which were more or less in disarray by this time. There were many gasps and pious ejaculations when we saw a large snake coiled up on the floor at the head of my bed, fast asleep and obviously very content with himself. I had foolishly neglected to tuck in the net at either the top or bottom ends of the bed, just letting it hang loosely to the floor. No wonder the snake had easy access to a comfortable niche for the night'.

I vividly remember her telling us that story and how we were all silent afterwards. I know that, for my part, I lived through her experience in my mind as clearly as if I had been there.

However, if you want to sit enthralled by 'snake stories' for a night you can do no better than listen to the tales of the locals who can hold you spellbound with stories handed down from their fathers and grandfathers. I am sure that many of those I heard were exaggerated just as the Irish storytellers – the sheanacháis – of the past embellished their stories about Kitty the Hare and head-less horsemen.

Gorillas in the Mist

The year 1994 saw the start of the mass murder of over a million people – mostly Tutsis – in Rwanda. It was another shameful chapter of human history from which we learned precious little in the way of handling these regular crises. I mention it at this point in connection with my visit to Ruhengeri, specifically to climb up the nearby mountains and see the gorillas made famous by the life and tragic death of Dian Fossey.

Dian was born in San Francisco in 1932, just two years before me. But, unlike me, Dian was reared in a loveless and harsh household. When she was six-year–old, her mother divorced her father and married a man who clearly had no time for his little stepdaughter to the extent that she was not even allowed eat at the same table as him. No wonder she turned to animals for the love she craved. Ultimately, she grew up to become the world's leading researcher on primates, with her specialty the gorillas in the mountains of Northeast Rwanda. She studied them, loved them and virtually lived with them, prior to her brutal murder, presumably by poachers, in 1985.

Her name and fame spread throughout the world after her death. And because of her love for these special gorillas, so like humans in many ways, the whole Dian Flossey story affair became a cause celebre.

Despite the terrible aftermath of the genocide and despite a very heavy workload, I was determined to take at least one day off and see the gorillas for myself.

I was staying in Kigali in a house rented by Refugee Trust, an Irish NGO with whom I was working at the time. There were just two of us in the house, Deidre Ruane – a red headed Irish nurse – and me.

Some African friends had arranged my trip to see the gorillas, but the night before I was due to go, I felt quite ill with a headache and fever, and was not sure that I could make it. I guessed that I had malaria and dosed myself with malarone, a powerful antimalarial drug, for I was determined to make this trip at all costs. Next morning, the jeep to bring me there arrived and I was feeling a lot better. The journey to Ruhengeri took less than two hours during which I slept most of the time.

There were no hotels or guesthouses in Ruhengeri in those days nor was there any place to eat or drink as far as I could see. But I was well prepared with a rucksack full of food and bottles of water. I knew that I would have to share this food with my guides and I also knew that I would have to give them some dollars which, I hasten to add, I was only too happy to do. Two other 'tourists' joined me: one an Italian photographer from the National Geographic and the other, a lady who was an American anthropologist. She was as thin as he was fat, but both were equally determined to see the gorillas and this common bond held the three of us together as we followed our guide up the mountain. I should explain that we had two guides, both armed, one leading in front the other and one bringing up the rear. The path was windy, narrow and slippery. It was bordered by lush green jungle foliage which had to be cut or beaten away with machetes so that we could pass. There seemed to be a constant trickle of water underfoot making the pathway slippery and the moisture-laden air was heavy with the smell of decaying undergrowth. Soon we were all sweating profusely, especially our fat Italian friend. Now and then, we would hear a rustling nearby, but we did not see any animals. The guides seemed more afraid of humans than of wild animals.

They told us that the mountain was infested with Hutus on the run, with poachers looking to acquire lucrative 'bush meat' and with common thieves who had acquired firearms during the genocide. Snakes, spiders and scorpions played second fiddle to the human hazards.

I fear our little band would have been easy prey for any robber. Our guides had stayed on without pay for the last year and a half and were completely loyal to the gorillas and – hopefully – to us as well. I was particularly lucky as I had been introduced as a doctor 'who was helping the ordinary people of Rwanda' and to whom special protection and special courtesy should be extended. But I do not think that would have counted for anything when facing the nozzle of a rifle or the blade of a machete. Oblivious to all these things and totally preoccupied with our own thirst and discomfort, we continued the slow trudge upwards.

The day got hotter as the sun rose higher, and the path seemed more tortuous and difficult with each step forward. But no one complained. In any case, we had been bound to silence from the start, so that we did not even communicate in whispers, but struggled along wordlessly. Every now and then, the front guide would stop, caution us to complete silence and examine a broken branch or point to some object or mark on the ground that told him we were on the right track. We could see nothing out of place in the dense foliage.

We had not really ascended very high before our guides motioned us to halt and be extra quiet. We had obviously come to a favourite feeding place for the gorillas, and now, on a sign from our guides, we crept slowly along with mounting excitement.

Then we saw them. There was a group of gorillas feeding off leaves less than twenty metres away. At least one was a large male silverback. The others were either children or females. We were motioned to stay absolutely still and not approach any closer. The Italian soundlessly perched his camera on a tree stump and started filming. The lady was looking at the gorillas through binoculars and was oblivious to anything else. I just lay there staring at the strange sight when, for some unknown reason, one of the gorillas spotted me and started to come towards where I was lying. I know that I felt no fear. Perhaps, it was the malaria, or perhaps it was the malarone. I do not know. But there was something in me that abolished all fear as the gorilla approached closer. Suddenly, he or she was beside me and was rubbing my hand. I remained still, and looked into the gorilla's eyes, which, at that moment, were unutterably sad. This lasted but a moment before the spell was broken and the gorilla turned and re-joined the group. It was a moment I will never forget, a moment I will cherish forever, a moment or both dream and reality when the one mixes intimately with something unexpected and wonderful.

There is little further to tell. We all trooped back down and I eventually got to Kigali about seven o'clock. In time for bed, dreams and peace.

Little Things with Big Bites

I have a recurrent fear of putting my foot into a shoe where a wasp is hiding.

This is a fear that I have had for many years probably due to my father telling me when I was a child that someone he knew had got stung repeatedly in this way many years previously.

It was routine then for me to check my shoes for unwanted visitors each morning before putting them on.

But it is easy to become careless when you are tired and know that nothing unforeseen has happened for the last hundred times. But I was always careful while overseas, perhaps too careful on one occasion.

It was about 4 a.m. when I heard the tap tap tap at my window. I was in Nigeria at the time and we had no phones. Instead, the nurse would come to my window and tell me in person whatever was troubling her. This particular morning, I did not need a torch since a full moon was bathing the room in a watery yellow glow.

O'K... I'll be across in a minute', I answered, while at the same time extricating myself from the mosquito net and stepping on the floor. I swung my legs over the side of the bed while tipping my shoes upright – as usual – to make sure that they were clear of insects. They were both empty, so I stood up straight and made to get my shirt and shorts from a nearby chair my shoes in my hand. As I stepped forward, I felt my foot crushing something soft and squelchy.

I almost screamed as a sudden pain seared up from my right heel to my hip. I hopped around in agony praying that the pain would ease and wondering what I had done. Had I stepped on a snake?, on an African hedgehog? on a poisonous lizard? on a nail? on what? One glance was enough. There was a lovely, though now partly mangled, specimen of an emperor scorpion. Perhaps nine inches long. I was lucky in that I had an emergency WHO first aid kit in my room and was able to inject novocaine into my heel within minutes. The relief was instantaneous and when I made it to the hospital, I told my tale to everyone including the patients.

Everyone had done the same thing in the past – many times.

From that day on when I got out of bed, I made sure not only to check my shoes but also to inspect the floor before planting my bare feet down.

A scorpion sting can kill a small child.

TROPICAL HAZARDS

Malaria

Sub-Saharan Africa, the Sahel, has more than its fair share of the tropical diseases that scourge Africa. Wherever I worked in the Sahel having 'fever' was synonymous with malaria and was as common as having a cold in Europe. The difference is that malaria can be lethal especially in the young, the elderly, the pregnant, the malnourished and the debilitated – that is most of the people. It is still a major problem, which is increasing in some countries because of drug misuse, drug resistance, overcrowding, globalisation and climate change. As with other headline diseases, governments and philanthropists in the West have made a huge impact on the push to eradicate malaria, but it is no easy task. My own direct experience in this regard is limited to seeing Sigma Tau, the Rome-based pharmaceutical company, developing the antimalarial drug eurartisim thanks to money from the Bill Gates foundation. Some day an effective vaccine will be found. Some day the vector mosquito will be eliminated or rendered incapable of carrying the dreaded parasite.

Blindness

The stiff wind that blows across arid sun-baked parts of Africa torments the locals from birth to death. One of the consequences is that people are constantly rubbing their eyes to remove sand, grit and particles of dust. Who can resist rubbing their eyes when they are itchy all the time? Those living in desert areas – and the Sahara is increasing in size year on year – are the ones most affected.

Where sanitation is poor, hygiene standards are low and people are crowded together, the causative organism, *chlamydia trachomatis*, spreads easily from one person to another so that eventually everyone in the house may become infected and eventually blind.

Trachoma is the leading cause of preventable blindness in the world. I was to see many cases of blindness from trachoma during the Ethiopian famine. It is one thing to write about it. It is another to see what it does to whole families and whole villages.

River Blindness, a neglected tropical disease or NTD, is far less common but just as serious as trachoma. It is so named because of its prevalence in those living near fast-flowing rivers where the vector, the black fly (simulium), breeds.

This little fly gives a painful bite as it injects the larvae of the offending parasite (*onchocerca volvulus*) under the skin. These develop into adult forms anywhere in the body, the females of which release tiny offspring called microfilariae. If the microfilariae are not picked up by another blackfly, then they die in the body causing an intense sclerosing reaction, especially in the eyes. Repeated attacks result in corneal opacity and blindness.

In mentioning River Blindness, I unreservedly pay tribute to all those who support its elimination, including Jimmy Carter the ex-President of the United States and the drug firm Merck which has donated millions of tablets of mectizan to affected countries all over the world. Not all multi-nationals are the self-aggrandising evil empires which so many politicians proclaim them to be.

Other Hazards

Access to water, especially clean water, is a pressing need in developing countries. So it is no surprise that outbreaks of infectious diarrhea, including dysentery and cholera occur all the time and are still a major cause of death, especially in small children.

Need I remind any of you who travel to the tropics, whether for work or holiday, that your best friend is clean water. Your three second best friends are loperamide, fluoroquinolone and azithromycin.

The viral haemorrhagic fevers such as Yellow fever, Lassa fever, Marburg, Ebola, Dengue, Chikungunya and Zika and many others are firmly rooted in warm climates. And because of their transmissibility, high mortality and ease by which they can be imported to the Western world, they pose a major threat to all of us. This is not just associated with returning travellers; it is part of the worldwide advance of disease bearing mosquitoes most notably the feared Asian tiger mosquito (*Aedes albopictus*) a vicious biter, who actively seeks out human blood. The media in the West have brought Ebola and Zika to everyones' attention because of the outbreaks in the 2010s, but these are just two of the frightening viruses that are straining to find new pastures in our increasingly globalised world.

Doctors know that many tropical diseases are clustered in specific geographical locations. This may be due to a microclimate or to local practices that facilitate the spread of a particular disease. For example, hydatid disease is far commoner in Turkana than anywhere else is in the world, simply because of the people live in such close proximity to infected animals. Calabar Swelling, caused by the 'eye worm', is confined to West Africa because that is where the vector lives. The examples are legion.

In the case of children, measles remains a big killer. This is particularly in children who are already malnourished and weakened from other diseases.

I mention rabies only because I have seen the terrible death it can cause. Once again it is children who are the most frequent victims and it is children in poorer countries who are most at risk.

It would be tedious to list those diseases which are more common in the tropics than elsewhere. They range from HIV/AIDS and typhus and TB (all common) to plague (rare). But other hazards, not strictly diseases, should also be mentioned.

There include road accidents, animal bites and physical violence. And for everyone, there are the rigours of the climate with periods of long hot dry spells and periods of drenching rain. Add to this the difficulty one finds in getting something simple done quickly and you can put 'frustration' on your list.

Simple Inexpensive Ways to Prevent Disease

Most infectious disease can be prevented by simple, inexpensive ways that do not require complicated research or advanced technology.

Basic health education, clean water, functional sanitation, decent housing and properly delivered vaccination programmes would demolish the high rate of disease and decimate mortality overnight. The quality of life would also change dramatically so that people would have a chance to fulfil their real potential.

OVERSEAS AID:
IS IT A WASTE OF MONEY?

What is overseas aid? Many would say that it is the transfer of money or of expert personnel from a rich country to a poorer one and add the caveat that in both cases strict monitoring is required.

As a general principle, 'aid' should be used only for projects that better the lives of people in the host country and personnel with expertise from developed ones should only stay temporarily in the poor country until an indigenous counterpart can take over.

Unfortunately, the reality does not match the ideal.

On the part of the donors, the self-interest of rich countries is promoted by imposing high tariffs on imports from developing countries and by investing chiefly in projects that boost the coffers of multinational companies. In poor countries, one can exploit cheap labour, turn a blind eye to child labour and earn access to growing markets by propping up corrupt regimes. In addition, technically advanced countries can recoup much of the aid they give by selling electronic equipment and armaments to poor countries on the pretext that they are sold for defense purposes only. This is an even uglier face than that of 'ordinary' corruption.

You might think that NGOs – by their very nature – are more perspicacious. And indeed some are. But there have been so many exposés of the misuse of funds in recent times that it is difficult for a disenchanted public to give money to any NGO. This is a shame as it tars all with the same brush.

On the part of receiving countries, there is also corruption. Contracts are bought and sold – often with overt 'sweeteners' – as part of the deal. Mismanagement of funds, diversion of funds into private pockets and gross incompetence at all levels of distribution means that much of the aid is lost.

At one end of the scale, one sees leaders of poor countries with massive fortunes stashed away in Western banks. At the other end of the scale, you find bags of rice and flour marked 'Gift from the USA' or 'Gift from the people of the EU' for sale in local markets, even in times of terrible distress. The rice or the flour has been pilfered and the proceeds diverted into someone's private pocket.

Corruption in the form of money laundering, false claims, fully funded projects that were never started or never finished and simple bribery are just some of the ways in which freely donated money is misused.

Add to this the heavy expenses in running an 'aid organisation'. It has to pay permanent staff, employ consultants to vet projects, send staff overseas on tours of inspection and maintain the whole superstructure of a corporate entity.

Common Pitfalls for Both NGOs and Government Agencies

On occasions, all agencies have been guilty of proposing projects with little reference to the actual needs of people they purport to help. Sometimes they fail to consult properly with the local authorities, and sometimes they embark on work that is already being done by another agency, occasionally they do work that is unnecessary, even harmful to the local economy.

One could cite many instances of projects in which both donor and host are at fault. I remember seeing a beautiful state-of-the-art hospital in Mogadishu, built by Western money, which lay empty and had equipment that was unused and unusable. The 'white elephant' stood side by side with people living in abject poverty, with no running water, no sanitation, no schooling for their children and no job prospects for themselves. The streets were dotted with rat-infested heaps of rotting garbage, and one wondered how the population avoided epidemics of cholera and typhus.

Surely, this project was a colossal mistake from its inception.

One might also cite the beautiful African Union building in Addis Ababa, a triumph of Chinese engineering, which on first sight seems a generous and useful gift. But many Africans tell me that this edifice is really a ploy to further political and economic influence among African leaders and that the money would have been better, if less ostentatiously, spent on projects designed to help ordinary people.

Emergency Aid

This is a different thing altogether and, although there may be waste and mismanagement, it is impossible to quibble with anyone or any organisation that engages in immediate crisis relief. We are slowly becoming more efficient at delivering a coordinated rapid response, and this is to be welcomed.

However, the constant showing of pictures of starving emaciated children on our TV screens – particularly in non-emergency situations – is losing its impact. The overuse of such images by development organisations is counter-productive and does not paint a true picture of things. This is readily apparent when visiting 'poor' countries where one is confronted with traffic jams, high-rise apartments, five star hotels, luxurious restaurants and all the usual Western amenities.

Starving children, forced labour, shantytowns, dire poverty and political oppression may not be far below the surface, but they do not dominate everyone's life as so many NGOs suggest.

Despite all the mismanagement and overt corruption, people still donate and donate generously. Nonetheless, more and more are asking the question 'When will it all end?... We have been donating now for the best part of 100 years and things seem to be getting worse, not better.' Donor fatigue is inevitable and understandable. So what do we do?

Nowadays, some people bypass NGOs and give money directly to someone going to work in a poor country or support a small practical project, such as sinking a well in a village. Others prefer to go overseas themselves for a short time and build houses or work in an orphanage. Many well-intentioned groups and individuals have channelled their efforts into small specific projects.

However, I seriously question the effectiveness of volunteers who go overseas for a few weeks to 'build houses'. These are viewed by the locals simply as tourists – which they are – and are often resented because they upset the local microeconomy. It is fairly obvious to all that the money each volunteer raises could be far more effectively spent if given to reliable indigenous charities.

Unless the volunteer has a specific skill which is not available locally, going overseas for a few weeks is of minimal benefit to anyone except perhaps the volunteer.

I finish on a depressing note. Since I first went to Africa in 1960, there has been little improvement in the lives of the majority of Africans where the average life expectancy is 25 years less than those living in developed countries. This is despite the enormous amount of aid that has flowed into Africa in the past 60 years. And it is despite the enormous advances in technology that have changed the way of life on every continent.

EPILOGUE

The storms of life are over for Doreen and me, for now we are sailing in calmer waters, thankful for our past and hopeful for the future.

If our lives have brought even the smallest comfort to anyone then we have a lot to be thankful for.

Doreen died of cancer in August 2016.

The Saints are in Heaven.